GUINNESS WORLD RECORDS 2016

GAMER'S EDITION

British Library Cataloguing-in-Publication Data: a catalogue record for this book is available from the British Library.

UK ISBN
978–1-910561-08-9

US ISBN
10: 1-910561-09-6
13: 978-1-910561-09-6

Check the official **GWR Gamer's Edition** website at: **www.guinnessworld records.com/gamers** for record-breaking gaming news as it happens, plus exclusive interviews and competitions.

ACCREDITATION:
Guinness World Records Limited has a very thorough accreditation system for records verification. However, while every effort is made to ensure accuracy, Guinness World Records Limited cannot be held responsible for any errors contained in this work. Feedback from our readers on any point of accuracy is always welcomed.

Guinness World Records Limited does not claim to own any right, title or interest in the trademarks of others reproduced in this book.

OFFICIALLY AMAZING

GAMER'S EDITION 2016

SENIOR MANAGING EDITOR
Stephen Fall

EDITOR
Stephen Daultrey

LAYOUT EDITORS
Tom Beckerlegge,
Bruno MacDonald

PROJECT EDITOR
Adam Millward

GAME CONSULTANT
Stace Harman

EDITORIAL CONSULTANT
Rob Cave

PICTURE EDITOR
Michael Whitty

DEPUTY PICTURE EDITOR
Fran Morales

PICTURE RESEARCHERS
Wilf Matos, Laura Nieberg

TALENT RESEARCHER
Jenny Langridge

ORIGINAL PHOTOGRAPHY
James Ellerker, Paul Michael
Hughes, Kevin Scott Ramos,
Ryan Schude

VP PUBLISHING
Jenny Heller

EDITOR-IN-CHIEF
Craig Glenday

DIRECTOR OF PROCUREMENT
Patricia Magill

PUBLISHING MANAGER
Jane Boatfield

DESIGN
Paul Wylie-Deacon, Richard
Page at 55design.co.uk

ART EDITOR
Paul Oakley

PRODUCTION CONSULTANTS
Roger Hawkins,
Dennis Thon

PRINTING & BINDING
MOHN Media Mohndruck
GmbH, Gütersloh, Germany

INDEX
Marie Lorimer

PROOFREADING
Matthew White

GUINNESS WORLD RECORDS

CORPORATE OFFICE
Global President: Alistair Richards

PROFESSIONAL SERVICES
Chief Financial Officer:
Alison Ozanne
Financial Controller: Zuzanna Reid
Account Receivable Manager:
Lisa Gibbs
Assistant Accountant: Jess Blake
Accounts Payable Manager:
Victoria Aweh
Management Accountants:
Shabana Zaffar, Daniel Ralph
Trading Analysis Manager:
Andrew Wood
Head of Legal & Business Affairs:
Raymond Marshall
Solicitor: Terence Tsang
Legal & Business Affairs Executive:
Xiangyun Rablen
Office Manager: Jackie Angus
Director of IT: Rob Howe
Desktop Administrator:
Ainul Ahmed
Developer: Cenk Selim
Junior Developer: Lewis Ayers

GLOBAL BRAND STRATEGY
SVP Global Brand Strategy:
Samantha Fay

GLOBAL PRODUCT MARKETING
VP Global Product Marketing:
Katie Forde
B2B Product Marketing Manager:
Tanya Batra
**Digital Product Marketing
Manager:** Veronica Irons
Online Editor: Kevin Lynch
Community Manager: Dan Thorne
Digital Video Producer:
Matt Musson
Designer: Jon Addison
Junior Designer:
Rebecca Buchanan Smith
  Product Marketing Assistant:
  Victor Fenes

TV & PROGRAMMING
**Director of Global TV Content &
Sales:** Rob Molloy
Senior TV Distribution Manager:
Denise Carter-Steel/Caroline Percy
Senior TV Content Executive:
Jonathon Whitton

RECORDS MANAGEMENT TEAM
SVP Records: Marco Frigatti
Head of RMT Operations:
Jacqui Sherlock
Records Managers: Sam Golin,
Sam Mason, Victoria Tweedy,
Chris Lynch, Corinne Burns,
Mark McKinley
Database & Research Manager:
Carim Valerio
Adjudications Manager:
Ben Backhouse
Specialist Records Manager:
Anatole Baboukhian
Customer Service Managers:
Louise McLaren/Janet Craffey
Senior Project Manager:
Alan Pixsley
Program Manager – Attractions:
Louise Toms
Project Manager:
Shantha Chinniah
Records Consultants:
Aleksandr Vypirailenko,
Sophie Molloy
Official Adjudicators: Eva Norroy,
Lorenzo Veltri, Pravin Patel, Anna
Orford, Jack Brockbank, Fortuna
Burke, Lucia Sinigagliesi, Şeyda
Subaşı Gemici, Chris Sheedy,
Sofia Greenacre, Evelyn Carrera,
Michael Empric, Philip Robertson,
Mai McMillan, Glenn Pollard,
Justin Patterson, John Garland,
Brittany Dunn

EMEA & APAC
SVP EMEA & APAC: Nadine Causey
VP Creative: Paul O'Neill
PR Director: Amarilis Whitty
PR Manager: Doug Male

Senior Publicist: Madalyn Bielfeld
UK & International Press Officer:
Jamie Clarke
B2C Marketing Manager:
Justine Tommey
B2C Marketing Executive:
Christelle BeTrong
B2B Marketing Manager:
Mawa Rodriguez
Head of Publishing Sales:
John Pilley
Sales & Distribution Manager:
Richard Stenning
Licensing Manager, Publishing:
Emma Davies
Head of Commercial Sales:
Sam Prosser
Commercial Account Managers:
Lucie Pessereau, Roman Sosnovsky,
Jessica Rae
Commercial Account Executive:
Sadie Smith
Commercial Representative, India:
Nikhil Shukla
Country Manager, MENA:
Talal Omar
Project Manager: Samer Khallouf
B2B Marketing Manager:
Leila Issa
Commercial Account Manager:
Muhsen Jalal

AMERICAS
SVP Americas: Peter Harper
**Publishing Sales & Product
Director:** Jennifer Gilmour
Head of Client Services:
Amanda Mochan
Director of RMT – Latin America:
Carlos Martinez
Head of RMT – North America:
Kimberly Partrick
Account Managers: Nicole Pando,
Alex Angert, Ralph Hannah
**Commercial Representative,
Latin America:** Ralph Hannah
Junior Account Manager:
Hanna Kubat

PR Manager: Kristen Ott
B2B Marketing Executive:
Tavia Levy
Project Manager: Casey DeSantis
Records Manager: Annie Nguyen
HR & Office Manager: Kellie Ferrick

JAPAN
VP Japan: Erika Ogawa
Office Manager: Fumiko Kitagawa
Director of RMT: Kaoru Ishikawa
Project Manager: Aya McMillan
Records Managers: Mariko Koike,
Gulnaz Ukassova
Designer: Momoko Cunneen
PR & Sales Promotion Manager:
Kazami Kamioka
**Digital & Publishing Content
Manager:** Takafumi Suzuki
**Commercial Sales & Marketing
Director:** Vihag Kulshrestha
Marketing Executive:
Asumi Funatsu
Account Manager:
Takuro Maruyama
Senior Account Executive:
Daisuke Katayama
Account Executive: Minami Ito

GREATER CHINA
President: Rowan Simons
HR & Office Manager: Tina Shi
Office Assistant: Kate Wang
Marketing Director: Sharon Yang
Digital Manager: Jacky Yuan
PR Assistant: Leila Wang
B2B Marketing Manager: Iris Hou
Marketing Executive: Tracy Cui
Head of RMT: Charles Wharton
Records Manager: Lisa Hoffman
**Records Manager/Project
Co-ordinator:** Fay Jiang
Content Director: Angela Wu
Commercial Director:
Blythe Fitzwilliam
Senior Account Manager:
Dong Cheng
Account Manager: Catherine Gao

Foreword

Hello readers, Smosh Games here!

As the people behind one of the biggest YouTube gaming channels – and now a games designer in our own right (see p.12) – it's a real privilege to contribute the first guest foreword to the *Guinness World Records Gamer's Edition* and to talk about the one thing that everyone loves – games!

We believe that gaming is the most exciting industry in the world. It has the most passionate fans and the most creative and imaginative people behind it. It's also the most rapidly evolving industry, too, with gaming channels attracting millions of viewers on YouTube and Twitch, eSports growing into a huge, global spectator sport, and the constant creation of new technology that changes the way we make and play games.

This is why the *Guinness World Records Gamer's Edition* is such an essential book. It not only brings recognition to the record holders, the fans, and the developers and professionals who drive the industry, but it's just so much fun to read. It's packed with great facts and records about the games you love. There is a giant, real-life game of *PAC-Man*, a 45-hr turn of *Hearthstone*, and even men jumping out of a plane playing *Skylanders*. But our favourite record is on the *Assassin's Creed* pages, where you'll discover that the most-viewed fan film based on an action-adventure game is "ULTIMATE ASSASSIN'S CREED 3 SONG [Music Video]" by…oh yeah, SMOSH!

This year we're hoping that Smosh Games videos will set more records so that we can come back and be in this book again next year. Being in this book feels great!

So without further ado, it is with massive pleasure that we welcome you to the *Guinness World Records Gamer's Edition 2016*. Whether your thing is for moustachioed plumbers, *League of Legends* champions or giant *Minecraft* cities, there's plenty to sink your teeth into here.

See you all next year. We're all off to play some games!

The Smosh Games team

Contents

Welcome to the ninth annual *Guinness World Records Gamer's Edition*! You have in your hands the world's **biggest-selling videogaming annual**, and as always it's packed with record-breaking high scores, speed-runs, technical achievements and gaming luminaries. New for this edition is our blockbustin' **mega *Minecraft* mini-section** starting on p.98 – as well as the ultimate record-breaking guide to the game, it's your chance to set some *Minecraft* records of your own. Good luck!

Helpful hints
Get the inside track on your favourite games with our handy Tips 'n' Tricks section.

In-depth features
Infographic features crammed with facts and figures give you the lowdown in game data.

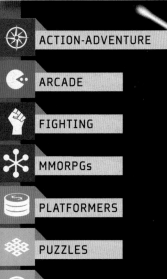

Genre icons
Listed below are the icons for each gaming genre represented in the book. You'll find them in the top left corner of each game-based page.

The last word in records
From best-selling games to the fastest speed-runs, the latest *Gamer's Edition* has them all.

- ACTION-ADVENTURE
- ARCADE
- FIGHTING
- MMORPGs
- PLATFORMERS
- PUZZLES
- RACING
- RHYTHM
- RPGs
- SHOOTERS
- SPORTS
- STRATEGY & SIMULATION

HALO

Meet the stars
More exclusive photo shoots than ever before showcase some of our most impressive record-breakers.

Meet the mobs
There are 22 pages of blocky action in our specially designed *Minecraft* section.

Be the best
Our *Minecraft* challenges could see you build your way into the record books.

BLOCK BUSTERS

Fast facts
Find out more about the best titles in gaming with our "Did You Know?" top trivia.

Killer quotes
Find out what GWR record-breakers and industry insiders really think about their feats.

INSIDE THE BOOK...
As you read the *Gamer's Edition*, keep an eye out for the special features running throughout the book. We explore the changing faces of Nintendo's gaming icon Mario (p.42), find out what's hot with reviews aggregator Metacritic (p.120) and talk to *Call of Duty* publisher Activision (p.88). Your New Favourite Games (p.164) will tell you what to look out for in the coming months.

The Hardware & Tech section (p.176) contains all you need to know about the latest hardware developments in the gaming industry – and exciting prospects on the horizon, such as Microsoft's HoloLens.

If that's not enough, from page 190 you'll find 10 pages of scoreboards from videogame record monitor Twin Galaxies, containing high scores and fastest times for games ranging from arcade coin-ops to Xbox.

Use your block
Turn to page 98 for the start of our *Minecraft* section. You can even attempt to set a record.

Introduction

The *Guinness World Records Gamer's Edition 2016* is the ultimate videogame guide. Our ninth annual edition is packed with new and updated records from all your favourite titles, plus news, high scores and feature reports from across all aspects of gaming.

Kurt J Mac – **longest journey in *Minecraft*** (pp.98–99)

Our expert consultants have searched high and low to bring you a selection of the very best records. Watch out, too, for insights from within the gaming industry in our exclusive interviews with the brains behind titles such as *Destiny, Hearthstone, League of Legends, Minecraft, Skylanders* and *Silent Hill*.

Kat Gunn – **highest-earning female gamer** (pp.64–65)

Shoot-'em-up

For this year's edition, our picture team arranged more photo shoots than ever before. Dotted around this introduction and the book itself you will meet some of the personalities setting records and making headlines playing the games they love.

We took the **highest-earning female gamer**, Kat Gunn, to the world-famous Vasquez Rocks in California, USA, for a stunning *Halo*-themed shoot, while multiple *NBA 2K* record holder Tristen Geren invited us to his local high-school gym in Fredericksburg, Texas, USA (see pp.124–25). We also travelled to Sweden to meet speed-runner Joel Ekman. To celebrate his *Legend of Zelda* record, Joel dressed up as Link

Game on!

Hello and welcome to *Gamer's Edition 2016*. We've squeezed more of your favourite games than ever before into this new book. Whether you love FPSs, MMOs and RPGs, or sports, strategy and arcade games, you'll find them all here – from *Assassin's Creed* to *WWE*. Plus, unique to this edition, is our 22-page *Minecraft* section – a blocky bonanza boasting a series of challenges in which you can attempt to set *Minecraft* records of your own.

Ken Hoang and Klayton Schaufler – **highest-earning *Super Smash Bros. Melee* player** and **most KOs on *Super Smash Bros. Brawl*** (pp.156–57)

François Federspiel – **fastest completion of *Assassin's Creed II*** (pp.16–17)

Joel Ekman – **fastest completion of *The Legend of Zelda: Ocarina of Time*** (pp.80–81)

Kenny Drews and Florian Fleissner – **longest marathon on *Need for Speed*** (pp.128–29)

himself in Stockholm's Ice Bar. Meanwhile, *Assassin's Creed* fan François Federspiel posed as Ezio on the streets of Prague, Czech Republic, and soccer fan Chris Cook (pp.48–49) took to the pitch at Sixfields Stadium in Northampton, UK, in honour of his 49-hr *FIFA* marathon.

Game changers

This year's edition has a theme of evolution. Our fresh new infographic features explore the ever-changing nature of the iconic platform-leaping plumber, Nintendo's Mario (pp.42–43), along with the progression of videogame controllers (pp.72–73) and in-game spaceships (pp.150–51). Other features include a close look at leading publisher Activision (pp.88–89) and online review aggregators Metacritic (pp.120–21).

There's also our fully updated Hardware & Tech section and 10 pages of high scores from our friends at Twin Galaxies, offering the authoritative low-down on landmark gaming achievements across every platform from arcade conversions to Xbox.

Still want more? Turn to p.164 to find out which games could be setting records in the next *Gamer's Edition*. And if you follow our guide to record-breaking on pp.8–9, maybe you can join them there!

Our picture editor, Michael, and videographer, Matt, have travelled the globe to secure amazing new images and footage. Visit www.guinnessworldrecords.com/bonus for exclusive access to unseen content, which portrays the stories behind some of the fantastic records in both the *GWR* and *Gamer's* book. Plus, you'll get a unique behind-the-scenes insight into the world of Guinness World Records.

The content is exclusive, so you'll need to solve the clues on the site. Find the answers in the book, in order to access the content.

Jason Camberis – **largest arcade machine** (pp.176–77)

Chris Cook – **longest marathon on a sports videogame** (pp.48–49)

GAIN ACCESS TO EXCLUSIVE:

📷 **BONUS IMAGE GALLERIES**

🎥 **BEHIND-THE-SCENES VIDEO FOOTAGE**

💬 **RECORD HOLDER INTERVIEWS**

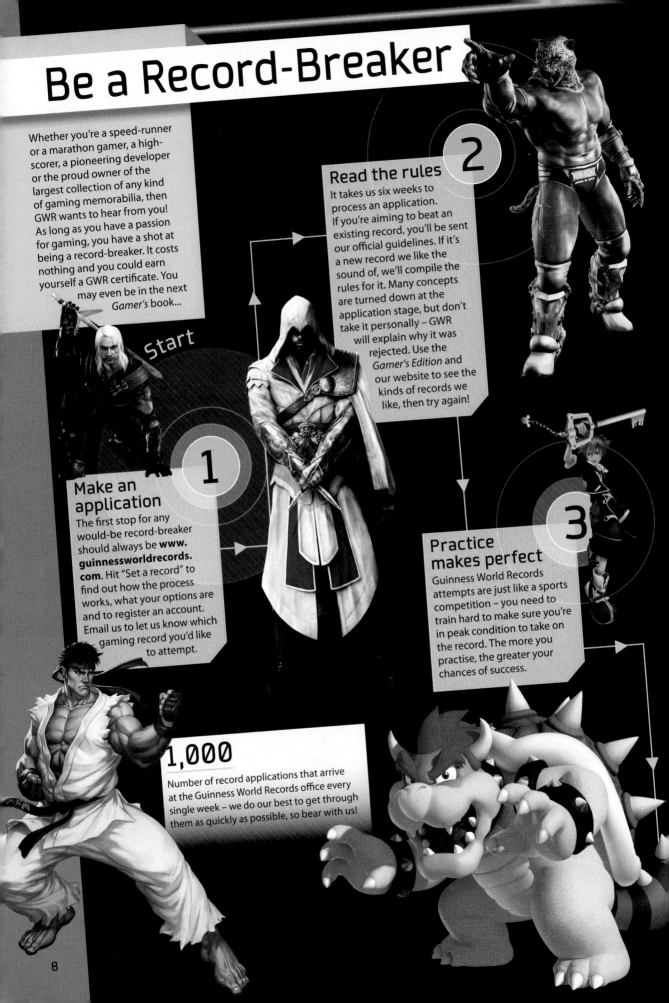

Be a Record-Breaker

Whether you're a speed-runner or a marathon gamer, a high-scorer, a pioneering developer or the proud owner of the largest collection of any kind of gaming memorabilia, then GWR wants to hear from you! As long as you have a passion for gaming, you have a shot at being a record-breaker. It costs nothing and you could earn yourself a GWR certificate. You may even be in the next *Gamer's* book...

Start

Read the rules 2

It takes us six weeks to process an application. If you're aiming to beat an existing record, you'll be sent our official guidelines. If it's a new record we like the sound of, we'll compile the rules for it. Many concepts are turned down at the application stage, but don't take it personally – GWR will explain why it was rejected. Use the *Gamer's Edition* and our website to see the kinds of records we like, then try again!

1 Make an application

The first stop for any would-be record-breaker should always be **www. guinnessworldrecords. com**. Hit "Set a record" to find out how the process works, what your options are and to register an account. Email us to let us know which gaming record you'd like to attempt.

Practice makes perfect 3

Guinness World Records attempts are just like a sports competition – you need to train hard to make sure you're in peak condition to take on the record. The more you practise, the greater your chances of success.

1,000

Number of record applications that arrive at the Guinness World Records office every single week – we do our best to get through them as quickly as possible, so bear with us!

Challenge addict

If anyone knows how to beat the best, it's Tristen Geren (USA). The serial record holder has set numerous records via our Challengers website, and on 1 August 2013 posted a video of himself scoring 2,100 points to set the **highest score** on *The Legend of Zelda: Phantom Hourglass*. Another record in the bag!

GWR Challengers

You can make an attempt to set a record right now. Visit **www.guinnessworldrecords.com/challengers**, pick the record you want to beat and follow the instructions for supplying video evidence. If it's a videogame record attempt, make sure that GWR can see every second of play. Adjudications are made every week, so you won't have long to wait.

5 Send your evidence

A bit of preparation can ensure your potential new record isn't missed or rejected because of technical issues. When filming videos, do a trial run to make sure that the lighting is right and that there are no obstructions. After you've successfully filmed your record attempt, simply package up the evidence and send it to GWR for assessment. It's that easy.

Finish

4 Make your attempt

Once you're certain you can't score another point or shave another second off your speed-run, you're ready to take on the record. Make sure you have everything in place to meet the guidelines – you will need a good-quality video recorder, witnesses and anything else we've specified you require for a valid claim.

6 Frame your certificate!

You did it! Successful record-breakers will be sent an official certificate to show off to their friends. If you're very lucky, you may even be one of the fortunate few to make it on to these pages next year. And if you've missed out there's no need to despair – you can always give it another shot. There's no limit to the number of attempts you can make.

Year in Gaming

News in brief

Legendary fantasy author Terry Pratchett sadly passed away on 12 March 2015. Pratchett's *Discworld* books spawned several games, including the point-and-click adventure *Discworld* for PC in 1995. In tribute, Frontier Developments created a starport in *Elite: Dangerous* entitled "Pratchett's Disc starport" (see far right for more on that game).

Harry Potter movie actor Daniel Radcliffe swapped potions for pixels to play Rockstar's Sam Houser in a BBC drama about *Grand Theft Auto*. The 90-min film, tentatively entitled *Game Changer*, examines the game's major cultural impact.

Social media king PewDiePie – the **highest-earning gaming contributor to YouTube** – has further expanded his megastar status with his first ever videogame. Developed by Outerminds, *Legend of the Brofist* was due to hit mobiles in summer 2015.

Unquestionably the shock news (or rumour) of the year was the revelation that *Metal Gear* creator Hideo Kojima would be ending his near 30-year relationship with Konami once his studio had finished *Metal Gear Solid V*. His impending exit also led to the cancellation of *Silent Hills*, the survival-horror game he was making with film director Guillermo del Toro.

Who said that gaming can't be good for you? *Assassin's Creed* publisher Ubisoft is currently developing a videogame that combats the "lazy eye" condition known as amblyopia. The innovative title requires players to wear stereoscopic glasses.

"Yes, we're being bought by Microsoft," announced Mojang after Microsoft snapped up the *Minecraft* developer for $2.5 billion (£1.65 billion) back in September 2014 – the **largest acquisition of a games studio**. A month earlier, e-tailer Amazon bought games-streaming site Twitch for $970 million (£639.3 million), making it a busy period for industry buy-outs.

New dimensions for LEGO®

With toys-to-life lines such as *Disney Infinity* and the groundbreaking *Skylanders* setting new standards in gameplay, it came as little surprise when LEGO announced that it too would be entering the ring. Due for release in September 2015, *LEGO Dimensions* will see a host of brick-headed megastars, such as Batman and Gandalf, reinvented as interactive figurines, who can then be jettisoned into a new range of videogames by way of a portal. Blocks away!

> "There are some very beautiful arthouse games and there are more traditional games. Our industry has become very broad and that's a great thing."
>
> **David Braben, OBE (creator *Elite*, *Elite: Dangerous*)**

Gamers go batty for limited-edition PS4s

When Sony launched its limited-edition grey PS4 units on 3 December 2014 to celebrate PlayStation's 20th anniversary, the 12,300 numbered units sold out quicker than it takes to unwrap the packaging. One unit even fetched $20,000 (£13,165) on eBay in April 2015. On 31 March 2015, Sony unveiled the Limited Edition *Batman: Arkham Knight* PS4 Bundle for release in June 2015, featuring a grey console with a sleek Dark Knight graphic.

A first for *Guitar Hero*

On 14 April 2015, Activision announced that its rhythm series *Guitar Hero* was returning as *Guitar Hero Live* – this time using a first-person perspective with live-action video. Due out in autumn 2015, the game's concert footage was shot using the robot camera technology from Peter Jackson's *The Hobbit* films, in which hobbit actors were filmed on smaller sets to make everyone else seem bigger. "We wanted to make sure we did something that people maybe weren't expecting," said developer FreeStyle Games.

Nintendo goes mobile

Ever wanted to see Mario on a smartphone? Your handheld dream should soon become reality. On 18 March 2015, Nintendo announced it was partnering with Japanese mobile company DeNA to make new games for mobile platforms based on its existing catalogue. Speaking to *Time*, Nintendo president Satoru Iwata revealed that his company would develop gameplay, while DeNA would handle the "service" operations. Nintendo had long resisted the temptation to move into mobile gaming, so the news came as a pleasant shock to everyone.

Danger! Danger! *Elite* is out!

Having earned the record for **longest development period for a videogame**, Frontier Development's *Elite: Dangerous* finally landed on PC on 16 December 2014 – 19 years 8 months after the last *Elite* game. The space-faring epic, which raised £1,578,316 through Kickstarter, is the third sequel to *Elite* (1984) – the **first open-world videogame**. Creator David Braben, OBE told GWR that his new game pushes the way games tell stories. "Think of it as a *Game of Thrones*-type game, where you can side with any character and the story evolves depending on your actions," he said.

Superheroes set for Marvel-lous tales

Telltale Games has been making a huge splash with episodic adventures such as *The Walking Dead* and *Game of Thrones*, pushing gaming close to an interactive, graphic novel-like experience. Now the US developer has struck a major deal with Marvel – home to Spidey and co. – to work on a new series for 2017. Given that Marvel Games' Bill Rosemann promised that future Marvel titles would be "exquisite" and "eye-popping", comic fans should be very excited.

A beastly prank

eSports hopefuls may have thought it was safe to play *Street Fighter* again when pro *Street Fighter* legend Daigo "The Beast" Umehara (Japan) – holder of several tournament records – announced that he was retiring to become a full-time accountant. However, eagle-eyed gamers soon observed the date of the news – 1 April 2015 – and realized it was an April fool's prank. D'oh!

Q&A

Eric Osborne – Bungie, developer of *Destiny*

Released in September 2014, *Destiny* became the biggest-selling debut of the year, with $500 million (£309 million) of stock shipped to retailers on day one. Its developer Bungie has revealed plans for a sequel, currently expected in 2016.

What's it like working at Bungie?
It's humbling. It makes you smile. It comes with a lot of pressure. We push ourselves to do better every day. A fundamental difference for Bungie is that we don't see players as fans – instead, we see them as being like us, each wanting to have uniquely rewarding entertainment experiences.

What feature were you most proud of in the original *Destiny* game?
For me, *Destiny*'s sandbox – the set of abilities and tools I use – are incredibly compelling. I love moving through the world and defeating enemies with the gear that I've earned. [But] it takes a multitude of systems, all working together, to pull that off.

Any new features you can reveal for the next *Destiny* game?
We're going to continue to watch what players do in the first game. Our live team has already delivered more updates [to the first game] than anything we've ever supported. We're also delivering more content, new ways to play and enhancements. We have several teams internally working on what's to come. We're really excited about the evolution of the world.

Year in Gaming

News in brief

When non-profit online library Archive.org added 2,400 playable MS-DOS retro games to its site in January 2015, gamers discovered that they could embed oldies such as *Wolfenstein 3D* into Twitter. Sadly, Twitter pulled the function in May 2015.

Leaked emails at Sony Pictures in late 2014 claimed that the movie mogul behind several Marvel films had been chasing film rights for Nintendo's characters. Top of his alleged wishlist was an animated feature film about *Super Smash Bros.*

On 28 April 2015, Mojang released a free female default skin for console versions of *Minecraft* to represent the "diversity" of its player base. The company revealed in a blog post that Alex would have "thinner arms, redder hair and a ponytail".

On 4 May 2015, eSports company ESL and *Counter-Strike* community ESEA launched the world's **largest *Counter-Strike: Global Offensive* league**. The Pro League offered a $1 million prize pot for the best players of Valve's tactical FPS.

Around 100 Atari 2600 cartridges, dug up in a New Mexico landfill, raised some $37,000 (£24,379) when they were sold on eBay in November 2014. The most desired title was a copy of *E.T. the Extra-Terrestrial* (1982), which fetched $1,537 (£1,012).

"Father of videogames" Ralph H Baer (Germany) passed away on 6 December 2014, aged 92. Baer invented the **first videogame console** – the Magnavox Odyssey – released in 1972 and later distributed in Japan by Nintendo.

On 17 August 2014, Syndicate became the **first individual videogame broadcaster with 1 million followers on Twitch!**

Cultured platformer

The collaborative result between developer Upper One Games and the Alaskan non-profit organization Cook Inlet Tribal Council, *Never Alone* became the world's **first commercial game developed with an indigenous culture**. The atmospheric platformer followed an Iñupiat girl and her Arctic fox through eight Alaskan folk stories and was released in November 2014. "*Never Alone* is a story of empowerment that shines a light on Alaskan people," its writer Ishmael Hope told Guinness World Records. "Its success has led to a world games initiative, which will tell stories of other under-represented communities around the world."

Pokémon tattoo goes viral

A self-drawn tattoo of the Pokémon character Charmander – widely dubbed "the worst Pokémon tattoo ever" – became an overnight viral sensation when it was posted to Reddit in April 2015. The bizarre artistry belonged to a 27-year-old man, who had etched the creature on to his own abdomen. Some viewers even created a range of spoof merchandise, including a Pokémon tattoo water bottle!

Grub's up

YouTube sensations SMOSH took a first foray into game development with the mobile gaming app *Food Battle: The Game* in November 2014. Developed with Roadhouse Interactive, the free2play action-adventure was based on the channel's long-running video series *Food Battle* and raised $250,000 through crowdfunding site Indiegogo. Gamers battled homicidal mutant donuts with weapons such as a "Celery Sword", sometimes wearing only their underpants. "It's completely insane and awesome at the same time," beamed Indian broadsheet newspaper *DNA*.

J-*Olli* good sport!

A studio of just seven people beat multiple sports giants to win a BAFTA gaming award for "Best Sports Game". Roll7 (UK), whose skateboarding game *OlliOlli* was released for PS Vita in January 2014, fended off rivals *FIFA 15*, *Forza Horizon 2* and *Football Manager* 2015. "It's unbelievable," the team told GWR. "We also had far less than a tenth of the budget of one of the other games we were up against."

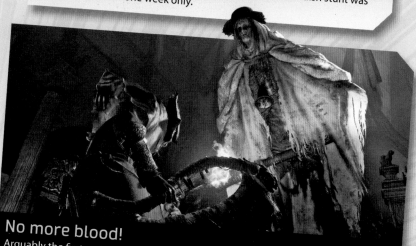

PAC your bags

PAC-Man holds numerous world records – now it can add **first arcade game to use Google's geometric data** to its growing list of accomplishments. On 31 March 2015, Bandai Namco teamed up with Google to create playable *PAC-Man* games in Google Maps, challenging gamers to gobble dots and evade ghosts on 2D maps anywhere in the world. This fiendish stunt was available online for one week only.

Rare NES game sells for thousands

If you've ever paid a lot for a videogame, the chances are it was just a small a fraction of the $35,100 (£24,034) forked out by an eBayer for a "factory-sealed" US edition of 1987 NES game *Stadium Events*. The ultra-rare "exergaming" sports title, known as *Running Stadium* in Japan, used a "running pad" designed to kick gamers into shape. However, the accessory was swiftly discontinued and only around 200 copies of the US version sold. The auction began on 5 January 2015 and was initially attracting fraudulent bids of $100,000 (£68,473).

No more blood!

Arguably the first major game of 2015, with a GameRankings score of 91.23%, Sony's *Bloodborne* was also one of the toughest. Fortunately, gamers quickly discovered a novel way of softening up its horrible bosses – let the game run for 12 hours! A memory glitch meant that leaving the RPG alone for a sustained period caused enemy AI to depreciate. As homage to the game's unrelenting difficulty, YouTuber "Irregular Dave" (aka Dave Jewitt) announced that he was donating £1 to the Leukaemia & Lymphoma Research charity (UK) for every time he dies in the game. His generosity should not go unnoticed!

Q&A

Tim Schafer – game designer of Double Fine Productions (USA)

After a 16-year hiatus from the genre, adventure designer legend Tim Schafer (*Grim Fandango*) returned to making point-and-click games in 2014 with the crowdfunded *Broken Age*, which raised $3,336,371 (£2,125,807) on Kickstarter – at the time, the most money ever pledged to a videogame. Its sequel was released on 28 April 2015.

Has making videogames changed over the years?

I started making games before the internet took off, so I was making them based on what I liked and what I thought people would like. Now developers are close to the audience, especially with free2play games, and through social media and YouTube. Developers are also trying to figure out how to make games streamable.

What are you currently most excited about in gaming?

It's not about new technology for me because I think there are so many game ideas we haven't yet explored that can be made with the existing technology. I'm just looking forward to my next game, which will have new worlds, characters and stories that people haven't seen before. That's all I can say on that for now.

Do you have any tips for young aspiring designers?

When I was younger you had to get a job at a company to make games, but now you can download one of many game engines. So my advice is to play a lot of games. Think about what you like. Then get one of the free engines and try to make your own game.

Awards Round-Up

MOBILE & HANDHELD:
Monument Valley

BEST PERFORMANCE:
Trey Parker (*South Park: TSOT*)

THANKS YOU GUYS.

BRITISH ACADEMY GAMES AWARDS

12 March 2015, London, UK

Award	Game
Best Game	*Destiny*
Artistic Achievement	*Lumino City*
Audio Achievement	*Alien: Isolation*
British Game	*Monument Valley*
Debut Game	*Never Alone*
Family Game	*Minecraft: Console Editions*
Game Design	*Middle-earth: Shadow of Mordor*
Game Innovation	*The Vanishing of Ethan Carter*
Mobile & Handheld	*Monument Valley* (see above)
Multiplayer	*Hearthstone: Heroes of Warcraft*
Music	*Far Cry 4*
Original Property	*Valiant Hearts*
Performer	Ashley Johnson (Ellie in *The Last of Us: Left Behind*)
Persistent Game	*League of Legends*
Sport Game	*OlliOlli*
Story	*The Last of Us: Left Behind*
BAFTA Ones to Watch in association with Dare to Be Digital	*Chambara*
BAFTA Fellowship in 2015	David Braben, OBE

4 March 2015, San Francisco, USA

Award	Game
Game of the Year	*Middle-earth: Shadow of Mordor*
Lifetime Achievement Winner	Hironobu Sakaguchi
Pioneer Award Winner	David Braben OBE
Ambassador Award Winner	Brenda Romero
Audience Award Winner	*Elite: Dangerous*
Innovation Award	Monument Valley
Best Audio	Alien: Isolation
Best Debut	The Banner Saga
Best Design	Hearthstone: Heroes of Warcraft
Best Handheld/Mobile Game	Monument Valley
Best Narrative	Kentucky Route Zero: Episode 3
Best Technology	Destiny
Best Visual Arts	Monument Valley

5 December 2014, Las Vegas, USA

Award	Game
Game of the Year	*Dragon Age: Inquisition*
Best Action-Adventure	*Middle-earth: Shadow of Mordor*
Best Family Game	*Mario Kart 8*
Best Fighting Game	*Super Smash Bros. for Wii U*
Best Independent Game	*Shovel Knight*
Best Role-Playing Game	*Dragon Age: Inquisition*
Best Shooter	*Far Cry 4*
Best Sports/Racing Game	*Mario Kart 8*
Best Mobile/Handheld Game	*Hearthstone: Heroes of Warcraft*
Best Narrative	*Valiant Hearts: The Great War*
Best Performance	Trey Parker (various voices in *South Park: The Stick of Truth*; see above)
Best Remaster	*Grand Theft Auto V*
Best Online Experience	*Destiny*
Best Score/Soundtrack	*Destiny*
Games for Change	*Valiant Hearts: The Great War*
Developer of the Year	Nintendo
Most Anticipated Game – Fan voted	*The Witcher 3: Wild Hunt*
Best Fan Creation – Fan voted	Twitch Plays Pokémon
eSports Player of the Year – Fan voted	Matt "NaDeSHoT" Haag
eSports Team of the Year – Fan voted	Ninjas in Pyjamas
Trending Gamer – Fan voted	TotalBiscuit
Industry Icon Award	Ken and Roberta Williams (Sierra Entertainment)

GAME OF THE YEAR:
Middle-earth: Shadow of Mordor

SXSW GAMING AWARDS

14 March 2015, Austin, USA

Award	Game
Videogame of the Year	Dragon Age: Inquisition
Mobile Game of the Year	Hearthstone: Heroes of Warcraft
Tabletop Game of the Year	Star Realms
Excellence in Gameplay	Middle-earth: Shadow of Mordor
Excellence in Art	Child of Light
Excellence in Animation	Middle-earth: Shadow of Mordor
Excellence in Technical Achievement	Destiny
Excellence in Visual Achievement	Far Cry 4
Excellence in Narrative	The Wolf Among Us
Excellence in Design and Direction	Middle-earth: Shadow of Mordor
Excellence in SFX	Alien: Isolation
Excellence in Musical Score	Transistor
Excellence in Multiplayer	Super Smash Bros. for Wii U
Excellence in Convergence	South Park: The Stick of Truth
Most Valuable Character	Ellie – The Last of Us: Left Behind
Most Valuable eSports Team	Cloud9
Most Valuable Add-On Content	The Last of Us: Left Behind
Most Anticipated Crowdfunded Game	Star Citizen
Matthew Crump Cultural Innovation Award	This War of Mine
Most Valuable Online Channel	Rooster Teeth
Gamer's Voice Award	SpeedRunners

LIFETIME ACHIEVEMENT:
Hideo Kojima

GOLDEN JOYSTICK AWARDS

25 October 2014, London, UK

Award	Game
Game of the Year	Dark Souls II
Best Original Game	DayZ
Best Online Game	Hearthstone: Heroes of Warcraft
Best Storytelling	The Last of Us: Left Behind
Best Visual Design	Assassin's Creed IV: Black Flag
Best Audio	Assassin's Creed IV: Black Flag
Playfire Most Played Game	Rust
Best Multiplayer	Battlefield 4
Best Indie Game	DayZ
Innovation of the Year	Oculus Rift DK2
Best Gaming Moment	"The Kiss" – The Last of Us: Left Behind
Handheld Game of the Year	Pokémon X and Y
Best Mobile Game	Hearthstone: Heroes of Warcraft
Most Wanted	The Witcher 3: Wild Hunt
Gaming Personality	PewDiePie
Studio of the Year	Ubisoft Montreal
Best Gaming Platform	Steam
Lifetime Achievement	Hideo Kojima (see above)

DICE 18ᵗʰ ANNUAL AWARDS

5 February 2015, Las Vegas, USA

Award	Game
Game of the Year	Dragon Age: Inquisition (see below)
Action Game of the Year	Destiny
Adventure Game of the Year	Middle-earth: Shadow of Mordor
D.I.C.E. Sprite Award	Transistor
Family Game of the Year	LittleBigPlanet 3
Fighting Game of the Year	Super Smash Bros. for Wii U
Handheld Game of the Year	Super Smash Bros. for Nintendo 3DS
Mobile Game of the Year	Hearthstone: Heroes of Warcraft
Outstanding Achievement in Animation	Middle-earth: Shadow of Mordor
Outstanding Achievement in Art Direction	Monument Valley
Outstanding Achievement in Character	Talion – Middle-earth: Shadow of Mordor
Outstanding Achievement in Game Design	Middle-earth: Shadow of Mordor
Outstanding Achievement in Online Gameplay	Destiny
Outstanding Achievement in Game Direction	Middle-earth: Shadow of Mordor
Outstanding Achievement in Original Music Composition	Destiny
Outstanding Achievement in Sound Design	Destiny
Outstanding Achievement in Story	Middle-earth: Shadow of Mordor
Outstanding Innovation in Gaming	Middle-earth: Shadow of Mordor
Outstanding Technical Achievement	Middle-earth: Shadow of Mordor
Racing Game of the Year	Mario Kart 8
Sports Game of the Year	FIFA 15
Strategy/Simulation Game of the Year	Hearthstone: Heroes of Warcraft
Role-Playing/Massively Multiplayer Game of the Year	Dragon Age: Inquisition

GAME OF THE YEAR:
Dragon Age: Inquisition

 # ASSASSIN'S CREED

Fastest completion of Assassin's Creed II

When François "Fed981" Federspiel (France) noticed that there were no *Assassin's Creed* speed-run records on Speed Demos Archive, he resolved to fill the gap. On 26 March 2011, he duly achieved the **fastest completion of Assassin's Creed II** in a total time of 5 hr 42 min 16 sec.

He went on to set records for the **fastest completion of Assassin's Creed: Revelations** – 2 hr 48 min 41 sec on 3 October 2012 – and the **fastest completion of Assassin's Creed: Brotherhood** – 2 hr 23 min 41 sec on 3 March 2013. On 8 April 2014, François recorded the **fastest 100% completion of Assassin's Creed II** – 7 hr 9 min 51 sec. "Even today, I cannot stop running the *Assassin's Creed* series," he admitted.

D.Y.K.?

For his lightning-quick run through *AC: Revelations*, François made great use of the hookblade and DLC expansion "The Lost Archive", which increased his ammo pouch capacity.

ASSASSIN'S CREED

Most watched E3 game trailer

Opening with a sweeping bird's-eye view of Paris during the French Revolution, Ubisoft's trailer for *Assassin's Creed: Unity* sees the assassins using their lethal skills to help the rioting people. Following its debut at E3 (the Electronic Entertainment Expo), the video was uploaded to YouTube on 9 June 2014 and had amassed an incredible 22,403,906 views as of 17 March 2015.

8

Number of months it took a designer, working on a 1:1 scale, to recreate the haunting Gothic architecture of Notre-Dame cathedral in Paris, France, for 2014's *Assassin's Creed Unity*.

Summary: Featuring a compelling mixture of historical adventure, stealth and swordplay, Ubisoft's stunning-looking *Assassin's Creed* has proved a winner with both critics and gamers alike. The series can boast worldwide sales of more than 73 million as of 18 March 2015.

D.Y.K.?

Ubisoft's Anvil engine – software designed to help the creation of the series' densely populated cityscapes – added "advanced reflection mapping, HDR (high-dynamic-range) graphics and volumetric lighting" – plus "a new breed of master assassin" – to *AC: Unity* (above), according to creative director Alex Amancio.

Publisher: Ubisoft
Developer: Ubisoft
Debut: 2007

Greatest aggregate time playing *AC III*

According to Ubisoft's assassinsnetwork.ubi.com, PlayStation 3 gamers had spent the equivalent of 164 centuries 75 years 20 days 9 hr 30 min playing the single-player mode on *Assassin's Creed III*, as of 27 March 2015 – more than 700 years ahead of their rivals on Xbox 360.

Highest score on *Assassin's Creed IV: Black Flag* "Wolfpack" on PS4

In the "Wolfpack" mode, assassins can work together to bring down targets. As of 29 April 2014, "Foniasophobia" sat proudly atop the leaderboards with a team score of 326,205 and an individual score of 82,070.

The **highest score on *AC IV: Black Flag* "Deathmatch" mode** is 22,250 points in 357 sessions, by "Hakuya13".

Most platforms supported by a stealth series in the 21st century

Since 2007, *Assassin's Creed* games have appeared on

Longest marathon on an action-adventure game

Belgian gamers Tony Desmet, Jesse Rebmann and Jeffrey Gamon played *Assassin's Creed: Brotherhood* for exactly 109 hr at the GUNKtv World Record Gaming Event in Antwerp, Belgium, on 18–22 December 2010. The marathon began with 20 participants, with the three record holders being the only gamers who lasted until the end.

no fewer than 16 different platforms, from eighth-generation consoles such as the Xbox One and PlayStation 4 to mobile devices. More unusually, there was a single-player, text-focused RPG for Facebook entitled *Assassin's Creed: Project Legacy*, which was released on 30 September 2010.

Highest K/D ratio for Xbox 360 *Assassin's Creed: Brotherhood* multiplayer

Gamer "ROCKY B 117" had achieved 75 kills per death from 2 days 15 hr 2 min of game time, as of 3 July 2011. The figures are even more impressive for the fact that the nearest rival only managed 27 kills per death.

Highest score on the "Short Kill" streak in *Assassin's Creed: Brotherhood*

On 10 November 2014, *Assassin's Creed* enthusiast "szurikata93" scored 1,156 points on the "Short Kill" streak challenge.

Most kills on *Assassin's Creed: Revelations* multiplayer (Xbox 360)

The third and final instalment of the "Ezio trilogy", 2011's *Assassin's Creed: Revelations* is an epic game spanning different continents and time periods, from 12th-century Masyaf in Syria, to 21st-century America. As of 17 January 2015, Spanish gamer "Junakar AC" had racked up a total of 117,266 kills on multiplayer mode for the Xbox 360.

Most successful multiplayer clan in *Assassin's Creed III*

With 487,912,060 assassinations successfully completed as of 12 August 2013, "The Invincible Clan" have lived up to their deadly moniker. The clan's star assassin, "Faith_89", can lay claim to 115,146 kills alone.

Most magazine covers for a game

Assassin's Creed II introduced the world to Ezio Auditore da Firenze, the deadly assassin of the Italian Renaissance. Between April 2009 and April 2010, the game and its iconic hero appeared as a lead cover story on 127 different publications in 32 different countries.

Most viewed fan film based on an action-adventure game

Released by the comedy duo Smosh, "ULTIMATE ASSASSIN'S CREED 3 SONG [Music Video]" was nominated for an award at the 2013 Webby Awards, and had racked up 61,991,336 views on YouTube as of 27 March 2015.

Largest range of bombs in a videogame

The "crafting" feature in *Assassin's Creed: Revelations* enables players to create more than 300 different types of bomb. Using a Hookblade weapon to grapple on to ziplines, gamers can navigate smoothly through cities and bomb them to devastating effect.

BATMAN

45

Metacritic percentage achieved by Catwoman, the **first female supervillain to star in her own videogame**, for the Xbox version of her self-titled 2004 bomb.

Most critically acclaimed superhero videogame

With a GameRankings rating of 95.94, based on 33 reviews, and a Metacritic score of 96 from 42 reviews, the PS3's *Batman: Arkham City* has put all other superhero titles in the Dark Knight's shadow. Its nearest rival is the X360 version, with 93.88 and 94 respectively.

Summary:
From beat-'em-ups and platformers to sleuthing adventures and even a Gotham City racer, Batman boasts the most eclectic gaming library of any superhero. Now with the brooding *Arkham* series under his (bat)belt, the Dark Knight's future looks "brighter" than ever.

Publisher: Various
Developer: Various
Debut: 1986

Most Batmobiles in a videogame

Arcade racer *Batman* (Specular Interactive, 2013) features 10 Batmobiles in which to screech around the streets of Gotham in search of The Joker, Bane and Mr Freeze. And in addition to cars from *Batman: The Animated Series*, *Batman Forever*, *Batman: The Brave and the Bold* and *Arkham Asylum*, it features aerial missions with "The Bat" from *The Dark Knight Rises*.

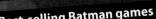

First 3D remaster of a console game

Batman: Arkham Asylum became the first console videogame to be re-released with additional 3D features. A "Game of the Year" edition, issued in March 2010, used the TriOviz system to add stereoscopic 3D to existing layers.

in July 2008, to be published by parent company Electronic Arts. However, design issues meant that the studio missed that first deadline, followed by a second target of December, intended to coincide with the film's DVD release. As EA's licence was also due to expire in December, the rights for making Batman games passed to Eidos. This reportedly cost EA around $100 million (£69 million). Pandemic was closed and 1,000 jobs were lost. Eidos enlisted Rocksteady for its first Batman game: *Arkham Asylum*.

Fastest completion of Batman: Arkham Asylum
Sean Grayson (USA) completed *Asylum* in 1 hr 57 min 8 sec

First *Batman: Arkham* game with multiplayer capability

Three games into the *Arkham* series, *Origins* tapped into the multiplayer market. In one multiplayer mode – a showdown between The Joker and Bane – the villains' gangs take each other on, while Batman and Robin pick off bad apples from both sides. In another, the gangs take on Batman alone.

First Batman videogame
It may seem primitive by today's standards, but Ocean's *Batman* (1986) was revolutionary for its time. Initially released on the Amstrad CPC and ZX Spectrum, it featured a groundbreaking isometric 3D playing world as players sought to rescue Robin by collecting items and solving puzzles. The game was developed by programming legend Jon Ritman and won numerous magazine awards.

Costliest missed deadline for a Batman game
The Australian branch of developers Pandemic began work on a game to accompany the movie *The Dark Knight*

First drivable *Arkham* Batmobile

Batman: Arkham Knight, the fourth *Arkham* outing, is the first to feature the caped crusader's car as a drivable entity. It's some debut, too, enhancing Batman's abilities in every respect, from criminal investigation to navigation. The game also has a Batmobile "Battle Mode", in which Gotham must be protected against Scarecrow's destructive minions.

on 16 August 2012, on "easy difficulty: single-segment" mode. The **fastest completion of Arkham City** was 1 hr 49 min 19 sec, by "RoboSparkle" (UK) on 21 November 2013.

First full Gotham City in a videogame
Rocksteady created a "full-sized" open-world Gotham for *Batman: Arkham Knight* – the first "complete" version of Gotham attempted or achieved in a videogame. Rocksteady describe the environment as being "five times the size of Arkham City", making it the most extensive area that the Dark Knight can explore in the *Arkham* series.

Best-selling Batman games

Game	Platform	Year	Publisher	Millions sold
LEGO Batman: The Videogame	Various	2008	Warner	13.12
Batman: Arkham City	PS3, X360, PC, Wii U	2011	Warner	10.59
Batman: Arkham Asylum	PS3, X360, PC	2009	Warner	7.84
LEGO Batman 2: DC Super Heroes	Various	2012	Warner	5.80
Batman: Arkham Origins	Various	2013	Warner	4.35
LEGO Batman 3: Beyond Gotham	Various	2014	Warner	2.63
Batman Begins	PS2, XB, GBA, GC	2005	EA	1.09
Batman: Vengeance	PS2, GC, GBA	2001	Ubisoft	0.99
Batman: Rise of Sin Tzu	PS2, XB, GBA, GC	2003	Ubisoft	0.59
Batman: Arkham Origins Blackgate	PSV, 3DS	2013	Warner	0.56

Source: VGChartz.com as of 19 March 2015

Lowest-rated game based on a comic character

Batman: Dark Tomorrow holds an average score of 27.83 on GameRankings and 29 on Metacritic. Published by Kemco and released on the Nintendo GameCube in 2003, it was described by *Game Revolution* as having "the worst camera and control in the history of videogaming".

BATTLEFIELD

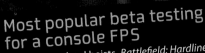

Most popular beta testing for a console FPS

With its gangland heists, *Battlefield: Hardline* (Visceral Games, 2015) was a thematic departure for the series. It attracted 7 million players for its public beta testing, which began on 3 February 2015 for the X360, Xbox One, PS3 and PS4. This was extended, owing to demand, and concluded on 9 February 2015.

Highest-earning player in *Battlefield 4*

This accolade is split between four pro gamers (shown left, top to bottom): Erik "2Easy" van Hoorn, Tom "Morte" Kerbusch (both Netherlands), Andrei "uNFixed" Leonov (Russia) and Hendrik-William "vallutaja" Kinks (Estonia). Competing as team "Fnatic", with "Morte" as captain, these fearsome militants have won four tournaments, each amassing individual earnings of $10,106.53 (£6,452.82), up to 23 November 2014.

5 Number of new, crime-themed game modes in *Battlefield: Hardline*, including "Blood Money", in which gangs vie to stash $5,000,000 of stolen cash in their trucks.

Summary: Strategic and action-packed, *Battlefield* has been a huge smash for EA. Since bursting on to the scene with the WWII-set *Battlefield 1942*, the FPS series has taken its team-focused warring to numerous conflicts and periods, barring 2015's *Battlefield: Hardline,* which featured cops fighting crime.

Publisher: Electronic Arts
Developer: Various
Debut: 2002

Highest score on *Battlefield 3*

As of 23 March 2015, a PC gamer known as "maberlin", from Berlin, Germany, had amassed 343,751,008 points in *Battlefield 3* multiplayer. He has played the game for 1,495 hr 2 min, which is a remarkable 9,700 hr less than the second-placed "MDA4iitep".

Highest score on *Battlefield 4*

An Austrian gamer playing under the tag "DIEMEXO" had scored 272,066,776 points on the PC version of *Battlefield 4* (EA DICE, 2013) as of 23 March 2015. According to the leaderboard at BF4stats.com, he had played the game for 2,153 hr 30 min and made 340,293 kills to 119,363 deaths.

First digital-only expansion pack

Sold via EA's Download Manager (now known as Origin), *Battlefield 2: Special Forces* was released in November 2005. The publisher subsequently released several *Battlefield* expansions that were exclusive to the digital distribution service. Although all of them were packaged for retail release, the boxes contained only a code used to download the game.

Most popular modification for *Battlefield 1942*

One of the first modifications released for *Battlefield 1942* was "Desert Combat", a fan-created add-on that turned the World War II game into one inspired by the first Gulf War. Winner of awards for best mod in 2002, 2003 and 2004, the developers so impressed the creators of *Battlefield* that they were made a subsidiary studio.

Largest cash prize won in a *Battlefield* tournament

An enviable sum of $250,000 (£144,000) was paid out to the aptly named gamers "Team Legends". They beat more than 200 rivals in *Battlefield 2: Modern Combat* to claim victory at the Best of the *Battlefield* tournament on 17 February 2006 in Redwood City, California, USA.

Most critically acclaimed *Battlefield* game

Released in 2005 for PC, *Battlefield 2* has amassed scores of 91% on Metacritic and 90.07% on GameRankings.

D.Y.K.?

Chinese authorities made *Battlefield 4* illegal on home soil after objecting to the game's plot, which featured a renegade general trying to overthrow the country.

Most jet kills in *BF3* air combat

As of 23 March 2015, the appropriately named "GrieferKiller" had shot down 185,809 enemy jets in *Battlefield 3* (DICE). The feared gamer topped the overall multiplayer leaderboard at battlelog.battlefield.com, and had been competing for 2,965 hr 46 min of total play time.

Largest living easter egg in a videogame

Measuring 16–18 m (52–59 ft) in length, the Megalodon is an extinct shark from 15.9–2.6 million years ago. On 4 April 2014, YouTuber "JackFrags" discovered the creature on the Nansha Strike map in the *Battlefield 4: Naval Strike* expansion pack. To make it appear, position 10 players around the floating buoy situated between flags A and B on the large Conquest configuration.

Fastest completion of *Battlefield 3* co-op

On 22 January 2015, buddies "promyy" and "phemocky" (both Poland) blasted through the PC version of *Battlefield 3* on "Co-Op Easy%" in 33 min 56 sec, as seen on "promyy"'s YouTube and Twitch channels.

First gamer to reach highest rank

The first person to rank as Supreme Commander – the highest position attainable in *Battlefield 2142*'s 44 ranks – was "Noobish-noob" in November 2006. There can only be one Supreme Commander at any one time.

Largest controllable vehicle in a shooter

Battlefield 2142's massive Titans are the largest controllable vehicles in any shooter. Not only can they be directed across a map by a team commander, but they can also be assaulted and defended by infantry units.

Tips 'n' Tricks

Teamwork is utterly key to a series such as *Battlefield*, and there are few better features to utilize in *Battlefield 4* than "spotting". Whenever your battle-weary eyes spot a target, simply click on it using the same button you use to bark squad orders. Marked targets will show up on your comrades' Mini Maps, making your team-mates aware of impending threats. And as a bonus, your selfless observancy will be rewarded with points. It's also worth noting that you should never take on tanks by yourself. If you do so, you will very quickly be destroyed.

BORDERLANDS

Summary: Often billed as a first-person role-playing shooter, *Borderlands* offers a frantic and humorous sci-fi experience, packed with trigger-happy mercenaries and giant mega-corporations. The series is notable for its striking art aesthetic and twisted characters, which lends its world a lavish, cartoonish feel.

Publisher: 2K Games
Developer: Gearbox Software
Debut: 2009

Most popular playable character in *Borderlands 2*

During a four-week *Borderlands 2* event known as the "$100,000 Loot Hunt", which ran from 12 October 2013, gamers were polled to find the most popular playable character. Top was Axton the Commando (left), chosen by 29% of players. The **least popular *Borderlands 2* character** was Krieg (far left). The buzz-axe wielding bandit-turned-Vault Hunter was chosen by a paltry 7% of competitors, placing him below Mechromancer Gaige in last place.

150

The number of Miss Moxxi's Good Touch guns that were listed on the Gearbox store in March 2015, priced at $700 (£460) each. The replicas were crafted in polystone and featured LED effects.

Fastest completion of *Borderlands: The Pre-Sequel!*

Released on 14 October 2014, *Borderlands: The Pre-Sequel!* sends players on a mission to take back a captured space station. On 19 March 2015, "TheFuncannon" (USA) posted a video of him blitzing the game in just 2 hr 18 min 36 sec (or 2:23:57 with loading screens taken into account).

Most *Borderlands* appearances

Appearing in the three main *Borderlands* games and three additional downloadable content packs, loudmouth robot Claptrap is the series' most prolific character. However, it wasn't until *Borderlands: The Pre-Sequel!* that he finally made his debut as a playable character – alongside Athena, Nisha, Jack, Aurelia and Wilhelm.

What happened to your arm? No one 'commandeers' my van!
Who are you people?

First adventure spin-off of a shooter

Developed by Telltale Games in conjunction with Gearbox Software and 2K Games, 2014's *Tales from the Borderlands* took the FPS/RPG sci-fi series and reimagined it as a cerebral point-and-click adventure.

Fastest completion of *Borderlands 2*

On 28 August 2013, speed-runner "Joltzdude139" completed the sci-fi sequel on the PlayStation 3 in 1 hr 43 min 22 sec. Using the "Ultimate Vault Hunter" mode, he beat his own world-record time.

Rarest *Borderlands 2* achievement

Taking its average across all platforms, just 6.1% of gamers had earned the "Challenge Accepted" achievement in *Borderlands 2*, as of 17 March 2015. The challenge requires players to complete Level 1 of all non-level-specific challenges with a single character.

First fan-inspired NPC in a *Borderlands* game

Developer Gearbox added a character to *Borderlands 2* named Michael Mamaril, in tribute to a gaming fan who passed away aged 22. His NPC namesake can be found giving out rare items such as E-tech weapons at various locations in Sanctuary. He also plays a key role in the "Tribute to a Vault Hunter" achievement.

Most viewed *Borderlands* video

Title song "Ain't No Rest for the Wicked", recorded by US rockers Cage the Elephant, had 4,350,623 YouTube views as of 2 April 2015. It was also a UK Top 40 hit in 2008.

Most downloaded PC mod for *Borderlands*

The "Oasis Map Hub" is a hub required to run all custom maps in the game. Uploaded to the NexusMods community by "gitface191" (UK), it had earned 732 unique downloads as of 7 May 2015.

The **most downloaded PC mod for *Borderlands 2*** is "Borderland 2 All Level 72 Character Games Saves" by "empxa", with 19,219 downloads.

Fastest completion of *Borderlands*

On 20 November 2014, speed-runner "pentaleks" (Brazil) completed *Borderlands* in just 1 hr 43 min 26 sec (minus loads). He played the PC version, using the female Siren character Lilith.

Most popular *Borderlands* fan art

John Su's (USA) "Borderlands YEAH" – featuring original series playable characters Brick, Lilith, Roland and Mordecai the Hunter – had earned 3,633 favourites and been downloaded 11,678 times from DeviantArt as of 17 March 2015.

First RPG shooter with four-player co-op

The original *Borderlands* (2009) took gamers to another dimension, combining RPG elements such as character-building with straight-up shooter mayhem. It also introduced the world's first four player cooperative role-playing first-person shooter.

First playable antagonist in *Borderlands*

Each new *Borderlands* title has introduced a new group of playable characters, but one in particular stands out in *Borderlands: The Pre-Sequel!* Wilhelm, an Enforcer working for Hyperion, is one of the main boss characters players must face in *Borderlands 2*.

CALL OF DUTY

125,000,000

Number of people Activision claims have played a *Call of Duty* game since its 2003 debut. This is more than the combined population of the eight largest cities in the USA.

Summary: Starting life as a rival to EA's *Medal of Honor*, *Call of Duty* has evolved into a global phenomenon. This military FPS series melds exhilarating action with engrossing narratives. Such is its popularity, no series has broken more sales records.

Publisher: Activision
Developer: Various
Debut: 2003

Most prolific *CoD* developer

Call of Duty – the game that would begin a juggernaut franchise – was the first title for Infinity Ward's 22-person team back in 2003. The studio was established by a core of game devs who had previously worked on World War II shooter *Medal of Honor: Allied Assault*, and it has since gone on to release a total of six full games in the *CoD* series.

Highest-earning *Call of Duty* player

As of 30 April 2015, FPS expert Damon "Karma" Barlow (Canada) had made $241,411 (£156,937) playing five *Call of Duty* titles on the Major League Gaming pro circuit. Barlow also won the *CoD* Championship in 2013 as a member of team "Impact" and in 2014 with "compLexity".

Fastest completion of "Extinction"

"Extinction" is the alien-killing survival mode on *Call of Duty: Ghosts*. It can be a tough task for a team to tackle, but "Jon The Chief" completed the "Extinction" campaign "Point of Contact" on his own in 39 min 53 sec in a video posted to YouTube on 10 July 2014.

Most popular Exo Ability in *Call of Duty: Advanced Warfare*

Exo Abilities are extra skills you can apply to your soldier's Exoskeleton in *Advanced Warfare*'s multiplayer and "Exo Survival" modes. Since the shooter's release in November 2014, 2.45 trillion Exo Abilities have been used. The most popular is the Overclock, which increases a player's speed. As of 3 April 2015, it accounted for 26% of Exo Abilities employed. The second most widely used is the Exo Shield, with 24%, followed by the Exo Cloak (22%), which makes gamers temporarily invisible.

Fastest completion of *Call of Duty: Black Ops*

"TheLongshotLegend", aka Oliver Smith (UK), made his way through *Call of Duty: Black Ops* in just 2 hr 54 min 28 sec on 26 May 2011 in Hitchin, Hertfordshire, UK. The 19-year-old played the game in the "Recruit" mode.

Best-selling FPS

Released in 2011 and developed by Infinity Ward and Sledgehammer (Treyarch for Wii), *Call of Duty: Modern Warfare 3* had amassed global sales of 30.43 million as of 24 April 2015, making it the most popular multi-format FPS of all time. It's also the single **best-selling FPS for the Xbox 360** with total platform sales of 14.5 million, according to VGChartz.

Breathing hotly down its neck in terms of overall sales is *Call of Duty: Black Ops II* (Treyarch, 2012), which boasted total platform sales of 28.22 million as of the same date.

Best-selling PS3 shooter

Call of Duty: Black Ops II had sold 13.42 million copies for the PS3 as of 24 April 2015. Impressively, eight of the PS3's top 10 shooters come from the *Call of Duty* franchise. The only other games in the list were *Battlefield 3* (with 7.1 million sales) and *Resistance: Fall of Man* (with 4.29 million sales), in sixth and ninth places respectively.

First free2play *Call of Duty* FPS

Designed as a *CoD* title for the Chinese market, *Call of Duty Online* is a free2play online game developed by Activision Shanghai and Raven Software and distributed by Chinese gaming giant Tencent. The game launched as an open beta on 14 January 2015.

Highest-earning player on *Call of Duty: Ghosts*

According to e-Sports Earnings, three pro gamers – Patrick "Aches" Price, Ian "Crimsix" Porter and Tyler "TeePee" Polchow (all USA) – had each earned $124,686 (£80,266) from *Ghosts* tournaments, as of 31 December 2014.

Best-selling FPS series

Game	Publisher	Years active	Sales
Call of Duty	Activision	2003–present	216.4 million
Halo	Microsoft	2001–present	60.21 million
Battlefield	Electronic Arts	2002–present	42.28 million
Medal of Honor	Electronic Arts	1999–2012	37.35 million
James Bond 007 (FPS titles only)	Various	1997–2012	21.81 million
Far Cry	Ubisoft	2004–present	17.84 million
BioShock	2K Games	2007–13	12.49 million
Doom	Various	1993–present	12.29 million
Resistance	Sony	2006–12	9.45 million
Killzone	Sony	2004–13	8.22 million

Source: VGChartz.com as of 24 April 2015

Largest charitable videogame endowment

Established in 2009, the *Call of Duty* Endowment is a non-profit-making public benefit corporation created by Activision Blizzard to help US military veterans find employment. In its most recent grant report, the endowment was valued at $12.3 million (£7.9 million).

eSports

With soaring prize money and sky-rocketing audience figures, organized competitive gaming is becoming a serious business. Thanks to online video streaming, live action from eSports tournaments for games such as *League of Legends* and *StarCraft II* can be watched around the world.

In 2014, gamers competed in ESPN's X Games and Winter X Games for the first time.

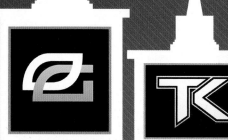

149,712

concurrent viewers watched the *StarCraft II* WCS finals at BlizzCon 2014

The 2014 *StarCraft II* World Championship Series was a series of gaming events with a $1.6-million (£1-million) prize pool. The global finals were held at BlizzCon on 8–9 November 2014 and achieved a peak of 149,712 concurrent viewers.

On 6–8 June 2014, the Summer X Games in Austin, Texas, USA, held its first ever eSports tournament. The game was *Call of Duty: Ghosts*, and it was "OpTic Gaming" who took the gold medal.

BIG MONEY, BIG SHOTS

As of 26 March 2015, *Call of Duty* and *Halo* each provided five of the top 50 most lucrative eSports games (according to e-Sports Earnings). The two franchises offered combined prize money of nearly $9 million (£6 million) across their 10 titles.

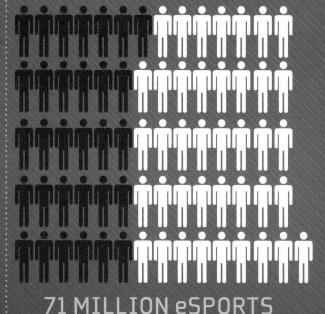

$9 MILLION

71 MILLION eSPORTS VIEWERS

According to market research experts Super Data Research and Newzoo, in 2013 eSports viewing figures doubled to 71 million in a single year. Nearly half that number – 31.4 million – came from just one country: the USA.

1 million US viewers =   *1 million viewers =*

BETTER NOT

Third-party site CSGOLounge. com allows players to bet in-game items with real-world value on the results of professional CSGO matches.

Controversy arose within the CSGO professional scene when some teams and players were accused of fixing matches to win bets, leading to several players receiving bans from major tournaments.

eSports in South Korea are governed by the Korea e-Sports Association (KeSPA), an agency founded in 2000 by the country's Ministry of Culture, Sports and Tourism.

Many KeSPA teams carry title sponsorships from electronics and telecommunications giants, with such teams including SK Telecom T1, KT Rolster and Samsung Galaxy.

LEAGUE OF LEGENDS

More than 27 million unique viewers tuned in to the Season 4 *League of Legends* World Championship finals on 19 October 2014, with a peak audience figure of 11.2 million.

Viewing figures in comparison:
2013 MLB ALCS Game 2: 8.26 million
Breaking Bad finale (2013): 10.3 million
Game 7 of the 2013 NBA Finals: 17.7 million
2015 Super Bowl: 114.4 million (average)

SUPER BOWL

| 8.26 m | 10.3 m | 17.7 m | 27 m | 114.4 m |

Eight teams.
Three days.
One game –
*Counter-Strike:
Global Offensive.*

$9,323,980

The prize pool for *DotA 2*'s The International 2014 tournament was swelled by $9,323,980 (£5,440,180), raised through fan purchases of the *Compendium*, an interactive book that unlocked rewards as the prize fund grew.

On 23–25 January 2015, "Team LDLC.com" won the Winter X Games *Counter-Strike: Global Offensive* tournament in Aspen, Colorado, USA. Silver went to "Ninjas in Pyjamas" and bronze to "Team Dignitas".

DESTINY

Summary: From the maker of *Halo* comes this ambitious brew of sci-fi FPS action and role-playing, set inside a massively multiplayer-shared world. Given the game's scale and the developer's pedigree, there were few eyebrows raised when it became the biggest series debut of 2014.

Publisher: Activision
Developer: Bungie
Debut: 2014

Largest budget for a first-person shooter

Developed by Bungie, *Destiny* cost a staggering $140 million (£93 million) to make. The total budget is pushed to an extravagant $500 million (£335 million) when infrastructure support, royalties and marketing and promotion costs are factored in. A big part of development costs went towards creating Bungie's new graphics engine and world-builder, both of which were written for the game.

3.37 Percentage of players to unlock the "Guardian Lord" trophy as of 11 May 2015 – the **rarest *Destiny* trophy on the PS4**.

"It's always a labour of love that we do because of the passion of the fans..."

Bungie President Harold Ryan accepting a British Academy award for "Best Game"

Most popular primary *Destiny* weapon

Revealed by Bungie on 9 January 2015, the most commonly used weapon in *Destiny* is the scout rifle Vision of Confluence. The developer listed it as number one in popularity based on user data. The fusion rifle Murmur was the **most popular special weapon in *Destiny***.

Most popular console beta for a debut game

With 4,638,937 players, *Destiny* became the most popular console beta for any game *not* based on an existing series or licensed from a franchise. The *Destiny* beta began on 17 July 2014 for the PlayStation 3 and PlayStation 4. It was then opened up for the Xbox 360 and Xbox One on 22 July 2014. The testing concluded on 27 July 2014.

First player to level-up without playing

Reddit user "yavin247" has built an ingenious device that allows him to level-up with *Destiny*

characters without him needing to be present. By applying tape and a crude motor to his Xbox One controller, "yavin247" can make his in-game avatar punch and move without human control. Using this method, AI-controlled enemies will eventually kill "yavin247"'s character, but *Destiny*'s respawn system causes the in-game character to reappear a minute later and repeat the process. As a result, "yavin247"'s character shot up from level 16 to level 20 in a single night.

Highest *Destiny* kill/death ratio in "Crucible"

According to Destinytracker. com, the player with the highest kill-to-death ratio

D.Y.K.?

Opening-day demand for *Destiny* was so fierce that more than 11,000 stores around the world held midnight openings. An ecstatic Activision said that it sold more than $500 million worth of *Destiny* stock to retailers on the first day alone.

First clan to beat Crota's End raid

A mere six hours after Bungie launched the "Crota's End" raid on 9 December 2014, gaming clan "Invigorate Gaming" had already beaten it. The "Crota's End" raid, which is a six-player co-operative mission set in Ocean of Storms, was released as part of the *Dark Below* expansion. Bungie announced the clan's super-fast completion via Twitter.

First solo completion without a gun

In an incredible feat of gaming, YouTuber "The HMO5" audaciously swept through the "Crota's End" raid solo on 8 March 2015 without firing a single gunshot. Instead, he used grenades and melee attacks to down the eponymous deity (above).

in "Crucible" matches is the USA's "Ilogain", with a ratio of 8.00 as of 19 February 2015. Across 3,548 games, "Ilogain" had racked up 51,921 kills and just 6,489 deaths. The most kills "Ilogain" had achieved in a single match was 48.

Most games played in "Crucible"

According to Destinytracker. com, the player who has competed in the most matches in the multiplayer mode "Crucible" is "Shes My Nerd". Across 7,588 confirmed games, "Shes My Nerd" had registered 169,242 kills and had been killed 48,930 times, as of 27 February 2015, sitting comfortably ahead of second-placed "RealKraftyy" (who had competed in 6,383 games).

Tips 'n' Tricks

There are three character classes in *Destiny*. For those who like to be nimble-footed and stealthy, the "Hunter" (right) is the one to choose. Pick the "Gunslinger" sub-class for knife-throwing and sniping at range. And if you like to creep up on foes, the "Bladedancer" will best suit your sly talents.

Best-selling debut series on eighth-generation consoles

Game	Platform	Publisher	Sales
Destiny	PS4/XO	Activision	7.12 million
WATCH_DOGS	PS4/XO	Ubisoft	4.92 million
Titanfall	XO	Electronic Arts	2.56 million
The Evil Within	PS4/XO	Bethesda	1.95 million
DRIVECLUB	PS4	Sony	1.57 million
The Crew	PS4/XO	Ubisoft	1.56 million
Knack	PS4	Sony	1.35 million
Ryse: Son of Rome	XO	Microsoft	1.14 million
ZombiU	Wii U	Ubisoft	0.83 million
Sunset Overdrive	XO	Microsoft	0.77 million

Source: VGChartz as of 24 March 2015

DIABLO

4 All 16 levels of the original 1996 *Diablo* game were intended to be playable in multiplayer mode, but the developer apparently ran out of time so only four of its 16 single-player levels ended up playable with fellow humans.

Summary: Diablo, the Lord of Terror, is a hellish deity exiled to the mortal realm. In the original game, players take on the role of a warrior, a rogue or a sorcerer to defeat him. *Diablo II* expands those scenarios, while *III* – set 20 years later – adds fresh layers of mythology.

Publisher: Blizzard
Developer: Blizzard North
Debut: 1996

Fastest-selling PC videogame

More than a decade after 2000's *Diablo II*, the much-anticipated sequel *Diablo III* (2012) became the **fastest-selling PC game**, shifting 3.5 million copies in the first 24 hours. A further 1.2 million fans received the game for free as part of a *World of Warcraft* promotion, meaning that with 4.7 million players from the off, it's also the **largest PC game launch.**

D.Y.K.?

Despite *Diablo*'s grim premise, Blizzard has injected humorous elements: *Diablo II* has a secret cow level, dubbed "Whimsyshire" when it resurfaces in the third instalment, and game director Jay Wilson stars as a dungeon boss.

Longest development for an RPG

After production duties began in 2001, *Diablo III* ended up in the works for 11 years before it was released in May 2012 to huge acclaim. The game underwent three redesigns and *Diablo* originator David Brevik described the result as "a very different game than I would have created".

First completion of *Diablo III*

Just 5 hr 30 min after the *Diablo III* server opened on 15 May 2012, South Korean clan EHG had completed the game and killed the final boss. Server problems meant that they were unable to collect some of the finest loot – such as weapons and armour – along the way. Nonetheless, they earned an unbeatable place in the game's history.

Longest *Diablo III* killstreak

On the prerelease beta version of *Diablo III*, unleashed eight months before the game hit the shelves, were loopholes and shortcuts excised from its final incarnation. Gamer "Lastea" took advantage of them to rack up a killstreak of 11,391 in 1 hr 46 min of playing time on 4 March 2012.

Fastest completion of *Diablo II: Lord of Destruction*

The fastest *Lord of Destruction* completion, as the assassin, was by Sören "FraGFroG" Heinrich: 58 min 52 sec on 11 October 2009. The **fastest completion as the druid** was by Ricky "LeWoVoc" Mitchell: 1 hr 11 min 43 sec on 12 November 2009. The **fastest completion as the sorceress** was by Alan "Siyko" Burnett (USA): 4 hr 22 min on 14 November 2008.

Fastest time to reach level 60 in *Diablo III*

To level-up his Demon Hunter, Swedish gamer "Djhunterx" used a technique known as "leeching". He joined friends' *Diablo III* games as they reached the ends of specific quests and levels, then immediately left to minimize his playing time. This careful organization paid off: he progressed to level 60 in just 15 min of in-game play, as logged on 9 October 2012.

Fastest RPG completion

Diablo games can last for several hours, but on 16 January 2009 Poland's Maciej Maselewski took advantage of glitches and tricks to speed his sorcerer character to the ending in just 3 min 12 sec. This established a record not just for *Diablo*, but for any role-playing game.

First completion of *Diablo III*'s "Hardcore Inferno"

Canadian gamer "Kripparrian" and his USA-based "wizard friend" "Krippi" claimed a major victory in the millions-strong *Diablo III* community when they achieved the first "Hardcore Inferno" completion of the game. The appropriately diabolical "Inferno" is the title's highest difficulty level, while the "Hardcore" mode means that, when a character dies, the game ends and the player cannot reload his or her last save point. Kripparrian and Krippi scored their milestone victory on 19 June 2012, just 35 days after the game's launch.

Tips 'n' Tricks

Don't get too excited about grey items in *Diablo III*: their only value is as junk to be sold. In ascending order of desirability and value, the items to go for are white (usable but not enchanted), blue (boasting at least one magical property), yellow (rare items with enchantments aplenty), then orange (specially generated legendary items, with unique names and specific properties). Best of all are green items, whose environmental qualities are open to debate, but which are parts of a legendary matching set. Collecting a whole set of the latter earns players a special bonus.

♞♙ DotA

Most chosen hero in *DotA 2*

Rubick the Grand Magus tops DatDota's statistics for the hero selected in most tournament matches, garnering 4,368 picks on the professional *DotA 2* scene as of 22 April 2015. A ranged Intelligence hero, the Grand Magus offers players the ability to copy the spells of his enemies and use them as his own – a useful asset in the heat of battle.

6,000,000

Cost in dollars (£3.83 million) of the *DotA* team "Catastrophic Cruel Memory" when purchased by Wang Sicong (China) in 2011. The team became the eSports powerhouse "Invictus Gaming".

Summary: Originally a *Warcraft III* mod based on a *StarCraft* map, the MOBA *DotA* has become the most lucrative title on the eSports circuit. Its sequel, *DotA 2*, has paid out at least $28 million (£18.6 million) in tournament winnings – the **most prize money for a videogame**.

Publisher: Blizzard/Valve
Developer: Various
Debut: 2003

Most *DotA 2* matches played

As of 15 April 2015, the pro *DotA 2* gamer "VPP.Scandal" had played 7,055 competitive matches according to Dotabuff, winning an impressive 58.02% of them. This was 527 matches more than second-place "FD.Meracle".

Largest eSports prize pool for a single tournament

Taking place in Seattle, Washington, USA, on 8–21 July 2014, The International 4 boasted a glittering prize pot of $10,931,103 (£6,395,000). As with previous competitions in the series, the pool had been heavily augmented with funds raised from the fan purchase of a digital compendium.

Most kills in a *DotA 2* game

Danil "Dendi" Ishutin (Ukraine) of "Natus Vincere" racked up 40 kills in a single game on 20 November 2012.

Highest average gold per minute in *DotA 2*

"Mski.Jay Gigabyte" of "Team Mineski" (Philippines) had earned an average of 599 gold per min from 121 matches as of 22 April 2015 – more than anyone else who has played a minimum of 100 competitive matches.

Most expensive item in *DotA 2*

Animal couriers can be a great asset in *DotA 2*, allowing players to remain in the thick of battle while their item purchases are ferried to them. On 6 November 2013, "July.24" bought an ultra-rare pink Ethereal Flame War Dog from "PAADA" on Dota2Trade for $38,000 (£23,739).

Highest total gold earned in *DotA 2*

While professional *DotA 2* players compete for increasingly large real-world cash prizes, the most in-game gold gained in a single match is 111,918, achieved on 20 March 2013 by "QwisTa", playing as Strength hero Bristleback.

Highest-earning eSports player

Given that *DotA* tournaments pay out some of the biggest prize money, it's no surprise that the **highest-earning *DotA 2* player** is also the highest-earning eSports pro overall. As of 5 May 2015, 24-year-old Chen "Hao" Zhihao (China), who has competed predominately in the eSports team "Newbee", had earned $1,207,857 (£770,661) from 39 tournaments on the pro *DotA* circuit. Of this total, $1,201,416 (£766,551) came exclusively from *DotA 2* tournaments.

D.Y.K.?

In 2014, "Sajedene" was the victim of an armed robbery while live-streaming *DotA*. Fellow gamers alerted the police, who caught one robber before they could escape.

Most *DotA 2* game wins

Gamer Airat "Silent" Gaziev (Russia) had achieved a total of 611 competitive victories as of 15 April 2015.

Most wins for a *DotA 2* hero

According to *DotA* data aggregator DatDota, Rubick (see main picture) had triumphed 2,646 times from 5,297 battles as of 12 May 2015 – a win rate of 50%. In second place, with fewer victories but a higher win percentage (51.7%), was "Nature's Prophet" with 1,940 wins from 3,753 matches.

Greatest aggregate time playing *DotA 2*

DotA 2 players tend to be incredibly dedicated, but as of 15 April 2015 nobody could match "Sonic", who had clocked up 283 days 9 hr 35 min playing an astounding total of 11,165 matches.

Most assists in a *DotA 2* match

In *DotA*, "assists" are given to players who deal damage to opponents who are subsequently killed. In a team game, assists can be crucial in setting up the win for the team. On 20 March 2015, "HR.ArtStyle" achieved 68 assists in a single match playing as Zeus, the mighty Lord of Heaven.

Highest win rate on *DotA 2*

Player	Matches	Time played	Win rate
"Newbee.Rabbit"	1,130	27 days 12 hr 47 min	74.87%
"Fire.TC"	1,386	33 days 15 hr 45 min	73.95%
"@inphinity123"	2,510	61 days 15 hr 11 min	72.51%
"Fire.FLUFFNSTUFF"	1,527	39 days 2 hr 25 min	71.71%
"EG.Aui_2000"	3,577	88 days 20 hr 20 min	71.43%
"MVP.FoREv"	3,146	76 days 11 hr 32 min	71.33%
"EHOME.Ohaiyo`"	2,150	55 days 16 hr 46 min	71.26%
"Newbee.Mu"	1,369	34 days 8 hr 28 min	70.85%
"Secret.Puppey"	1,761	44 days 13 hr 13 min	70.76%

Source: Dotabuff as of 16 April 2015 (players with 1,000 verified competitive matches or more)

Longest *DotA 2* competition match

With no limit to the potential duration of games, *DotA 2* matches are a true test of competitors' stamina. On 15 April 2014, a marathon match at the Fragbite Masters 2014 tournament between "4 Friends + Chrillee" and "Team Dog" lasted 2 hr 5 min 26 sec.

DRAGON AGE

Best-selling eighth-generation RPG

Released in November 2014, second sequel *Dragon Age: Inquisition* swiftly outsold all other RPGs on eighth-generation consoles. By 7 April 2015, it had shifted 1.42 million units on PS4 and 0.65 million units on Xbox One, making for combined sales of 2.07 million. Nearest rival *Diablo III* had sold 1.26 million across both platforms as of the same date.

Summary: Since finding fame with *Baldur's Gate* in 1998, BioWare has established itself as one of the finest RPG developers in the business. *Dragon Age* is the company's latest endearing series, packing adventurers into Tolkien-inspired worlds of magic, monsters and intrigue.

Publisher: Electronic Arts
Developer: BioWare
Debut: 2009

D.Y.K.?

The first *Dragon Age* game, *Origins*, features more than 54 hr of dialogue. Behind that there were 144 voice actors contributing those lines for the English-language version.

165,000

Number of golden nugs killed by players during the *Dragon Age: Inquisition* Multiplayer Weekend Event from 30 January to 2 February 2015. Nugs are small, harmless creatures with long ears and pig-like snouts.

Fastest completion of *Dragon Age: Origins*

Selecting a Mage for superior firepower, Eli "Smilge" Chase completed the first *Dragon Age* game in 33 segments in 35 min 30 sec on 25 February 2010. "Smilge" played the game on the "Easy" difficulty and took advantage of glitches that allowed his character to level-up quickly.

Fastest completion of *Dragon Age: Inquisition*

BioWare speed-run specialist "LettersWords" (USA) completed an any% speed-run of *Dragon Age*'s second sequel *Inquisition* in 2 hr 29 min 19 sec (excluding loading screens), using the Day 1 patch. He streamed this feat on Twitch on 4 February 2015.

Most dragons killed in *Dragon Age*

As of 15 January 2015, a total of 2,602,377 dragons had been slain by players in *Dragon Age: Inquisition*. Players can hunt 10 different breeds of fiery beast, with the Ferelden Frostback the most commonly killed.

First action RPG to use the Frostbite engine

BioWare has traditionally built and used its own gaming engines, but for *Dragon Age: Inquisition* it employed EA DICE's Frostbite 3. This engine, used for the *Battlefield* FPS series, offers powerful terrain-generation tools.

Fastest completion of *Dragon Age II*

Eager speed-runner "Pallytankful" boosted his credentials by smashing his way through *Dragon Age II* in 2 hr 17 min 33 sec (minus loading screens) on 19 January 2015.

Fastest any% completion of *Dragon Age: Inquisition* on "Nightmare" difficulty

On 1 February 2015, Sweden's Kevin "DashingSplash" Johansson raced through the most recent *Dragon Age* iteration in 3 hr 43 min 54 sec, beating the game on its toughest difficulty setting. The ambitious gamer believes that the time can still be shaved by a further 30 min by sticking to his current route.

First videogame to enable customizable "world states"

Via the DragonAgeKeep.com website, gamers can export and customize the outcome of 300 narrative choices from previous *Dragon Age* games into 2014's *Dragon Age: Inquisition* – effectively enabling them to tailor the "world states" they had created. This feature was supported by cross-platform functionality.

Most advanced character face generator

In addition to 24 character options, *Dragon Age: Inquisition* lets players alter jowls, nostrils, Adam's apples and horns, while a "make-up" tool edits eyelashes and lip shine. It means that you, too, can create stars as handsome as the chap above.

First *Dragon Age* 24-hour marathon winner

On 28 October 2009, six days before the release of *Dragon Age: Origins*, Electronic Arts staged a 24-hr gaming tournament in London, UK, with a cash prize of $50,000 (£30,395) at stake. Ten four-man teams comprising fans from around the globe competed in the anticipated RPG's Warden's Quest, scoring points for mission completion, enemies killed, achievements unlocked and areas explored. Team Hungary won the event, with each of its members returning home with $12,500 (£7,598.75). A team selected from BioWare's own community came second, and Canada finished third.

Most critically acclaimed BioWare games

Game	Platform	Release date	Rating
Mass Effect 2	Xbox 360	Jan 2010	95.77%
Star Wars: Knights of the Old Republic	Xbox	Jul 2003	94.21%
Baldur's Gate II: Shadows of Amn	PC	Sep 2000	93.97%
Mass Effect 3	Xbox 360	Mar 2012	92.17%
Baldur's Gate	PC	Dec 1998	91.94%
Mass Effect	Xbox 360	Nov 2007	91.24%
Dragon Age: Origins	PC	Nov 2009	90.63%
Dragon Age: Inquisition	PS4	Nov 2014	89.68%
Jade Empire	Xbox	Apr 2005	89.46%
Neverwinter Nights	PC	Jun 2002	88.98%

Source: GameRankings as of 7 April 2015

Tips 'n' Tricks

Got achy feet and looking for a mount to ride? You'll be pleased to know that ridable creatures can be obtained early in *Dragon Age: Inquisition*. Seek out the side quest "Master of Horses", which can be found in the west of the Hinterlands map. If you agree to help make the road traversable for the Horsemaster's steeds, the gracious NPC will gift you a Ferelden Forder all of your own. You'll find plenty of other mounts throughout the game – 30 different types in total – that can be purchased, found in the wild or won by completing specific side-quests.

Most unique NPCs in a videogame

The Elder Scrolls Online (2014) has 10,202 unique non-player characters, i.e., those controlled by the game instead of the player. Notable examples include "King of Worms" Mannimarco; gifted commander Jorunn the Skald-King; goddess of love Dibella; powerful god Arkay; Thieves Guild patron Nocturnal; and the enslaving prince Molag Bal.

1 Position reached by *The Elder Scrolls* in a vote to find the "Greatest Game Series of the Decade" on website GameSpot in 2013. It beat *Grand Theft Auto* in the final with 52.5% of the vote.

Summary: The huge, intricate open worlds of *The Elder Scrolls*, from Morrowind to Skyrim, offer engrossing adventures. Fans and critics alike laud the series for its freedom: players can be whoever they wish and do whatever they like… be it heroic or villainous.

Publisher: Bethesda
Developer: Various
Debut: 1994

Best-selling RPG for Xbox

The Elder Scrolls III: Morrowind (2002, above) had sold 2.86 million copies worldwide on the original Xbox as of 26 March 2015. The **best-selling RPG for Xbox 360**, meanwhile, is *The Elder Scrolls V: Skyrim* (2011). It's also the **fastest-selling RPG for Xbox 360**, with first-week sales of 1.82 million and overall sales of 8.36 million.

First player to be crowned Emperor in *The Elder Scrolls Online*

On 30 March 2014, during *The Elder Scrolls Online*'s Early Access period, "Morkulth" was crowned Emperor on the Dawnbreaker campaign. "It was," he admitted, "a little nerve-wracking."

Most critically acclaimed first-person RPG

As of 16 March 2015, *The Elder Scrolls V: Skyrim* (which can be played in first- or third-person), scored 95.15% from 75 reviews on GameRankings. This places it in the site's top 30 All-Time Best chart. "An absolutely captivating experience," enthused Destructoid.com.

Fastest completion of *Morrowind*

On 7 May 2014, a gamer named "Fatalis" raced through *The Elder Scrolls III: Morrowind* in just 3 min 14 sec, following a similar path to previous record holder "Pendrokar" (Latvia) and making use of levitation spells and jumping through walls.

Longest RPG marathon

"The Great Falls Gamers" (Jeff Nation, J J Locke, Casey Coffman, George Vogl and Jeff Sagedal of the Montana State University College of Technology, USA) spent 48 hr 14 min on 6–8 May 2012 playing *The Elder Scrolls V: Skyrim*. They previously held an FPS marathon record, having played *Battlefield: Bad Company 2* for 51 hr.

First *Elder Scrolls* action-adventure game

Not all *Elder Scrolls* have been epic RPGs: Bethesda's *The Elder Scrolls Adventures: Redguard* (1998) was a linear action-adventure inspired by *Prince of Persia* and *Tomb Raider*. It was also the first – and so far only – *Elder Scrolls* game that did not allow players to make their own characters.

Most readable books in a videogame

The Elder Scrolls Online contains a total of 2,235 readable books, including tantalizing titles such as *Desert Delicacies* and *Alchemical Misconceptions*. If you took the time to read them all, you would digest about 480,000 words in total – approximately 25,000 more than are in the first *Lord of the Rings* book, and five times as many as are in *The Hobbit*.

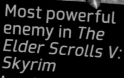

Most powerful enemy in *The Elder Scrolls V: Skyrim*

Appearing only on Level 81 or higher, the fearsome Ebony Warrior can inflict paralysis, is 50% resistant to all status effects, and uses a sword that drains the player's powers while renewing his own.

D.Y.K.?

At the time of the first *Elder Scrolls* game – 1994's *Arena* – Bethesda was best known for its hockey and FPS *Terminator* titles. There was therefore little rejoicing when *Arena* hit the shelves, not least thanks to a misleading title: arena combat was dropped before the coding stage, and designer Vijay Lakshman had no more idea than anyone else what "The Elder Scrolls" meant. Nonetheless, the game overcame a mixed reception to earn a cult following and a sequel.

Least-completed *Skyrim* achievement on Steam

The PC version of *The Elder Scrolls V: Skyrim* is one of Steam's most popular titles. However, as of 16 March 2015, of the tens of thousands of players enjoying the game every day, only 2% have earned the Dragonrider achievement, awarded for taming and riding five dragons in the *Dragonborn* add-on.

The **most completed *Skyrim* achievement on Steam**, as of the same date, is Unbound, earned by 86.6% of players. This achievement is unlocked by finishing the introductory section, which means 13.4% of wannabe Elder Scrollers didn't even get that far.

Largest playable area in an RPG

The Elder Scrolls II: Daggerfall (1996) used a map of randomly generated terrain covering a virtual 161,600 km² (62,394 sq mi, or about the size of Tunisia) – the largest fixed map size of the entire series. It contained 15,000 towns and dungeons, and 750,000 non-player characters. The area with the most locations is the Wrothgarian Mountains.

Best-selling Xbox 360 RPGs

Game	Publisher	Year	Global sales
The Elder Scrolls V: Skyrim	Bethesda	2011	8.36 million
Fable III	Microsoft	2010	5.04 million
Fallout 3	Bethesda	2008	4.54 million
The Elder Scrolls IV: Oblivion	2K	2006	4.27 million
Fable II	Microsoft	2008	4.23 million
Fallout: New Vegas	Bethesda	2010	3.79 million
Mass Effect 2	Electronic Arts	2010	3.08 million
Mass Effect 3	Electronic Arts	2012	2.97 million
Mass Effect	Microsoft	2007	2.88 million
Dragon Age: Origins	Electronic Arts	2009	2.53 million

Source: VGChartz as of 13 March 2015

FABLE

Summary: You've got to love a game that features dialogue such as, "Chicken chasing, that makes you a true hero." From the mind of Peter Molyneux, these beautifully crafted, very English RPGs are enjoyed by millions of fans. The news that *Fable Legends* is set to be a free2play game heralds an exciting new chapter for the series.

Publisher: Microsoft
Developer: Lionhead
Debut: 2004

Farthest distance to kick a chicken in a videogame

Fable tasks players with kicking virtual chickens into scoring zones, and records the greatest distance of these feats. Gamer Mike Morrow reigns supreme with a 52.24-yd (47.77-m) boot recorded on 10 April 2005.

First RPG to win a PETA award

PETA (People for the Ethical Treatment of Animals) named *Fable II* "the most animal-friendly game" of 2008, owing to it awarding players "purity" points for eating non-meat products and "corruption" points for eating meat.

The overall record for the **first videogame to win a PETA award** was set by *Nintendogs* in 2006.

First asymmetric multiplayer *Fable* game

Previous titles in the series have featured co-operative play, but *Fable Legends* (due out in 2015) is taking a different route with a multiplayer mode that pitches four playable heroes against a single playable villain. The heroes can be controlled from a traditional third-person perspective by up to four individual players, with a computer AI taking control of any for whom there is not a player available. But the villain has a wider, god-like perspective and is able to select and place enemy units for the heroes to fight around the map.

D.Y.K.?

In *Fable*'s Lychfield Graveyard there's a reference to *Pirates of the Caribbean*, with one tombstone reading: "Capt. J. Sparrow. A wind at your back forever, sir." This refers to a quote from *Blow* (2001) by a character played – as is Sparrow – by Johnny Depp.

D.Y.K.?

Fable III boasts one of the most star-studded voice casts in RPG history, with a line-up of 80 stars including Michael Fassbender, Ben Kingsley, Simon Pegg, Naomie Harris, Stephen Fry and John Cleese.

Fastest single-segment completion of *Fable*

On 18 March 2015, US gamer "KJFreshly" whizzed through *Fable: The Lost Chapters* in 1 hr 25 min 50 sec. This extended version of the original offers extra quests and features (none of which make any difference to fastest any% runs).

Don't bother looking for an acorn to become an oak in *Fable* – it isn't there. Designer Peter Molyneux promised players could knock one off a tree and watch it grow; an innocuous claim that became a yoke around his neck when it didn't happen. Even after he apologized on the game's messageboard ("Every feature I have ever talked about WAS in development, but not all made it"), he became, as he told Kotaku, "someone who promised acorns that didn't grow into trees".

Most viewed fan film based on *Fable III*

Fable III certainly divided reviewers. Its GameRankings score was 80.23% as of 26 March 2015, but the less complimentary "Top 32 Reasons *Fable III* Sucks!" by "AngryJoeShow" had earned a total of 3,053,283 YouTube views as of the same date.

50 Number of gargoyles you must kill in *Fable II* to be rewarded with a crossbow topped with a ram's head.

Largest criminal fine in *Fable*
You don't have to be law-abiding in *Fable*, but failure to do so will attract large fines that keep growing as long as you keep breaking the rules – at least until you're caught. Bad boy gamer Mike Morrow (see above left) had amassed fines totalling 1,019,050 in gold, as of 10 April 2005.

On the same date, Morrow also achieved the **highest score in *Fable*'s knothole archery contest**. In-game prizes are offered to anyone scoring over 200, and Morrow won a whopping 617 points.

Fastest completion of *Fable II*

"DarkLightBoco" from Quebec, Canada, finished *Fable II* in just 3 hr 10 sec on 20 December 2014, beating his previous record by 8 min 28 sec. "I'll take a little break from this game for now," he wrote on YouTube. "But I want to beat it one more time to get it under three hours."

Evolution of Mario

The world's most famous game character turns 35 in 2016 – that's three-and-a-half decades of coin collecting, mushroom chomping and Koopa stomping! Here, we pick out some of the highlights from Mario's career.

MAKING A BUNDLE

When *Super Mario Bros.* was bundled together with the NES in 1985, it proved an irresistible combination. The result was sales of 40.24 million, making it the best-selling *Mario* game.

Sibling rivalry

Wii U expansion pack *New Super Luigi U* (2013) was released to celebrate the 30th anniversary of the debut of Mario's brother, Luigi. It's the **first platformer in the *Mario* series not to feature Mario.** As of 15 April 2015, it had sold 2.06 million units.

SHINING STAR

As of 7 April 2015, Mario had **appeared in a staggering 265 videogames.** According to review aggregator GameRankings, the most critically acclaimed *Mario* game is 2007's *Super Mario Galaxy*, with a score of 97.64%. The innovative 3D platformer broke the rules of gravity as Mario ventured into space and explored other planets.

HANDHELD HIT

Taking Mario on a quest to rescue Princess Peach from Bowser, 2006's *New Super Mario Bros.* boasted sales of 29.66 million as of 15 April 2015 – **making it the best-selling non-bundled *Mario* game and also the best-selling DS game overall.**

1981
DONKEY KONG
(Atari 2600)
Mario made his debut in this arcade game, designed by Shigeru Miyamoto.

Sales
1.46
million

1983
MARIO BROS.
(Atari 2600)
This title saw Mario change profession from carpenter to plumber.

Sales
1.59
million

1985
SUPER MARIO BROS.
(Famicom/NES)
The game that propelled Mario to global stardom.

Sales
40.42
million

1989
SUPER MARIO LAND
(Game Boy)
For Mario's first handheld outing, 12 fun-packed levels were crammed on to one Game Boy cartridge.

Sales
18.14
million

1990
SUPER MARIO WORLD
(Super Famicom/SNES)
The arrival of a certain blue hedgehog made Nintendo nervous. But *Super Mario World* went on to sell more copies than the first two *Sonic* games combined.

Sales
20.61
million

1992
SUPER MARIO KART
(Super Famicom/SNES)
Mario traded in platforms for crazy racetracks, and the result was a pioneering kart-racer that spawned a stream of imitators.

Sales
8.76
million

Disaster movie

Released on 28 May 1993, *Super Mario Bros.* was the **first feature film based directly on a videogame.** Despite its strong cast and box-office returns of $20 million (£12.83 million), production costs of $50 million (£32 million) meant it was a huge flop.

This Ain't No Game.
SUPER MARIO BROS.

CHAIN REACTION

Over the course of his career, Mario has faced off with 1,925 different types of enemies and 588 bosses. Some of the enemies have been inspired by real-life characters and events. For example, Shigeru Miyamoto got the idea for the chain chomp baddies in *Super Mario Bros.* 3 from a dog on a chain who tried to chase him when he was a child.

GHOST STORY

The ghostly Boos in *Super Mario 64* were based on the wife of designer Takashi Tezuka. "His wife is very quiet normally, but one day she exploded, maddened by all the time he spent at work," said Shigeru Miyamoto.

What's in a name?

Mario was originally called Jumpman, before Nintendo changed his name in honour of their landlord, Mario Segale. The plucky plumber's nemesis is Wario (right), whose name is a simple combination of "Mario" and the word "warui", Japanese for "bad".

1995

SUPER MARIO WORLD 2: YOSHI'S ISLAND
(SNES)
Mario's dinosaur-like companion Yoshi proved so popular that he got his own instalment as he carried around an infant Mario on his back.

2002

SUPER MARIO SUNSHINE
(GameCube)
In this game, Mario could travel vertically for the first time with the help of FLUDD (Flash Liquidizer Ultra Dousing Device).

2006

NEW SUPER MARIO BROS.
(DS)
Returning to their roots for this handheld smash, Mario and Luigi set off to rescue Princess Peach from Bowser.

2007

MARIO & SONIC AT THE OLYMPIC GAMES
(Wii)
The old console rivals were united for the first time in this licensed sports outing for the 2008 Beijing Olympics.

2009

NEW SUPER MARIO BROS. Wii
(Wii)
Featuring simultaneous multiplayer, this was also the first side-scrolling *Mario* game to feature four-player action.

2011

SUPER MARIO 3D LAND
(3DS)
This game mixed side-scrolling and free-roaming level designs to create another unique instalment in the series. It also presented Mario's environment in stereoscopic 3D.

Sales
4.12
million

Sales
6.31
million

Sales
29.66
million

Sales
7.97
million

Sales
27.94
million

Sales
10.08
million

FALLOUT

Fastest completion of *Fallout 3*

A French gamer known as "Rydou" achieved a single-segment run in a super-fast time of 18 min 53 sec, as recorded on 25 March 2015. With such fine margins at stake, Rydou exploited several glitches. "Every time you quickload, the collision detection doesn't work for about 10 frames, allowing me to clip through objects and walls," he explained.

D.Y.K.?

The super mutants in *Fallout* were created by "The Master", whose birth name, Richard Moreau, was inspired by the scientist in H G Wells' *The Island of Dr Moreau* (1896).

4 *Fallout* appearances by Harold, a human whose Forced Evolutionary Virus mutates him into a living tree with a face in its trunk – the **most character appearances in the *Fallout* series**.

Summary: The *Fallout* series is set in a post-apocalyptic USA, where nuclear war has left the country a wasteland populated with mutants and ghouls, and sparse pockets of humanity cower in fallout shelters known as "Vaults".

Publisher: Interplay/ Bethesda Softworks
Developer: Various
Debut: 1997

Most crowdfunded *Fallout* project

The second season of the popular *Fallout: Nuka Break* web series raised $130,746 (£83,719) by 17 June 2012, via crowdfunding platform Kickstarter. Series producers Wayside Creations had asked for $60,000 (£38,419), but interest in the project saw them double their target.

Rarest RPG for a seventh–gen console

The limited-edition *Fallout 3: Survival Edition* (2008), exclusive to Amazon, offered a host of goodies including a DVD, art booklet, a Pip-Boy 3000 replica and Vault Boy bobblehead, and a Vault-Tec lunchbox. By 2014, sealed versions were fetching more than $700 (£400).

Most popular fan-made *Fallout* film

Wayside Creations' *Nuka Break* follows ex-Vault dweller Twig (Zack Finfrock) and his companions Scarlett (Tybee Diskin) and ghoul Ben (Aaron Giles) as they travel the *Fallout* wastelands in search of a bottle of Nuka-Cola. The film had been viewed 2,873,316 times on YouTube as of 25 March 2015.

Most popular mod for *Fallout: New Vegas*

It might not be the most downloaded *F:NV* mod (see right), but as of 25 March 2015 *Project Nevada* had received the most endorsements on the Nexus mods website – 40,154. It offers a host of features including enhanced vision modes and "Bullet Time", which can slow down in-game time.

Most-downloaded mod for *Fallout: New Vegas*

As of 24 March 2015, a total of 2,385,731 users of the Nexus mods site had downloaded *Weapon Mods Expanded – WMX*. Coded by Joseph Lollback, it brings further enhancements to *Fallout: New Vegas*'s weapons-modding system.

Largest world in a *Fallout* game

Set in the year 2277 – 200 years since war laid waste to the Earth – *Fallout 3* (2008) presents a gamescape of traversable land estimated at 15 sq mi (24 km²). Known as the Capital Wasteland, the area comprises the ruined remnants of Vaults and other settlements in Washington DC, USA.

Fastest completion of *Fallout 2*

On 10 January 2014, French gamer "ZombySpootchy" (aka Florent) steered the Chosen One hero through the post-apocalyptic sequel, saving the villagers of Arroyo in a blistering single-segment time of 14 min 59.33 sec.

Most prolific developer of RPG sequels

When it comes to producing sequels to other companies' role-playing games, California-based developer Obsidian has worked up an impressive CV. As of February 2015, Obsidian had developed sequels for four RPG franchises: *Star Wars: Knights of the Old Republic II* (2004), *Neverwinter Nights 2* (2006), *Fallout: New Vegas* (2010) and *Dungeon Siege III* (2011).

Fittingly, in 2014 Obsidian was also involved in the development of *Wasteland 2* – the long-awaited sequel to the seminal 1987 post-apocalyptic RPG that is widely considered to be the "spiritual godfather" of the *Fallout* series.

Most lines of dialogue in a single-player RPG

Fallout: New Vegas boasts 65,000 lines of dialogue, including those delivered by famous actors such as *Hellboy* star Ron Perlman.

Fastest-selling *Fallout* game

On 28 October–4 November 2008, *Fallout 3* sold an incredible 4.7 million copies worldwide during its first week of sale.

Fastest segmented completion of *Fallout*

On 22 July 2010, Vault-dweller Jakub "Fex" Surma (Poland) raced across the post-apocalyptic wastelands of Southern California, USA, and out-fought mutants, deathclaws and the Master himself to complete the original *Fallout* in an astonishing 6 min 54 sec. The super-fast run was completed in five segments.

Most played RPGs by the TrueAchievements Xbox community

Game	Publisher	Players	Players unlocking all achievements
Fallout 3	Bethesda	165,182	14.13%
Fable II	Microsoft	163,520	8.49%
The Elder Scrolls V: Skyrim	Bethesda	160,836	7.36%
Borderlands	2K Games	155,819	10.86%
Fable III	Microsoft	154,839	4.40%
Mass Effect	Electronic Arts	144,815	8.40%
The Elder Scrolls IV: Oblivion	Bethesda	134,114	22.95%
Borderlands 2	2K Games	127,612	8.57%
Dead Island	Deep Silver	127,046	5.80%
Mass Effect 2	Electronic Arts	119,194	11.63%

Source: www.trueachievements.com as of 11 May 2015

Tips 'n' Tricks

Whether it's *Duck and Cover!*, *Pugilism Illustrated* or even *US Army: 30 Handy Flamethrower Recipes*, useful books are scattered throughout the *Fallout 3* wasteland. Reading them will permanently raise a player's corresponding skill by one point. (By obtaining the Comprehension perk early in the game, this can be increased to two points.) Most skill books are considered to have no owner, even when found in someone's belongings, so taking them will not result in a loss of Karma.

FAR CRY

Summary: An open-world first-person shooter series, *Far Cry* challenges gamers to survive in exotic and dangerous locations, ranging from the snowy peaks of the Himalayas to the sun-baked African savannah. A map-editing program allows players to shape and share their environment.

Publisher: Ubisoft
Developer: Crytek/Ubisoft
Debut: 2004

First game to use CryEngine technology

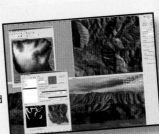

The now-widespread CryEngine tech was used to develop the first *Far Cry* game in 2004. It has since spawned two major engine lineages in the form of CryEngine and Ubisoft's Dunia Engine, which have powered all *Far Cry* games since.

Tips 'n' Tricks

The natural world plays a key role in the *Far Cry* series, and in *Far Cry 4* animals can be both friend and foe to the unwary gamer. They might not be the quickest mode of transportation, but elephants can be a safe and sturdy vehicle once you've learned how to ride them – and they can also tip enemy vehicles over the cliffs with their trunks. The honey badger might sound cute but, in fact, it is a fast and savage predator, to be avoided at all costs.

9
Number of lead characters to choose from in *Far Cry 2*, each with their own backstory, after the original's hero Jack Carver was deemed insufficiently engaging and replaced.

Most weapons in a *Far Cry* game

The original *Far Cry* featured 19 different weapons, but as the series has developed so has the choice of armaments. *Far Cry 4* included everything from handguns and C4 explosives to rocket launchers and bows and arrows (above), totalling 52 types – 13 more than *Far Cry 3*'s previous record of 39.

Most viewed *Far Cry* video

VanossGaming's fan-made video for *Far Cry 4*, entitled "Far Cry 4 Funny Moments – Crocodile, Honey Badger 1v1, Body Glitch (Next Level Hunting)", is the most popular *Far Cry* video on YouTube, and had earned a total of 7,548,554 views as of 11 March 2015.

Highest-altitude game console session on land

William Cruz (USA) won a Ubisoft competition to travel to the Himalayas, the setting for *Far Cry 4*. On 11 October 2014, he played the game on an adapted console at an altitude of 5,660 m (18,569 ft) at Kala Patthar, Nepal.

Worst-rated Wii videogame

A remake of the Xbox's *Far Cry Instincts: Evolution* – which aggregated 76.62% on GameRankings – *Far Cry Vengeance* for Wii (2006) was criticized for its graphics, and the full-motion video was deemed overly compressed. As of 19 March 2015, it had a score of just 37.71%.

Fastest completion of *Far Cry*

Gamer Vladimir "Knu" Semenov set the speed-run record for the original *Far Cry* on 20 January 2006, with a super-fast time of 1 hr 7 min 2 sec. The **fastest any-percentage completion of *Far Cry 3: Blood Dragon*** is held by "ZanderGothSRL", who sprinted through the futuristic standalone game in 47 min dead on 6 September 2013.

Most active *Far Cry* community

As of 11 March 2015, the PS4 community had collectively played *Far Cry 4* for a total of 6,107 years 310 days – way ahead of Xbox One gamers, who had played for 3,134 years 63 days.

The **most accurate *Far Cry* shooting community** is on the PC. Collectively, PC gamers had scored a 40% accuracy headshot rating as of 11 March 2015, compared with 20% on both PS4 and Xbox One.

Best-selling *Far Cry* game

With global sales of 7.15 million as of 10 March 2015, according to VGChartz, *Far Cry 3* is the series' most successful game.

Most XP earned for outpost challenges in *Far Cry 3*

Far Cry 3 player "Gar3th_26" had racked up a mammoth 1,000,010,129 total XP during the game's outpost challenges as of 11 March 2015.

Most popular weapon class in *Far Cry 4*

Assault rifles are the weapon of choice for *Far Cry 4* gamers. They had been used to log 3,431,820,773 kills across all platforms, as of 11 March 2015. Sniper rifles take second place, with 1.62 million kills.

Rarest *Far Cry 4* trophy/achievement on PS4

Typically, "Platinum" achievements are the rarest trophies in PlayStation games as they require players to collect every other trophy in the game first. As such, *Far Cry 4*'s coveted "Master of Kyrat" platinum trophy on PS4 had been achieved by just 2.7% of players as of 19 March 2015.

Most downloaded mod for *Far Cry 3* on PC

With 90,355 unique downloads as of 11 March 2015, "Ziggy's Mod" is the most downloaded player-made addition to *Far Cry 3* for PC. Released on the Nexus Mods site by "Dziggy" in 2013, it adds a number of tweaks to the game and unlocks all content at the start.

The **most downloaded mod for *Far Cry 4*** is "FC4 Attachments Mod" by "jvarnes", which allows players greater customization of their original weapons. It has clocked 2,503 unique downloads.

D.Y.K.?

When Ubisoft published a teaser video for *Far Cry 3: Blood Dragon* on 1 April 2013, it led some gamers to think that the retro-futuristic game was an elaborate April Fools' joke.

 # FIFA

Summary: Debuting in 1993, when top-down soccer games were all the rage, EA's *FIFA* has been honing sporting realism and TV-like presentation for more than 20 years. The series is packed with licenced clubs and stars, while its addictive "Ultimate Team" mode lets you manage fantasy teams online.

Publisher: EA
Developer: Various
Debut: 1993

Longest marathon on a soccer videogame

On 5–7 November 2014, Chris Cook (UK) played *FIFA 15* for an incredible 48 hr 49 min 41 sec at the Loading Bar gaming café in Dalston, London, UK. The event was organized to raise money for SpecialEffect, a charity for disabled gamers. Despite losing the feeling in his hands as his marathon wore on, Chris rallied to win his final two matches. His excursion is also the **longest marathon for a sports videogame**.

D.Y.K.?

One of *FIFA 15*'s major innovations is Emotional Intelligence. On-pitch events can cause players to feel 600 emotions, which play a key role in determining whether or not they're celebrating come the final whistle.

991,000

Number of in-game goals scored every 90 min by *FIFA 14* players, according to figures released by publisher EA Sports in the run-up to the 2014 World Cup.

Most consecutive ball juggles in one minute in *FIFA 14* (multi)

On 19 August 2014, Shawn Alvarez (USA) managed 166 consecutive ball juggles. Along with Edoardo Lo Baido (Italy), Shawn also holds the title for **most consecutive crossbar hits in one minute** – four, achieved on 22 September 2014.

Top goalscorer in *FIFA 14*

As of 21 November 2013, *FIFA 14* players had scored 35.2 million goals using Portugal's Cristiano Ronaldo – ahead of his Real Madrid team-mate Karim Benzema (France) in second place, with 26.7 million.

Highest-earning *FIFA* videogame player

In 2013, Ivan "BorasLegend" Lapanje (Sweden) pocketed $145,378 (£93,735) from two *FIFA 13* tournaments and one *FIFA 14* event. The majority of his earnings – $140,000 (£90,267) – came from winning the EA Sports FIFA Challenge 2013 in Las Vegas, Nevada, USA, on 9 February 2013.

Highest margin of victory against the computer on *FIFA 14*
Patrick Hadler (Germany) managed to win a 90-min game by 322 goals on 31 March 2014. This betters his own mark of 307 goals that he set playing the previous *FIFA* game – the **highest margin of victory against the computer on *FIFA 13***.

Most licenced leagues in a sports simulation game
Improving on *FIFA 14*'s quota of 33, *FIFA 15* features 35 licenced leagues from around the globe, ranging from Italy's Serie A to the South Korean K League. The game also boasts more than 600 clubs and 16,000 players.

Highest margin of victory in *FIFA Street*

FIFA Street takes the beautiful game back to the streets. On 8 June 2007, Jonathan Mee (UK) thrashed the computer by a 22-goal winning margin. The **highest score on *FIFA Street*** is held by Jonathan's brother Andrew, who scored 222,774 points in a 12-min game on 7 August 2006.

Most controllable players in a sports videogame

Since *FIFA 11*, gamers have been able to participate in 11-versus-11 matches in which every player on the pitch can be controlled, including goalkeepers. These 22-person matches are limited to the "Online Team Play" multiplayer mode and can only be played with an internet connection.

Highest-rated player in *FIFA 15*
At the launch of *FIFA 15*, Lionel Messi of Barcelona and Argentina had a rating of 93 out of 100, one higher than long-standing rival Cristiano Ronaldo (Portugal).
The **highest-rated midfielder in *FIFA 15*** is Arjen Robben (Netherlands) with 90, one point higher than Andrés Iniesta (Spain).

Longest-running soccer videogame series
As of May 2015, *FIFA* had been running for 22 years, with yearly updates since 1993, making it the veteran of the genre.

Most transferred *FIFA 14* "Ultimate Team" player

Introduced in *FIFA 09*, "Ultimate Team" mode challenges players to assemble their best real-life squads on a budget and compete in online and offline tournaments. According to EA stats released in the build-up to the 2014 World Cup, Belgian striker Christian Benteke was the most transferred player.

Best-selling sports videogame series

As of 29 April 2015, EA's *FIFA* series had generated net-busting global sales of 146.13 million, according to VGChartz. Its nearest rival is EA's own *Madden NFL* series, with sales of 110.56 million across all platforms. *FIFA 14* has sold 16.55 million copies alone, making it the **best-selling soccer videogame**.

FINAL FANTASY

Summary: Since its debut in the late 1980s, this innovative and record-breaking fantasy RPG – created by Hironobu Sakaguchi – has spawned a series of highly successful games and offshoots that include movies, a radio station and even an eatery.

Publisher: Square/ Square Enix
Developer: Square/ Square Enix
Debut: 1987

87

In 2001, *Final Fantasy* character Aki Ross was voted 87 in Maxim magazine's "Hot 100" – making her the first computer-generated character ever to make the list. She also featured on the cover.

First all-female playable cast in an RPG

Released for PlayStation 2 on 13 March 2003, *Final Fantasy X-2* revolves around three main playable characters: Yuna and Rikku from *Final Fantasy X*, plus new character Paine (below). Together they form a group known as the Gullwings, who hunt the world of Spira for precious spheres. All three characters are female, marking the first time that an RPG has offered a line-up exclusively comprised of heroines.

D.Y.K.?

A new playable character in *Final Fantasy X-2*, Paine (above) sports a "punk" appearance. However, the developer was initially considering a softer "pop-star" look.

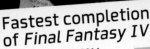

Best-selling Final Fantasy games

Game	Platform	Release date	Units sold
Final Fantasy VII	PS	1997	9.72 million
Final Fantasy X	PS2	2001	8.05 million
Final Fantasy VIII	PS	1999	7.86 million
Final Fantasy XII	PS2	2006	5.95 million
Final Fantasy IX	PS	2000	5.30 million
Final Fantasy X-2	PS2	2003	5.29 million
Final Fantasy XIII	PS3	2009	5.26 million
Final Fantasy III	SNES	1994	3.42 million
Crisis Core: Final Fantasy VII	PSP	2007	3.14 million
Final Fantasy XIII-2	PS3	2011	2.65 million

Source: VGChartz as of 6 March 2015

Fastest completion of Final Fantasy IV

On 28 November 2014, David "the_roth" Rothall completed Final Fantasy IV (known originally as Final Fantasy II outside of Japan) in an astounding time of just 2 hr 52 sec.

Most prolific Final Fantasy creature

The chicken-like Chocobo has been a recurring feature of the Final Fantasy series since 1988. It has appeared in 62 games in total as of 22 April 2015, including games outside of Final Fantasy, such as Kingdom Hearts and Dragon Quest VI.

First complete Final Fantasy remake in another game

LittleBigPlanet player and avid RPG fan Jamie Colliver didn't want to wait for an official remake of Final Fantasy VII. Instead, he decided to spend two years recreating the entire game using the creation tools in LittleBigPlanet – a mammoth task that involved making 107 separate videos.

Largest budget for a JRPG

With a reported $45 million (£27.3 million) spent on production, and a $100-million (£60.6-million) promotion campaign with adverts in prime-time slots during Saturday Night Live and The Simpsons, 1997's Final Fantasy VII had the biggest JRPG budget. Adjusted for inflation, the 2015 equivalent figure is closer to $215 million (£144 million).

Longest development period for a JRPG

Originally intended as the spin-off title Final Fantasy Versus XIII, the enormously anticipated Final Fantasy XV has been in development for almost nine years, having first entered the studio in May 2006. As of March 2015, it was still without a release date.

Technically impressive and hugely ambitious, the game will be the first title to use Square Enix's Luminous Studio middleware engine. In 2011, the studio developed a tech demo to show off the new engine's capabilities. From conception to finish, the showcase took a year to create, making it one of the longest ever development periods for a tech demo.

Most wanted PlayStation remake

In a poll by Sony in December 2014, a total of 10,000 gamers voted Final Fantasy VII as the series entry they would most like to see remade.

First RPG music used at the Olympics

The American synchronized swimming team of Alison Bartosik and Anna Kozlova were awarded bronze medals at the 2004 Olympic Games in Athens, Greece, for their performance to two Final Fantasy VIII tracks – "Fithos Lusec Wecos Vinosec" and "Liberi Fatali".

Best-selling Japanese RPG

With worldwide sales of 9.72 million as of March 2015, Final Fantasy VII is the best-selling single-edition JRPG. It is also the second best-selling game on the original PlayStation, after Gran Turismo.

Most expensive animated film inspired by a videogame

Final Fantasy: The Spirits Within (2001) cost $137 million (£96.7 million) to make, but it recouped only $85.1 million (£58.6 million). The overall **most expensive videogame-inspired film** is Prince of Persia: The Sands of Time (2010) – shot for some $200 million (£129.3 million) according to The Numbers, it made $314.6 million (£212.6 million).

FORZA

Summary: Driving lessons? Road tax? Fuel price rises? No, thank you. Keep the real cars in the garage and put the pedal to the metal with this critically acclaimed and multi-million-selling motorsports sim. Alongside Polyphony Digital's *Gran Turismo* franchise, it's *the* series for discerning drivers.

Publisher: Microsoft
Developer: Turn 10, Playground, Sumo
Debut: 2005

Fastest speed in a sim version of a real car

In *Forza Motorsport 5* (Turn 10, 2013), players can choose a fully upgraded and tuned Nissan GT-R R35 Black Edition, then enjoy their nerves being shredded by the greatest speed available for a simulated version of a genuine car: 284 mph (457 km/h).

Longest set-distance race in a racing game

At 20.99 km (13.04 mi), the Nürburgring Nordschleife in *Forza Motorsport* is slightly longer than the real thing's regular simple configuration of 20.8 km (12.9 mi). The track also appears in *Gran Turismo*, *TOCA Race Driver* and *Project Gotham Racing*.

Highest-earning players on *Forza Motorsport 2*
According to standings on eSportsEarnings.com, David "Daveyskills" Kelly and Dean "Picaso" Sutton (both UK) – competing as Birmingham Salvo – each earned $62,500 (£43,165) from sealing the top spot in the 2008 Championship Gaming Series season.

"Daveyskills" also bagged himself a further $7,000 (£4,525) from competing in *Forza Motorsport 3* at the 2010 World Cyber Games.

Most sim-racing videogames in one decade

Boasting Ford's GT supercar, Mustang Shelby GT350 and F-150 Raptor, 2015's *Forza Motorsport 6* celebrates the series' 10th anniversary. Since it got into gear in May 2005 with *Forza Motorsport* on the original Xbox, a further seven games have joined the race: *Forza 2* (2007), *3* (2009), *4* (2011), *Horizon* (2012), *5* (2013), *Horizon 2* (2014) and *6* (2015).

138 Track configurations in *Forza 3*, as listed on Forza Wikia. With 18 at Tuscany's Sidewinder Proving Grounds alone, it has the **most track configurations in any racing sim game**.

A questionable honour perhaps, but *Top Gear*'s love-him-or-hate-him host Jeremy Clarkson has been associated with the series since *Forza Motorsport 4* (Xbox 360, 2011). Clarkson offers commentary in the game's Autovista mode.

Most participants in a racing game relay

A total of 49 participants took part in a racing videogame relay on 5 June 2014. Audi AG set the record at Audi City Berlin in Germany.

First team garages in a racing game

Players once formed alliances by adding prefixes to their gamertags. *Forza*, however, offers an in-game garage environment, so you can drive alone or as part of a team. Share a garage with other members of a "Forza Club" and you can paint your vehicles in team colours. As with social networking, you can constantly enlarge your circle of allies.

Most downloadable cars

Since *Forza Motorsport 4* shot off the starting line in October 2011, a total of 176 vehicles have been added to the game via monthly instalments of downloadable content. These include the 1995 Ford Mustang SVT Cobra R, the 1956 Lotus Eleven (in real life, Lotus' most successful race car) and the 1958 Austin-Healey Sprite Mark I, aka the "Frogeye".

Fastest completion of *Forza 5*'s Triple Crown (team of two)

This record was set in 3 hr 4 min 38 sec by race drivers Ho-Pin Tung (Netherlands) and David Cheng (USA), who beat 21 other two-driver teams at an Xbox *Forza* event at Shanghai's World Financial Center on 7 November 2014.

Highest-rated *Forza* game

As of 16 March 2015 the best-rated *Forza* games are the first and third, sharing a 92% rating on Metacritic. The **worst-rated *Forza* game** is *Forza 5*: criticized for lacking much of 4's best content, it has a still-impressive score of 79%. This reduces *Forza*'s overall average to 85.78, just behind that of the *Gran Turismo* series.

First racing community recognized by a governing body

The Online Racing Association (TORA) is an online community for *Forza Motorsport, Need for Speed: Shift 2 Unleashed* and *F1 2010* players on the Xbox 360. In May 2010, the UK's Motor Sports Association made TORA the first sim organization to be officially recognized by a motorsports governing body.

Most complex cars in a racing game

Owing to increased processing power, there are 1 million polygons – the discrete 2D shapes used to build the cars – for every vehicle in *Forza 5*, complementing the game's 1080p resolution.

Best-selling Xbox driving videogame sim series

When it comes to beating the racing competition, *Forza* is the king of the Xbox grid. Since *Forza Motorsport* revved on to Xbox in 2005, the franchise had shifted 20.26 million units as of 13 March 2015, with biggest seller *Forza Motorsport 3* amassing sales of 4.43 million on Xbox 360. The series offers detailed decal editors, presenting untold possibilities for personalizing your dream car.

Tips 'n' Tricks

Utilizing Microsoft's Kinect technology to its fullest, the fourth *Forza Motorsport* title is the **first racing simulator to track players' head motions** and reflect it in the game. ("One of the first proper uses for Kinect outside ass-shaking and party tricks," noted Kotaku.com approvingly.) Move your head to the left or right, and the Kinect peripheral translates it directly into the game. This enables you to inspect the cars thoroughly, and gives you more control of what you see on screen, with fewer blind spots and better visibility when using the bonnet-cam view.

GEARS OF WAR

Fastest-selling TPS

According to VGChartz, *Gears of War 3* sold 3 million copies in its first week on sale following its release on 20 September 2011 – more than the combined first-week sales of *GoW* and *GoW2*. In fact, the game was breaking records months before players could even get their hands on it. More than a million fans had placed pre-orders for the game by May 2011, making it the **most pre-ordered Xbox 360 videogame**.

Summary: The fictional planet of Sera provides the backdrop for a bitter war between the burly heroes of Delta Squad and the vicious subterranean swarms of the Locust Horde in this highly acclaimed sci-fi third-person shooter.

Publisher: Microsoft
Developer: Epic Games/ Black Tusk Studios
Debut: 2006

780 Number of rounds carried by the Locust Horde-manufactured Hammerburst Assault Rifle, making this the **largest ammunition capacity for a Gears of War weapon**.

D.Y.K.?

On 15 December 2006, *Gears of War* became the **fastest-selling Xbox 360 game from a new series**. The game sold more than 2 million copies in its first six weeks after release.

" *...Gears of War was the first multiplayer game for me that I enjoyed...*"

Game designer Tim Schafer

D.Y.K.?

In 2010, Epic used sales of two digital T-shirts for Xbox avatars to decide whether Clay Carmine would live or die in *Gears of War 3*. Luckily for Carmine, sales of the "Save Carmine" T-shirt outsold those with the slogan "Carmine Must Die".

Tips 'n' Tricks

Cover plays a crucial role in *Gears of War*, and gamers can use their surroundings to protect their character from incoming fire. All the inhabitants of the planet Sera are right-handed, giving smart players an opportunity to take advantage. Keeping characters to the far right-hand side of all cover ensures that they present the smallest possible target to an enemy, while also offering the best shot back. This is especially true in one-on-one battles, where even the slightest edge could mean the difference between life and death.

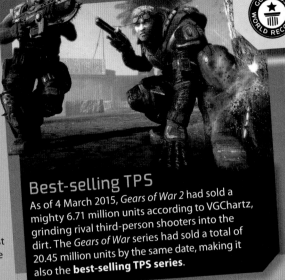

Best-selling TPS

As of 4 March 2015, *Gears of War 2* had sold a mighty 6.71 million units according to VGChartz, grinding rival third-person shooters into the dirt. The *Gears of War* series had sold a total of 20.45 million units by the same date, making it also the **best-selling TPS series**.

Most MLG National Championships wins for a *Gears of War* team
The pioneering eSports organization MLG hosted *Gears of War* 4v4 (2007–08) and *Gears of War 2* 4v4 (2009) contests at its National Championships. After finishing runners-up to US team Infinity at the 2007

Championships, TH3 NSAN3Z (USA) won in 2008 and 2009, when both tournaments were contested online and known as the $1000 Online Fragking Championships.

In terms of an individual gamer, the **highest-ranked *Gears of War* player** is "JamesyyFitz" (Ireland), who was top of the pile at MLG for *Gears of War 3*. As of 17 March 2015, he had clocked up 1,718 points with 579 wins and 65 losses.

Fastest co-op completion of *Gears of War*
Veteran speed-runners "Youkai" (aka William Welch) and "Brassmaster" (aka Andrew Meredith) completed the co-op campaign on *Gears of War* in 1 hr 34 min 38 sec on 28 November 2011.

The **fastest completion of *Gears of War 2* on "Casual" difficulty** was set on 19 May 2013 by Canada's "zzDAZZLEzz", who stormed through the game, with no restarts, in 3 hr 56 min 48 sec. The same gamer also achieved the **fastest single-segment completion of *Gears of War: Judgment* on "Casual" difficulty**, in 2 hr 25 min 58 sec on 5 May 2013.

First Xbox 360 game to sell out in Japan
Given the previous lack of popularity for shooters in Japan, it was no small achievement when *GoW* sold out following its release on 18 January 2007. The game also became the **first Xbox videogame in the Japanese top 10**, selling 33,212 units in its first week and reaching a chart position of #7.

First playable female in *Gears of War*

It wasn't until *Gears of War 3* that a female character was able to break into the super-macho world of Delta Squad. Private Samantha Byrne was voiced by Claudia Black, best known for sci-fi TV shows *Farscape* and *Stargate*.

D.Y.K.?

In March 2012, the BBC reported that various departments within the US government would adopt the Unreal Engine used in *Gears of War* in an attempt to save the vast sums of money needed to develop their own technology for training personnel.

Mobile Gaming

The popularity of mobile phone gaming has exploded, allowing players the ability to access their favourite games on the move. Independent developers are thriving, fuelling creativity and innovation, and producing global hits such as *Clash of Clans*.

CLASH OF CLANS

"The technology is simple, but it works. The art is very simple, but it's pretty. Gameplay is simple, but it has lots of depth."

Supercell, creator of Clash of Clans

$1.64 MILLION PER DAY

- *Clash of Clans* is the **top-grossing app in the Apple App Store**, as of February 2015, earning $1.64 million (£1,050,120) in daily revenue.

- *Clash of Clans* first appeared in July 2012 in Canada, in beta form and released under the code name "Magic".

CROSSY ROAD

Travel too slowly in *Crossy Road* and you'll be picked off by an eagle. To date, 185 million characters have been swept away.

As of February 2015, 40 million players had downloaded *Crossy Road*.

40 MILLION

As of January 2015, Mojang's *Minecraft: Pocket Edition* had been downloaded 30 million times.

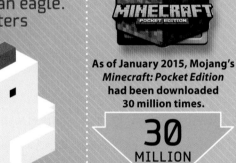

30 MILLION

Angry Birds Go! players have collectively travelled 2.1 light years (20 trillion km; 12 trillion mi) in the game.

Angry Birds players across all versions have earned 150 billion in-game reward stars. That's more stars than in our own Milky Way.

THE SIMPSONS: TAPPED OUT

On 5 November 2014, *Simpsons* creator Matt Groening was made available to *The Simpsons: Tapped Out* players as a limited-time character. Completing the "Writers Building" enabled gamers to add the legendary animator to their town.

TOP GAME PUBLISHERS OF 2014

(iOS & Google Play Game)

BY DOWNLOADS

1 KING (UK)

2 GAMELOFT (FRANCE)

3 ELECTRONIC ARTS (USA)

4 ROVIO (FINLAND)

5 GLU (USA)

6 SUPERCELL (FINLAND)

7 DISNEY (USA)

8 TENCENT (CHINA)

9 OUTFIT7 (UK)

10 LINE (JAPAN)

Source: AppAnnie

★ MOST DOWNLOADED ★
MOBILE GAMES 2014

★ TOP-GROSSING ★
MOBILE GAMES 2014

	Rank		
CANDY CRUSH SAGA (King, 2012)	1	**CLASH OF CLANS** (Supercell, 2012)	
SUBWAY SURFERS (Kiloo/SYBO Games, 2012)	2	**PUZZLE & DRAGONS** (GungHo Online Entertainment, 2012)	
MY TALKING TOM (Outfit7, 2013)	3	**CANDY CRUSH SAGA** (King, 2012)	
FARM HEROES SAGA (King, 2014)	4	**MONSTER STRIKE** (Mixi, 2013)	
CLASH OF CLANS (Supercell, 2012)	5	**GAME OF WAR: FIRE AGE** (Machine Zone, 2013)	
POU (Zakeh [aka Paul Salameh], 2012)	6	**HAY DAY** (Supercell, 2012)	
DESPICABLE ME: MINION RUSH (Gameloft, 2014)	7	**FARM HEROES SAGA** (King, 2014)	
TEMPLE RUN 2 (Imangi Studios, 2013)	8	**DISNEY TSUM TSUM** (LINE Corporation, 2014)	
DON'T TAP THE WHITE TILE (Umoni Studio/Hu Wen Zeng, 2014)	9	**THE WORLD OF MYSTIC WIZ** (COLOPL, 2013)	
HILL CLIMB RACING (Fingersoft, 2012)	10	**BRAVE FRONTIER** (A-Lim, 2013)	

Source: AppAnnie

CANDY CRUSH SAGA

"It was a bright idea that my team had. Everyone has a fondness for candy from a very early age, and it's very accessible to people because it's an inexpensive treat. It's also an international thing: flavours are different in different countries, but the colours are universal and make for a strong visual component."

***Tommy Palm, co-creator of* Candy Crush Saga**

$1.33 BILLION

In 2014, *Candy Crush Saga* players spent an amazing $1.33 billion (£832 million) on in-app purchases.

Candy Crush Saga makes a cameo in PSY's video for "Gentleman", the follow-up to the **most-viewed video ever**, "Gangnam Style".

In 2014, games made up 75% of revenue on Apple's App Store and 90% of Google Play revenue.

GOD OF WAR

Best-selling PlayStation action-adventure series

The *God of War* series has achieved global sales of 23.51 million units since the original's PS2 debut in 2005.

Meanwhile, within the series itself, *God of War III* (2010) is the **best-selling God of War game**, with sales of 4.77 million as of 6 March 2015.

Summary: Exclusive to PlayStation, this thrilling-but-bloody videogame draws upon the history and mythology of ancient Greece. Spartan hero Kratos wields his double-chained blades to brutal effect as he takes the fight to gods and monsters alike.

Publisher: Sony/Capcom
Developer: SCE Santa Monica Studio
Debut: 2005

Highest kill-to-death ratio in *God of War: Ascension*

The kill-to-death (K/D) ratio represents the average number of kills a player has achieved per single in-game life. Turkish gamer "jackaliso" holds the highest K/D ratio in the game, with 8.8 (9,448 kills and 1,080 deaths) as of 24 March 2014.

26

Number of bonus costumes available for Kratos throughout the *God of War* series – including the "Spud of War", which makes the fearsome Spartan warrior look like a giant potato.

D.Y.K.?

In 2010, music label Roadrunner released a heavy metal homage to the *God of War* series, featuring blistering tracks from Trivium, Opeth and Killswitch Engage. Entitled *God of War: Blood & Metal*, it was available as DLC and through iTunes.

"If all those on Olympus would deny me my vengeance, then all of Olympus will die."

Kratos, God of War II

Most revisited fantasy roles in a videogame series

The *God of War* series has seen a number of big names voicing its characters, including five actors reprising roles from other film and TV series. These include Kevin Sorbo (left), who first played the Greek god in the TV series *Hercules: The Legendary Journeys* (left), providing the voice of Hercules (right), and Harry Hamlin, who starred as Perseus in the classic 1981 fantasy film *Clash of the Titans*.

Tips 'n' Tricks

God of War: Chains of Olympus features one of Kratos' most devastating secondary weapons in the form of the Gauntlet of Zeus. As potent as that brooding moniker suggests, the Gauntlet is at its most powerful when charged up for heavy attacks and can cause unprecedented damage against enemy hordes. While it may be cumbersome and slow, it can be upgraded for quick special attacks, including the "Lightning Thrash" and the "Olympic Strike", which are especially formidable when combined with an aerial assault.

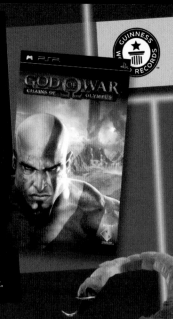

Most critically acclaimed PSP videogame

In the pantheon of PlayStation classics, *God of War: Chains of Olympus* – the series' fourth release – reigns supreme on the PSP with a GameRankings score of 91.44%, based on 80 reviews as of 27 February 2015.

First high-definition remastering of a PlayStation 2 game

The first instance of a PlayStation 2 game being remastered in high definition for a PlayStation 3 release took place in November 2009, when *God of War* and *God of War II* were re-released on a single Blu-ray disc under the title *God of War Collection*.

First PSP videogame remastered in HD with trophy support

Released on PlayStation 3 in September 2011, *God of War Collection: Volume II* (known in the USA as *God of War: Origins Collection*) included fully remastered versions of Kratos's two PSP adventures, *God of War: Chains of Olympus* and *God of War: Ghost of Sparta*.

Greatest aggregate time playing *God of War: Ascension*

US gamer "milliejacqueson" had spent 1,326 hr 30 min on *God of War: Ascension* as of 25 March 2014 – equating to some 55 days of combat.

Highest score on *God of War: Ascension*

In 1,200 or so hours of play, gamer "Rudda-Johnny2011" (UK) has earned the most experience points (XP) in *God of War: Ascension*, with a total of 10,941,690 XP as of 25 March 2014. The same player holds the record for **most multiplayer kills in *Ascension***: 75,700, as of the same date.

Fastest completion of *God of War II*

On 21 December 2007, gamer "shenminiu" (aka Li Lihong) managed to complete *God of War II* in a blistering time of 3 hr 7 min 25 sec. The record was set over 38 segments on the sequel's fiendish "Titan" difficulty mode, which can only be unlocked once an easier mode has been completed.

Most prolific Olympian slayer in a videogame

God of War's Kratos had killed a record 23 Greek gods as of 25 February 2015. But thankfully there were no fatalities when he took to the greens in PS3's 2007 release, *Everybody's Golf: World Tour* (above).

First *God of War* game to feature unarmed combat moves

Despite being widely revered for its fighting mechanics, the seventh instalment in the *GoW* series – *God of War: Ascension* – was the first that allowed players to punch and kick foes, courtesy of a revised combat system.

Fastest completion of *God of War*

The fastest completion time for the original *God of War* is 2 hr 16 min 23 sec, achieved by Philip "ballofsnow" Cornell on 4 April 2006. The time is more impressive for the fact that Cornell completed the game on "God mode" – the most difficult of all modes.

GRAN TURISMO

Highest-rated racing game ever

The original *Gran Turismo* boasts a seriously impressive Metacritic score of 96%, making it the highest-rated racing game of them all. The popular PlayStation title set a new benchmark for driving simulations, and proved that the genre could work on home consoles.
With a score of 95%, *Gran Turismo 3: A-spec* (below) is the **highest-rated racing game of the 21st century**.

Best-selling driving simulator series

With total series sales of 71.35 million games as of 1 April 2015, according to VGChartz, *Gran Turismo* is the most successful racing sim around. *Gran Turismo 3: A-spec* has sold 14.98 million copies alone, making it the **best-selling driving simulator game**.

335 Total number of circuits in the *Gran Turismo* series as of 1 April 2015, from real-world tracks such as Nürburgring's Nordschleife to original creations such as Deep Forest Raceway.

D.Y.K.?

In 2013, the Spanish city of Ronda named a street "Paseo de Kazunori Yamauchi" after the *GT* visionary (see below left). The Japanese racing legend described the dedication as "very special".

Summary: The original *Gran Turismo* revolutionized driving simulations, bringing an unprecedented element of realism while offering a vast range of high-performance vehicles. Subsequent sequels have built on that heritage, packing in additional modes, more detail and greater speeds.

Publisher: Sony
Developer: Polyphony Digital
Debut: 1997

Longest-serving designer of a racing videogame

Kazunori Yamauchi (Japan) began work on the original *Gran Turismo* back in 1992, although it was another five years before the game was released. A pro racing driver, Kazunori had applied his expertise to every game in the series as of April 2015.

Largest virtual-to-reality competition

The NISMO PlayStation GT Academy offers *Gran Turismo* players the chance to drive real-life racing cars and vie to become a racing driver for Nissan under its motorsport arm NISMO. Since the inception of the GT Academy in 2008, there have been some 5 million entries from 20 countries.

Most real-world cars in a videogame

Choosing from a garage of hundreds of real vehicles has always been a major part of *Gran Turismo*'s appeal. Including updates, *Gran Turismo 6* (2013) has upped the vehicle count to 1,237 – from 109 different car manufacturers – beating the previous record of 1,074 vehicles held by *Gran Turismo 5*.

Fastest lap of Laguna Seca in *Gran Turismo 5*

On 25 July 2014, Lewis Appiagyei (UK) completed a lap in exactly 44 sec. The **fastest lap of Laguna Seca in GT 5 (two players)** is 1 min 38.20 sec, achieved by Callum McGinley and Olajide Olatunji (both UK) on 8 August 2013.

First PlayStation 3 game to reach 1 million pre-orders

According to the PlayStation Universe website, *Gran Turismo 5 Prologue* – an extended demo for the fifth entry in the racing car series – generated 1 million pre-orders before its release in Japan on 13 December 2007. As of 1 April 2015, the game had sold 4.18 million copies.

Most podium finishes for a gamer in real-life driving competitions

Since winning the 2011 GT Academy – an initiative for *Gran Turismo* gamers to race pro racing cars – Jann Mardenborough (UK) had achieved 16 podium finishes in real-life racing competitions as of 8 April 2015. This included two podium spots in the 2014 GP3 series, which is aimed at aspiring Formula One drivers. Jann is also the **youngest GT Academy champion**, winning the competition at the age of 19.

Most expensive virtual sports racing car

The Jaguar XJ13 can be purchased in-game by players of *Gran Turismo 6* on the PlayStation 3, but only those with 20 million credits to spare. Alternatively, racers can pay with real-world cash – $196 (£119.95) will allow you to add the Jaguar to your garage.

Fastest car in a videogame

The Red Bull X2011 Prototype, which first appeared as DLC in *Gran Turismo 5*, is a hypothetical concept car developed by Red Bull Racing's Chief Technical Officer Adrian Newey and *Gran Turismo* producer Kazunori Yamauchi. It was engineered with the sole purpose of delivering ferocious speeds, and boasts a 1,635-hp engine. A YouTube video shows the in-game prototype burning up the road at an amazing 622 km/h (386 mph). While faster speeds may have been recorded in arcade games, or in gamer-modded cars, the Red Bull X2011 Prototype is the fastest car grounded in real-world physics to appear in a racing sim.

Longest racetrack in a videogame

Released as DLC for *GT 5* and *GT 6*, the oval test track "Special Stage Route X" runs to 30.28 km (18.8 mi) in length. This is even longer than the famous German track (and *Gran Turismo* staple) Nürburgring Nordschleife, the **longest real-life circuit in a videogame**, which measures 20.8 km (12.9 mi).

Most courses in a *Gran Turismo* game

Gran Turismo 6 has 86 courses, beating its predecessor *Gran Turismo 5*'s record of 60.

Best-selling PS game

With worldwide sales of 10.95 million according to VGChartz, 1997's *Gran Turismo* is the highest-selling game for Sony's PlayStation console.

Longest racetracks in *Gran Turismo 5*

Track	Location	Length	Corners
Special Stage Route X Oval	n/a (fictional)	30,283.2 m	2
Nürburgring 24h	Nürburg, Germany	25,359 m	89
Special Stage Route 7	n/a (fictional)	23,280 m	24
Circuit de la Sarthe 2005	Le Mans, France	13,650 m	38
Chamonix Main	France (fictional)	8,262.4 m	24
Eiger Nordwand K Trail	Bernese Alps, Switzerland	7,167.3 m	38
Cape Ring	n/a (fictional)	7,070 m	28
Circuit de Spa-Francorchamps	Francorchamps, Belgium	7,004 m	21
Suzuka Circuit	Suzuka, Japan	5,807 m	20
Autodromo Nazionale Monza	Monza, Italy	5,793 m	10

Source: www.gran-turismo.com

Tips 'n' Tricks

The red-and-white "rumble strips" that line the edge of the racetrack are a safety feature designed to warn drivers of their proximity to potential hazards. But for armchair racers they also offer a helpful guide to the racing line – the fastest path around the circuit. Keep to the rumble strips on the outside of the track and turn into corners in time to make sure that your apexes coincide with the appearance of the rumble strips on the inside of the course. You'll be setting a new PB in no time.

GRAND THEFT AUTO

Summary: Vast, violent and utterly addictive, *Grand Theft Auto* takes gamers deep into the sinister and sleazy world of crime. Developed by Rockstar, this trailblazing open-world action-adventure has grown into a bona fide global phenomenon and become the **best-selling action-adventure series**, with 153.75 million sales.

Publisher: Rockstar Games
Developer: Rockstar Games
Debut: 1997

Most successful *GTA Online* multiplayer crew

As of 12 August 2014, five-man crew "Violent Pacification" had an unrivalled 1,171 wins and zero losses on the PS3 edition of the game. Leader "tb4u01" has spent more than 1,108 hr on the game, killing 7,930 other players.

D.Y.K.?

Grand Theft Auto has become renowned for the number of celebrities providing voices in the game – including (clockwise from top left) singer Axl Rose, rapper Ice-T, and actors Dennis Hopper and Samuel L Jackson, the latter of whom won an award at the 2004 Spike TV Video Game Awards for his role as Officer Tenpenny in *GTA: San Andreas*.

Best-selling action-adventure game

Its estimated budget of $135 million (£90.3 million) may have made *GTA V* the **most expensive action-adventure game**, but three days after its release on 17 September 2013 it also became the **fastest entertainment property to gross $1 billion**. As of 19 March 2015, *Grand Theft Auto V* had sold an incredible 43 million units across its platforms – more than any other action-adventure game.

80,000

Lines of dialogue in *Grand Theft Auto V* – some of which were voiced by real-life gang members to establish characters' authenticity.

Best-selling game on the PS2

With sales of 20.81 million units as of 29 April 2015, *Grand Theft Auto: San Andreas* (2004) had outsold every other PS2 game according to VGChartz. The franchise's amazing popularity is further underlined by *Grand Theft Auto V* – the **best-selling PS3 game**, it has sold 19.45 million copies.

Tips 'n' Tricks

The streets of *Grand Theft Auto Online* can be pretty mean, so why not leave the others to fight it out among themselves and take to the skies in a helicopter? If you take the stairs to the Flight School and jump over the wall, you'll find airport security a lot more relaxed than in single-player mode. Once you're in the air, you'll see that there is a parachute waiting for you at the top of the tallest building downtown. If you've got the nerve, you can BASE-jump from the building back down to the streets below.

Most critically acclaimed 2D open-world game

With a Metacritic review score of 93% on DS, 91% on iOS and 90% on PSP, *GTA: Chinatown Wars* is the undisputed boss of 2D open-world gaming.

Highest-rated game on eighth-generation consoles

Grand Theft Auto V is the highest-ranked game on both PS4 and Xbox One, with a Metacritic rating of 97% on both platforms as of 9 March 2015. As the game is a re-release of the original PS3 and Xbox 360 versions, these critical rave reviews also ensure that *Grand Theft Auto V* is the **highest-rated re-release**.

Largest playable area in a *Grand Theft Auto* game

The San Andreas locale that provides the setting for *Grand Theft Auto V* roughly totals 71.2 sq km (27.5 sq mi) – making the game bigger than *GTA IV*, *GTA: San Andreas* and *Red Dead Redemption* combined.

Longest survival on a 6-star wanted level on *GTA IV*

On 13 April 2009, Henrik Lindholm (Denmark) managed to evade the clutches of the police, federal agents and even a helicopter gunship for a felonious 16 min 16 sec at the Copenhagen eSports Challenge in Copenhagen, Denmark.

Fastest completion of *GTA: San Andreas*

On 18 January 2008, Daniel "CannibalK9" Burns finished the game in 6 hr 9 min. His time was set on the PC edition, with only the main narrative missions of the game requiring completion.

Largest in-game soundtrack

Including expansion packs *The Ballad of Gay Tony* and *The Lost and Damned*, *Grand Theft Auto IV* features 340 commercially released songs.

Most formats for a handheld open-world videogame

Grand Theft Auto: Chinatown Wars (2009) appeared on four different handheld formats – the DS, PSP, Android and iPhone.

Fastest Classic% completion of *Grand Theft Auto V*

On 10 January 2015, Dates Lupastean (Belgium) completed a Classic% run using no taxi trips or failed mission skips in just 7 hr 19 min 58 sec.

Most popular user-created job in *GTA Online*

One of *GTA Online*'s most popular features, user-created "jobs" allow players to build their own challenges and share them with the *GTA* community. Designed by "GSXR01570", the "Obstacle What?" job – a race filled with jumps and blockades – had been played 28.6 million times as of 10 March 2015, and received 5.1 million "likes".

Most vehicles in a *GTA* game

With methods of transportation ranging from cars and trucks to helicopters, planes, submarines and speedboats, *Grand Theft Auto V* boasted 217 different vehicles upon its launch on 17 September 2013. Subsequent add-on content and the arrival of the PS4 and Xbox One editions in 2014 saw the number increase to 244.

HALO

Highest-earning female gamer

Growing up in a gaming-mad household, Katherine (Kat) "Mystik" Gunn (USA) honed her competitive skills playing against her family before the growth of eSports allowed her to turn pro. Since 2007, she has earned $122,000 (£77,094) from gaming, specializing in FPS and fighting games. Kat's biggest tournament victory came in the final of the US reality-TV show *World Cyber Games Ultimate Gamer Season 2* on 3 October 2010. In the race to be the first to achieve 15 kills on *Halo: Reach*, Kat blitzed her opponent 15–1.

D.Y.K.?

Kat Gunn is also a keen player of *Dead or Alive 4*, and credits much of her success as a professional gamer to her adaptability, which allows her to react to ever-changing technology.

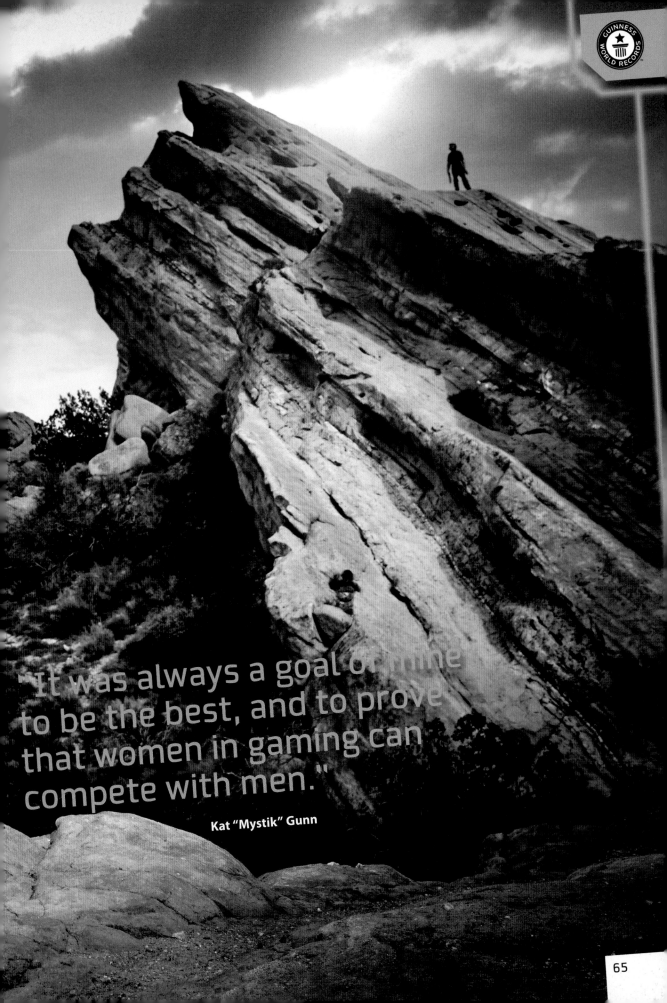

"It was always a goal of mine to be the best, and to prove that women in gaming can compete with men."

Kat "Mystik" Gunn

HALO

First web series to debut on the *Halo* Channel

Halo: Nightfall was a five-episode live-action series that introduced fans to *Halo 5: Guardians* hero Agent Jameson Locke (played by Mike Colter, above, in both the series and forthcoming game). The first episode was shown on 11 November 2014 at the launch event of the *Halo* Channel in Los Angeles, USA. The *Halo* Channel is an interactive digital hub that provides content from the *Halo* universe, including live streams of multiplayer matches.

39,000

Lines of dialogue written for *Halo 3* – a sharp increase from the 14,000 lines in *Halo 2*, and a positively giant leap from the taciturn 3,000 lines of dialogue in the original game.

Summary: Debuting with a launch title for the Xbox back in 2001, *Halo* is an iconic sci-fi shooter series set in the 26th century. Players are thrust into an interstellar war, in which cybernetically enhanced supersoldiers known as Spartans defend humanity against a deadly alien alliance.

Publisher: Microsoft Studios
Developer: Bungie/ 343 Industries
Debut: 2001

Longest-running machinima series

Debuting in April 2003, Rooster Teeth Productions' comedy web series *Red vs Blue* was first created using the multiplayer modes in *Halo: Combat Evolved*. As of 31 March 2015, there had been 12 seasons and 160 episodes produced, with each routinely achieving viewing figures in excess of 1 million.

Highest-earning *Halo* player

Pro *Halo* hotshot Aaron "Ace" Elam (USA) had won $243,087.50 (£162,279.58) from 23 *Halo* tournaments as of 23 April 2015.

Aaron's older brother, Kyle "Elamite Warrior" Elam (USA), is the **highest-earning *Halo 3* player**, with career winnings of $130,000 (£86,784.98) as of the same date.

Smallest development team on *Halo*

While 343 Industries has more than 200 people in its *Halo 5* dev team, former Microsoft VP of game publishing Ed Fries (USA) programmed a version of the game himself. Comprising just 64 screens, *Halo 2600* was designed for second-gen console Atari 2600.

Highest-grossing sci-fi shooter (24 hours)

Upon its launch on 6 November 2012, the much-anticipated *Halo 4* grossed $220 million (£137.6 million) in just one day.

Fastest single-segment completion of *Halo: Combat Evolved*

On 4 November 2014, a gamer known as "vetroxity" (USA) completed the first *Halo* game in a time of 1 hr 16 min 46 sec.

Fastest completion of *Halo 2* on "Legendary" difficulty

On 20 October 2014, "Mister Monopoli" (USA) completed the sci-fi sequel on the highest difficulty setting in a time of 1 hr 43 min 11 sec.

Highest-charting game soundtrack on the US albums chart

The musical score to *Halo 4* entered the US albums chart at No.50 on 10 November 2012. Composed and produced by Massive Attack producer Neil Davidge (UK), the haunting soundtrack features a 16-voice male choir, 10 female Bulgarian vocalists and a 50-piece orchestra.

Most critically acclaimed Xbox game

Halo: Combat Evolved had a GameRankings rating of 95.54% as of 15 April 2015, ahead of Tecmo's *Ninja Gaiden Black* in second place with 94.76%.

Most active *Halo 4* player

As of 11 January 2015, gamer "SHOOTemUUp325" had started 40,805 online games – and given that their overall win percentage is an impressive 71%, practice obviously makes perfect. Their favoured game type was "Regicide", on which they had a K/D ratio of 2.06.

Fastest single-segment completion of *Halo 4*

Set in 2557, four years after *Halo 3*, *Halo 4* sees Master Chief and Cortana sparring once more with the Covenant and the Warrior-Servant Prometheans. On 17 December 2014, speed-runner "HaoleCake" (USA) completed a single-segment run-through of the game in 1 hr 24 min 37 sec.

First FPS to sell 10 million

On 8 August 2009, sales of *Halo 3* soared past the 10 million mark. With worldwide sales of 12.02 million as of 15 April 2015, *Halo 3* is also the **best-selling *Halo* game** and the only title in the series to pass the magical 10 million threshold.

Longest spaceship in the UNSC fleet

Making its debut in *Halo 4*, the UNSC *Infinity* measures 5,694 m (18,681 ft). This makes it even longer than the Covenant's *CAS-class Assault Carrier*, which is 5,346 m (17,539 ft) in length.

Highest K/D ratio on *Halo 4*				
Gamer	Games played	HaloTracker score	Site ranking	K/D ratio
"legize"	253	7,510	52,779	113.00
"Med Kuz Bed"	613	831,359	2	53.24
"iBullz3ye"	204	6,749	59,140	32.89
"Boss Juliano"	246	89,192	1,011	27.12
"drearguide90835"	300	7,609	52,051	23.46
"t rextum"	416	10,380	36,332	23.37
"the p00dle"	207	23,297	11,647	21.70
"t wrecks em"	585	13,153	26,795	20.32
"Respctful"	1,388	451,437	19	19.36
"lumpierbird125"	703	230,659	125	18.89

Source: HaloTracker as of 16 April 2015

Tips 'n' Tricks

You can take the fight up close and personal in *Halo 4* by assassinating other players. A total of 140 kills will see you achieve the rank of Assassin Master, unlocking some cool Venator armour. Select the multiplayer gametype "Team Swat" – as the absence of radar makes stealthy ambushes easier – and zero in on unwary players who are focused on other targets. Some gamers use a tactic known as "camo camping" – hiding out while cloaked and lying in wait for victims. But for many *Halo* players, this is a sneaky step too far.

HEARTHSTONE

Summary: Existing within Blizzard's *Warcraft* universe, *Hearthstone: Heroes of Warcraft* is a free2play digital collectible card game that pitches players into a head-to-head battle. It became an instant success, racking up millions of players worldwide.

Longest turn on *Hearthstone*

On 25 March 2015, 25-year-old Florian "Mamytwink" Henn (France) took an incredible 1 day 21 hr 18 min to complete a single *Hearthstone* turn. The average turn in *Hearthstone* takes around 1 min 30 sec. However, "Mamytwink" exploited a loophole that enabled him to fire 28,752 arcane missiles, triggering an animation that took 45 hr 18 min to finish. The turn was streamed live on Twitch.tv.

Publisher: Blizzard Entertainment
Developer: Blizzard Entertainment
Debut: 2014

Eric Dodds, Lead Designer on *Hearthstone*

Q&A

Hearthstone has a reported 25 million player accounts as of January 2015. What's the secret?
A lot of our innovation has been making the game work extremely well for the digital space while making sure it's a game literally everybody can play.

What do you see as *Hearthstone*'s strengths as a multiplayer game?
Many players can find multiplayer a little intimidating – *Hearthstone* focuses on making these people feel welcome. Our game is easy to learn, and new players can complete short matches and move on without feeling tension.

Where next for the series?
We're releasing *Hearthstone* on Android and iOS phones. This version will be a deeply strategic game that players play for a long time.

Tips 'n' Tricks

New *Hearthstone* players should start out with the Mage character – the core cards offer versatility and the play mechanics are reasonably simple to pick up. Mages are also fun to play and are adept at casting spells. Cards such as Frostbolt and Fireball in the Mage deck have great potential for inflicting damage or clearing boards. You can use the Mage to win early games and unlock more class cards, mastering the basics before you try other classes as you progress further into the game.

D.Y.K.?

Unlike many other card games, *Hearthstone* does not operate a trading system. Unwanted cards are "disenchanted", producing a substance known as "Arcane Dust" that helps players craft new cards.

Fastest one mana kill

Bachir "Athene" Boumaaza (Belgium) gained idol status among the game's fans by winning a battle on his very first turn using just one mana. As of 8 May 2015 he had 181,201 subscribers to his Twitch channel.

Rarest *Hearthstone* card

The Golden Elite Tauren Chieftain was made available as a promotional gift to players who purchased a ticket or virtual ticket to BlizzCon 2013. The exact number of Golden Elite Tauren Chieftain cards in existence is unknown. They are soulbound and cannot be crafted or disenchanted.

Most popular Legendary card in *Hearthstone*

When pro *Hearthstone* players were quizzed by *PC Gamer* to find their favourite Legendary card in a January 2015 survey, 90% of them cited Dr Boom.

Most popular *Hearthstone* deck

Submitted to *Hearthstone* website Hearthpwn by veteran player Travis "Flood" Mays (Canada), the "Miracle Rogue" deck had amassed 1,307 community endorsements as of 19 March 2015.

Country with the most successful *Hearthstone* players

With four names in the top 10 highest-earning players as of 19 March 2015, China is top of the *Hearthstone* tree. In total, the four Chinese players had amassed career earnings of $267,589 (£170,897). The next most successful country was the USA, with three entries.

Most popular *Hearthstone* player

As of 17 March 2015, *Hearthstone* professional Jeffrey "Trump" Shih (USA) claimed a total of 421,544 YouTube subscribers and a mighty 425,406 followers on his "TrumpSC" Twitch. tv channel, where he provides advice for players across multiple skill levels.

First digital collectible card game to win at the Games Awards

Hearthstone walked away with the award for "Best Mobile/Handheld Game" at the Game Awards, held on 5 December 2014 in Las Vegas, Nevada, USA. And the awards didn't stop there – on 12 March 2015, *Hearthstone* won in the "Multiplayer" category at the British Academy Games Awards, becoming the **first digital collectible card game to win a BAFTA**.

Most money won in a *Hearthstone* tournament

Professional *Hearthstone* player James "Firebat" Kostesich (USA) won the inaugural *Hearthstone* World Championship on 7–8 November 2014, taking home $100,000 (£63,866) into the bargain. He defeated Xieyu "Tiddler Celestial" Wang in the final, winning the best-of-five match 3–0.

JUST DANCE

Summary: A rhythm game series that's jam-packed with pop tunes and slick dance routines, *Just Dance* isn't only great fun to play – it can also help you keep fit. The game is now so globally successful that even President Barack Obama has been snapped buying it. Not bad for a series inspired by a prototype for a *Raving Rabbids* title…

Publisher: Ubisoft
Developer: Ubisoft
Debut: 2009

Largest online virtual dance battle

Courtesy of *Just Dance 2014*'s "world dance floor" – the series' first online multiplayer mode – 66,101 dancers connected on 25 December 2013. Just the thing to sweat off those extra Christmas calories…

Best-selling dance game on Wii U

With over 470,017 copies sold as of 17 March 2015, *Just Dance 2015* is the best-selling dance game currently available for the Wii U. *Just Dance 2014* comes a close second, with 465,496 copies sold.

30

UK chart position of *Just Dance* when it debuted in late 2009. By January 2010, the game had waltzed its way to No.1, where it remained for five months. Its success was attributed to word-of-mouth and fan videos on YouTube.

Best-selling dance game series

Forty *Just Dance* games, including the same titles packaged for different platforms, totalled 52.13 million sales as of 17 March 2015. The series' biggest rival, *Dance Dance Revolution*, has been around since 1998 but lags behind with 21.58 million. *Dance Central*, launched in 2010, is up to 6 million, while *Pump It Up* (1999) has yet to hit a million.

First player-choreographed dance game routines

Just Dance 3, on the Xbox 360, boasts a "Just Create" mode that allows players to video themselves performing moves they have created using the Kinect camera.

Best-selling rhythm videogame on a single platform

The 10.07 million sales of the Wii version of *Just Dance 3* (as of 19 March 2015) make it the most popular rhythm game based on figures for a single platform. *Just Dance 2* is just behind with 9.42 million Wii sales. For comparison, the best-sellers in other rhythm game series are *Guitar Hero II* on the PS2 (5.12 million), *Rock Band* on the Xbox 360 (2.45 million sales) and *Dance Dance Revolution X2* on the PS2 (2.23 million).

Most prolific dancing game high scorer

Elizabeth "Kitty McScratch" Bolinger (USA) holds more high-score records for *Just Dance*, *Just Dance 2* and *Dance Central* than any other player on the Twin Galaxies achievements site: she is top of the leaderboard for more than 85 songs. Kitty has also enjoyed success on YouTube, with videos demonstrating her *Just Dance* prowess while blindfolded.

Most popular *Just Dance* game in Japan

As of 9 March 2015, *Just Dance Wii* (2011) is the most popular release in the series, with more than 720,000 copies sold. Its tracklisting is dominated by the country's J-pop acts, but does find room for Rihanna, Britney Spears and the Spice Girls.

Oldest song in a dancing videogame

"Jingle Bells" – a trio routine in *Just Dance Kids 2* – was written by James Lord Pierpont (USA) in 1857 and was originally titled "The One Horse Open Sleigh".

The overall **oldest music in a videogame** is "Winter", from Vivaldi's *The Four Seasons*, which features in the Xbox rhythm game *Fantasia: Music Evolved* (2014). It was composed in 1725.

Most viewed *JD*-themed video

A "Wii rip" of *Just Dance Kids 2*'s colourful routine for Gummibär's "I'm a Gummy Bear (The Gummy Bear Song)", uploaded by YouTuber "beyre83" on 20 November 2011, had been viewed 38,706,750 times as of 6 March 2015. Other uploads of the same clip, starring *Girl Meets World* actress Sabrina Carpenter, take its total views close to 50 million.

Most appearances in *Just Dance* by one artist

With 11 songs – including "Hot N Cold", "Teenage Dream" and "Firework" – across the series as of 13 February 2015, the most prolific artist in *Just Dance* is Katy Perry (USA).

Longest dance game marathon

Carrie Swidecki (USA) played *Just Dance 4* for 49 hr 3 min 22 sec at Otto's Video Games & More! in Bakersfield, California, USA, on 15–17 June 2013. "People ask all the time, 'Why marathon world records on dance games?'" wrote the formerly overweight, but now slim Carrie. "I know the power of 'exergaming', because it changed my life."

First World Cup based on a rhythm videogame

In 2014, Ubisoft and the Electronic Sports World Cup staged the inaugural *Just Dance* World Cup. Heats began on 13 July and finals took place from 30 October to 1 November in Paris, France, featuring 20 of the finest movers dancing to tracks by Lady Gaga, Arianna Grande and Rihanna. The victor was 24-year-old Diego Dos Santos Silva (Brazil, shown centre). Carrie Swidecki (see above right) also took part.

D.Y.K.?

The frog who turns into a prince in *Just Dance 2015*'s "Love Is All" isn't the song's only wildlife. It also features a Raving Rabbid: one of the bonkers bunnies who graduated from the *Rayman* games to a series of their own.

Evolution of Controllers

As consoles have grown more powerful, so controllers have grown more complex to match the demands placed on them by increasingly advanced gameplay. In recent years, manufacturers have introduced features that have impacted the way we play games, from simple rumble feedback to motion control. This choice selection illustrates how controllers are constantly evolving.

1993

Atari Jaguar
D Pad + Pause, Option buttons + 3 action buttons + 12 numeric keys

1982

1972

Atari 5200 SuperSystem
Joystick + Start, Reset + Pause buttons + 16 action buttons

1988

1996

Magnavox Odyssey
First gaming console.
2 dials + Reset button

Sega Mega Drive
D Pad + Start button + 3 action buttons

Nintendo 64
Analog stick + D Pad + Start button + 9 action buttons

Nintendo Entertainment System
D Pad + Start, Select buttons + 2 action buttons

Super Nintendo Entertainment System
D Pad + Start, Select buttons + 6 action buttons

Atari 2600
Joystick + 1 action button

1983

1990

PlayStation
D Pad + Start, Select buttons + 8 action buttons

1977

1994

FIRST RUMBLE CONTROLLER FOR A GAME CONSOLE

The Rumble Pak was launched in April 1997 to coincide with the release of the Nintendo rail shooter *Star Fox 64*. It slotted into the N64's controller's memory cartridge slot, typically making the controller vibrate at key moments in the gameplay to enhance tension. This rumble feedback has since become an industry-standard feature.

FIRST DUAL ANALOG CONTROLLER FOR A GAME CONSOLE

First released in Japan in April 1997, the PlayStation "Dual Analog Controller" (SCPH-1150) boasted a dual-stick set-up that allowed precise control in 3D environments. The **first console game requiring a dual analog controller** was PlayStation platformer *Ape Escape*, released on 31 May 1999.

1998

Dreamcast
Analog stick +
D Pad + Start button
+ 6 action buttons

2001

GameCube
2 analog sticks +
D Pad + Start button
+ 7 action buttons

2005

Xbox 360
2 analog sticks + D Pad
+ Home, Start, Back buttons
+ 8 action buttons

2013

PlayStation DualShock 4
Touchpad + 2 analog sticks
+ D Pad + PS, Share, Options
buttons + 8 action buttons

PlayStation DualShock
2 analog sticks + D Pad
+ Start, Select buttons +
8 action buttons

Wii
Motion control + D Pad +
6 action buttons + Home +
speaker + Nunchuk (analog
+ 2 action buttons)

Wii U
Motion control + camera
+ touchscreen + 2 analog
sticks + D Pad + Home,
Start, Select, Power, TV +
8 action buttons + NFC +
microphone + speaker

1998

Xbox
2 analog sticks + D Pad
+ Start, Back buttons +
8 action buttons

2006

2012

2001

2010   **Kinect**
Motion control + microphone

"We made it as light as possible without causing durability problems."

Nintendo's Satoru Iwata on the Wii U controller

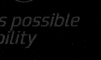

Best-selling crossover RPG series

A "crossover" is a combination of two franchises – in this case, Square Enix characters and Disney. As of 6 March 2015, the *Kingdom Hearts* series had sold 22.22 million units. And with *Kingdom Hearts III* in the works, the series looks set for even greater success.

Summary: In this popular crossover RPG, hero Sora's search for his missing friends takes him on a series of wild adventures, during which he encounters Disney characters and the denizens of Square Enix games *Final Fantasy* and *The World Ends with You.*

Publisher: Square Enix
Developer: Square Enix
Debut: 2002

D.Y.K.?

Along with Sora and Donald Duck, Disney's Goofy is an ever-present in the *Kingdom Hearts* series. Despite his position as Captain of the Royal Knights of King Mickey's court, Goofy favours a shield over weapons and tries to avoid combat wherever possible.

D.Y.K.?

The original *Kingdom Hearts* was the last title to feature the Squaresoft logo on the packaging before the publisher merged with rival house Enix in 2003 to become Square Enix. Subsequent *Kingdom Hearts* releases, including re-releases, had the new company logo.

Fastest completions of *Kingdom Hearts II: Final Mix*		
Gamer	Time	Date
TehRizzle	3 hr 41 min 28 sec	12 November 2014
Cyberman6	3 hr 47 min 10 sec	21 May 2014
Liquid WiFi	3 hr 48 min 31 sec	8 February 2015
KHfan169	3 hr 49 min 29 sec	5 February 2015
Bl00dyBizkitz	3 hr 49 min 34 sec	9 July 2014
Rupa	3 hr 55 min 09 sec	25 May 2013
Santana	3 hr 59 min 31 sec	1 April 2014
Sonicshadowsilver2	4 hr 01 min 55 sec	20 August 2014
Yulf	4 hr 05 min 57 sec	6 January 2015
Jensei	4 hr 12 min 08 sec	4 September 2014

Source: KH leaderboard as of 27 February 2015

1 Japanese chart position reached by "Hikari", the theme song for *Kingdom Hearts*. It was performed by pop star Hikaru Utada, who also wrote and co-produced the smash hit.

First censored Disney game

In order to secure a suitable age rating for its audience, *Kingdom Hearts II* had multiple scenes from the original Japanese game either cut or edited for the English-language version. These scenes included a wounded Hydra oozing smoke rather than green blood. In the *Pirates of the Caribbean* world "Port Royal", violence was toned down, with guns swapped for crossbows, and undead pirates *didn't* burst into flames when struck with fire magic. Elsewhere, a cutscene in which Daisy Duck spanked Donald was completely removed.

Fastest single-segment completion of *Kingdom Hearts: Chain of Memories*

Playing as Riku, Keith "The Quiet Man" Skomorowski completed the game in just 1 hr 29 min 5 sec on 2 January 2009. The sequel to *Kingdom Hearts*, *Chain of Memories* was made exclusively for the Game Boy Advance and was one of the first games to include full-motion video.

Fastest single-segment completion of *Kingdom Hearts*

On 24 June 2013, veteran *Kingdom Hearts* speed-runner Daniel "Sonicshadowsilver2" Tipton (USA) dashed through the Realm of Light in record time, completing the game in 5 hr 33 min 35 sec on the PS2.

Best-selling Disney videogame

With 6.4 million global sales as of 6 March 2015, according to VGChartz, the original *Kingdom Hearts* is the biggest-selling videogame licensed by The Walt Disney Company.

Fastest single-segment completion of *Kingdom Hearts HD 1.5 Remix*

A speed-runner going by the name "Themistmaster1" sprinted through the game in just 2 hr 49 min 36 sec on 27 November 2014. He achieved this by playing the *Kingdom Hearts: Final Mix* portion of the game on "Beginner" difficulty.

Most prolific Disney gaming character

Not counting numerous game & watch, educational and mobile games, *Kingdom Hearts* star Mickey Mouse has headlined more games than any other Disney character. Indeed, since debuting in 1983's *Sorcerer's Apprentice* for the Atari 2600, he has been the main star or co-star of no less than 30 titles. As of March 2015, his most recent headline appearance was in *Castle of Illusion Starring Mickey Mouse*, a Sega Studios remake of a Sega Genesis game from 1990. It was released on PlayStation Network, Live Arcade and PC in September 2013.

Strongest keyblade in *Kingdom Hearts 3D: Dream Drop Distance*

The Unbound's strength rating of 18 is two points higher than its nearest rival keyblade, Ultima Weapon. No wonder it's so hard to earn – in order to claim the Unbound, you have to clear every secret portal in the game.

D.Y.K.?

In 2002, Disney fans were surprised when Alice, the heroine of Lewis Carroll's classic 1865 novel *Alice's Adventures in Wonderland*, joined Snow White, Jasmine, Belle, Cinderella, Aurora and Kairi as a Princess of Heart in *Kingdom Hearts*. The mixed reaction was down to the fact that although Alice had appeared in a Disney film she was not a princess. In fact, she was a late replacement for Ariel from 1989's *The Little Mermaid*. Off with her head!

First fan to appear in a *Kingdom Hearts* game

Not to be mistaken for an obscure Disney villain, the character Kurt Zisa is, in fact, a US fan who won Square Enix's "Name-in-Game" competition. His prize was to star in *Kingdom Hearts* as a six-armed crustacean boss who can be found in the Agrabah desert.

THE LAST OF US

Most critically acclaimed PlayStation 3 game from a debut series

With a 95.09% average across 68 reviews on GameRankings, *The Last of Us* is the highest-rated non-sequel or licensed game released for the PS3, as of 12 March 2015. Similarly, the souped-up *The Last of Us Remastered* holds the same honour for PS4, with a score of 95.7% from 43 reviews.

Summary: From Naughty Dog, the highly respected developers of the *Uncharted* series, came this cinematic thriller. It follows the fortunes of Joel and Ellie, survivors in a *Walking Dead*-esque world of fungus-infected zombie-style unfortunates and dangerously militarized humans.

Publisher: Sony
Developer: Naughty Dog
Debut: 2013

D.Y.K.?

Actress Ellen Page (*Juno, Inception*) was unhappy with Ellie's resemblance to her. "I am acting in a videogame called *Beyond: Two Souls*, so it was not appreciated," she wrote in a Reddit Q&A. However, she was gracious to Ashley Johnson, whose portrayal of Ellie beat her in the 2014 BAFTA Games Awards' Performer category.

Fastest-selling debut game for the PlayStation 3

A total of 1,319,206 copies of *The Last of Us* were sold in its first week of worldwide release in June 2013. According to VGChartz, this record-setting figure rose to more than three million in eight weeks, making it the overall fastest-selling PS3 game in 2013.

D.Y.K.?

The Last of Us began as *Mankind*, in which women were infected and Joel had to deliver Ellie – the only immune female – to a lab to find a cure. However, Naughty Dog's Neil Druckmann rejected the concept as "misogynistic".

Most critically acclaimed PS3 DLC

Scoring 89.84% on GameRankings and 88% on Metacritic as of 11 March 2015, *Left Behind* (2014) is the highest-rated downloadable content (DLC) for the PlayStation 3 and the **highest-rated DLC for any action-adventure game**. The prologue to *The Last of Us* follows Ellie and her BFF Riley on a journey that pushes their lives and friendship to the brink.

Highest-ranked clan player for PlayStation 4

As of 12 May 2015, German gamer "secura2007" topped the clan leaderboard for the *The Last of Us Remastered* on the PS4. Clan mode is a team-based multiplayer element that includes three game modes: Supply Raid, Interrogation and Survivors. Secura2007's supremacy factors in performance across all three modes.

4

Number of issues in Dark Horse Comics' *The Last of Us: American Dreams* miniseries – a prequel to the game that began publishing before the latter was released.

Most viewed *The Last of Us* video

Swedish online personality Felix "PewDiePie" Kjellberg uploaded part one of his "The Last Of Us Gameplay Walkthrough Playthrough Let's Play (Full Game)" to YouTube on 14 June 2013 (the day of the game's release on PlayStation 3). As of 11 March 2015, it had received 12,524,117 views.

IGN GAME OF THE YEAR OVERALL WINNER 2013

Most "game of the year" awards

The Last of Us earned 249 "game of the year" awards when it was unleashed in 2013. These consist of 58 fan-voted honours and 191 critics' garlands, including major wins at the 2014 BAFTA Awards, the 14th Annual GDC Awards and the 2014 SXSW Gaming Awards.

Most BAFTA wins for a videogame

The Last of Us won five awards at the BAFTAs in London on 12 March 2014 and a further two for its *Left Behind* DLC on 12 March 2015. Nominated in eight categories in 2014, it collected Best Action & Adventure Game, Audio Achievement, Performer (Ashley Johnson, right), Story (Bruce Straley and Neil Druckmann) and Best Game. In 2015, *Left Behind* won in both its categories: Story (Druckmann) and Performer (Johnson).

First actor to win two Games Awards BAFTAs

Ashley Johnson (USA) won British Academy of Film and Television Arts "Best Performer" awards in consecutive years for her performance as Ellie in *The Last of Us*. Her first gong came in 2014, overcoming competition from co-star Troy Baker, who plays Joel. Johnson collected the same award a year later for reprising Ellie in the DLC *Left Behind*. Johnson not only provided Ellie's voice for the games, but was also fully motion-captured.

Game	Publisher	Year	Millions sold
Grand Theft Auto V	Rockstar	2013	19.45
Grand Theft Auto IV	Rockstar	2008	10.36
Uncharted 3: Drake's Deception	Sony	2011	6.65
Uncharted 2: Among Thieves	Sony	2009	6.58
Assassin's Creed III	Ubisoft	2012	6.34
Red Dead Redemption	Rockstar	2010	6.33
Metal Gear Solid 4: Guns of the Patriots	Konami	2008	5.95
Assassin's Creed II	Ubisoft	2009	=5.49
The Last of Us	Sony	2013	=5.49
Batman: Arkham City	Warner Bros.	2011	5.26

Best-selling PlayStation 3 action-adventure games

Source: VGChartz as of 7 May 2015

LEAGUE OF LEGENDS

Most played online videogame

According to figures from Riot Games, *League of Legends* is played by 67 million people worldwide every month, with an average 27 million logging in daily – the largest active playerbase of any current title. Furthermore, it reports 7.5 million concurrent players at its peak. As of February 2015, online gaming platform Raptr also revealed that *LoL* topped its chart with 19.97% of the PC market.

27,087,098

The number of YouTube views of Imagine Dragons' "Warriors", the official theme tune of 2014's *League of Legends* World Championship as of 1 April 2015.

Summary: For many, *League of Legends* is king of the ring when it comes to multiplayer online battling. This free2play MOBA offers serious prize money and stages global championships. Players known as "Summoners" pit their unique champions in strategic, magic-laced brawls.

Publisher: Riot Games
Developer: Riot Games
Debut: 2009

Q&A

The *League of Legends* development team collecting a 2015 BAFTA for "Best Persistent Game"

League of Legends currently has 67 million players. Happy?
There are definitely a lot of people playing it! It excites us. A lot of our fans have different interests, so it's a big challenge to keep everyone engaged and playing our new content.

You've said that fans inspire you. Do you listen to their ideas and suggestions?
Absolutely. Our mission is to be the most player-focused company in the world.

Can *LoL* grow even more?
Our hope is finding ways of attracting new players to the game and improving everyone's experience. We're less worried about filling bigger stadiums, but we always joke about hiring a Moon base for staging tournaments in order to outdo our rivals.

Will there ever be an eSports Olympics?
That would be awesome. As players, we'd love to watch that!

"Royal Club" (China), attracted 11.2 million concurrent viewers, making it the most-watched live eSports match, as of 1 April 2015. The final, which took place on 19 October 2014, was hosted in the Seoul World Cup Stadium in South Korea, with 40,000 fans watching the virtual carnage unfold – the **largest live attendance for a** *League of Legends* **tournament**.

Most minion kills in *League of Legends*

"CompLexity Black" player Robert "ROBERTxLEE" Lee killed 719 minions (foot soldiers in *LoL*) on 12 July 2014. He achieved this feat in the **longest professional** *League of Legends* **game**, which clocked in at 1 hr 20 min 34 sec and took place against "Curse" at the 2014 North America LCS.

Largest eSports prize pool in *League of Legends*

Riot Games fronted up an astonishing prize pool of $5 million (£3.23 million) for its *LoL* Season 2 World Championship, with money going to local, national and international tournaments.

Highest-earning *League of Legends* player

Bo Wei (Chinese Taipei) had earned $275,869.52 (£178,691.07) as of 1 April 2015. Since 2012, the arena-hardened 24-year-old has been victorious in 10 *League of Legends* tournaments. Bo's biggest victory came in the *LoL* Season 2 World Championship on 13 October 2012, when he scooped $200,000 (£124,548). That triumph alone accounts for 72.5% of his total career earnings.

Most concurrent viewers for an eSports tournament

The final of 2014's *League of Legends* World Championship, which saw "Samsung White" (South Korea) take on

Largest audience for an eSports tournament

With eSports fast becoming a massive spectator sport, few videogames draw crowds quite like *League of Legends*. The Season 3 World Championship, which ended on 4 October 2013, was streamed live on Twitch and was watched by 32 million people. At its peak, the tournament had 8.5 million viewers tuning in at the same time.

Fastest movement speed in *LoL*

Using the "Tank" champion Malphite (above), Daniel "FrockSaints" Santos (Portugal) hit 31,102,888 Movement Speed (MS) on 12 April 2015. The intuitive schemer hatched a complex plan in which two Malphites were stealing MS from each other in a loop.

The **highest attack damage (AD) in** *League of Legends* is 8,725 AD, achieved on 5 August 2014 by Mathew "Feantugelha" Callaghan (UK). "Feantugelha" used the towering champion Hecarim: "I would love to be a competitive player but competition is high," he said. "At the moment my focus is on breaking unusual *LoL* records!"

Highest-ranked *League of Legends* team

As of 1 April 2015, "Edward Gaming" (China) had battled their way to a rating of 1,362, placing them top of the GosuGamers table – 74 points ahead of the second-placed "yoe Flash Wolves" (Chinese Taipei). Edward Gaming had an all-time win rate of 70% and were on an eight-match winning streak as of the same date.

Tips 'n' Tricks

If you're a relative newbie to *League of Legends*, finding a champion to suit your playing style can be a daunting prospect. Below is a brief guide:
• "Ranged" is for players who like to attack from range with fewer risks.
• "Pushers" are adept at dealing with large minion waves.
• "Junglers" are used for ridding the jungle of monsters, but are also great at backing team-mates in a fight.
• "Carry", for those who like a challenge, starts off weak but can be developed into a fearless foe who "carries" others to victory.

Fastest completion of *The Legend of Zelda: Ocarina of Time*

Having played videogames from the age of three, it is no surprise that Joel "Jodenstone" Ekman (Sweden) has become a talented speed-runner. A fan of *Zelda* for its atmosphere, aesthetics and mixture of puzzles and combat, Joel set the any-percentage record (non-tool-assisted) for completing *Ocarina of Time* in just 17 min 55 sec on 16 March 2015. The speed-run was live-streamed to 1,300 people. "This run was amazing, and the first sub 18 ever!" said Joel. "I love repeating something until it is perfect," he adds – the ideal attitude for a successful speed-runner.

5,000

Number of times "Jodenstone" has started a fresh run-through of the game, completing it more than 1,000 times. In all, he estimates he has spent 2,000 hr playing as Link – that's 83 days of solid gaming!

D.Y.K.?

A programming glitch in *Ocarina of Time* means that Link runs faster backwards than forwards, hence why the top speed-run videos often show their hero facing the other way.

THE LEGEND OF ZELDA

Summary: Name-checked by *The Simpsons Game*, featured in *How I Met Your Mother* and referenced in *Forza*, the series that gave Link to the world is a multi-million-selling, critically acclaimed classic. A mooted live-action TV series is being billed as a family version of *Game of Thrones*.

Publisher: Nintendo
Developer: Nintendo
Debut: 1986

Fastest completion of *Skyward Sword*

"Joshantel" raced through this thrilling Wii action-adventure in 5 hr 14 min 44 sec, recording the feat on 7 November 2014. "Great run, still improvable," he wrote on his YouTube page. "Might beat [it] in the future…"

Fastest completion of target practice

On 10 September 2011, Cameron Jones of Washington, USA, completed target practice on *Majora's Mask* in 24.58 sec. Jones briefly also held the record for the fastest completion of Dampé's race in *Ocarina of Time*.

Most critically acclaimed videogame

As of 30 April 2015, *The Legend of Zelda: Ocarina of Time* (1998) for N64 holds an unrivalled score of 99% on review site Metacritic. "We can't think of any game that we'd rather play," enthused IGN.

The adventure's 3DS remake *The Legend of Zelda: Ocarina of Time 3D* (2011), co-developed with Grezzo, is the **most critically acclaimed 3D game remake**, with a score of 94%.

535,000

Number of copies *The Legend of Zelda: Skyward Sword* sold in its first week on sale in North America – the **fastest-selling Zelda game**.

Largest bead sprite

Kevin Gillespie (USA) used 57,344 beads to create an exact replica of *Zelda*'s title screen. The piece is 1.25 m (4 ft 1 in) wide and weighs 2.3 kg (5 lb).

Most viewed *Zelda* fan film

"*The Legend of Zelda* Rap" by comedians Smosh had earned 55,315,871 YouTube views by 12 March 2015.

First hospitalization from a *Legend of Zelda* injury

On 2 March 2014, Local 2 news in Houston, Texas, USA, reported that cosplayer Eugene Thompson, scuffling with his girlfriend's estranged husband, used a replica Master Sword to stab his opponent in the chest and leg. Thompson was hit over the head with a flower pot.

First *Sonic/Zelda* crossover

Sega and Nintendo united their mascots in *Mario & Sonic at the Olympic Games*, but the tie-in gained a new twist when *Sonic Lost World* was issued for the Wii U. A level called *The Legend of Zelda Zone*, released as free DLC on 27 March 2014, sees Sonic explore Hyrule's fields and dungeons in Link's green hat and tunic, swapping rings for rupees.

Biggest-selling action-adventure videogame on Wii

As of 11 March 2015, the Wii version of *Twilight Princess* had sold 7.08 million. The first *Zelda* game to be simultaneously released on two consoles (Wii and GameCube, in 2006), it is also Wii's **most critically acclaimed action-adventure game**, with a GameRankings average of 94.58%.

Rarest *Zelda* game

In 2013, game memorabilia collector Tom Curtin sold an NES cartridge on eBay for $55,000 (£35,480). Thought to be unique, it contained a fully playable, pre-release prototype of *The Legend of Zelda*.

Also of interest to collectors is an "Adventure Set" of *Majora's Mask*, with the game, a soundtrack CD, a watch, a T-shirt and two pin badges. This desirable box-set was limited to 1,000, each with a numbered certificate. *Retro Gamer* magazine called it "the jewel in the crown" of any N64 collection and, on the rare occasions it is listed on online auction sites, it usually sells for in excess of $1,540 (£1,000).

Most prolific action-adventure character

As of 2015, Link is the most ubiquitous action-adventure icon, starring in 19 official *Zelda* games and three CD-i spin-offs, and making cameos in titles such as *Super Mario RPG: Legend of the Seven Stars*, *Mario Kart 8*, *Sonic Lost World* and *SoulCalibur II*.

First Easter egg appearance awarded as a prize

In 1990, *Nintendo Power* ran a contest in which the winner would feature in a future NES game that turned out to be *The Legend of Zelda: A Link to the Past*. Hidden in the game is a highly elusive room containing 45 blue rupees and a plaque that reads: "My name is Chris Houlihan. This is my top secret room. Keep it between us, OK?"

Best-selling *The Legend of Zelda* games

Game	Platform	Release date	Millions sold
The Legend of Zelda: Ocarina of Time	N64	1998	7.60
The Legend of Zelda: Twilight Princess	Wii	2006	7.08
The Legend of Zelda	NES	1986	6.51
The Legend of Zelda: Phantom Hourglass	DS	2007	5.05
The Legend of Zelda: A Link to the Past	SNES	1991	4.61
The Legend of Zelda: The Wind Waker	GameCube	2002	4.60
Zelda II: The Adventure of Link	NES	1988	4.38
The Legend of Zelda: Skyward Sword	Wii	2011	3.88
The Legend of Zelda: Link's Awakening	Game Boy	1993	3.83
The Legend of Zelda: Ocarina of Time 3D	3DS	2011	3.61

Source: VGChartz.com as of 20 March 2015

D.Y.K.?

It may be the most acclaimed game ever, according to Metacritic's database, but for a while N64's *The Legend of Zelda: Ocarina of Time* could have offered players a very different experience. It's reported that Nintendo was considering making it a first-person action-adventure inspired by the James Bond FPS *GoldenEye*.

In 2014, a crafty mod was created that let gamers play an emulated version in first-person using the Oculus Rift. Footage of it in action was demoed to an excited fanbase by gaming YouTuber "Chadtronic".

LEGO ®

Most prolific developer of toy videogames

UK studio Traveller's Tales (TT) has been making LEGO videogames since 2005's *LEGO Star Wars: The Video Game*. As of 5 March 2015, it had released 24 titles in the franchise, including two *Harry Potter* games and two *Indiana Jones* games, with further *LEGO* games due in 2015 for *Marvel's Avengers*, *Ninjago* and *Jurassic World*. But it's not all bricks, though: TT also developed the tie-in game to *Transformers: The Movie* in 2007.

Summary: Filled with humour and adventure, the ever-popular LEGO toys have been spawning hugely imaginative videogames for nearly 20 years. Some of the world's most iconic heroes (and villains) have now been immortalized in brick form.

Publisher: Various
Developer: Various
Debut: 1997

Tips 'n' Tricks

Lost in LEGO City? In a Middle-Earth muddle? Then visit videogames.lego.com, which posts tips and tricks. *The Lord of the Rings* players, for example, are advised:

• "Gimli can be thrown to reach places he can't normally reach"
• "Don't try to work out which Dwarves are female or male. Even they don't know"
• Stuck in a level? "Try destroying everything around you. That may reveal a helpful object. Don't try this at home!"
• "If you can't quite reach something, try using an Elf."

180

Heroes, sidekicks and villains in *LEGO Marvel Super Heroes*, giving it the **most playable characters in an action-adventure videogame**; its customizer system means that players can create a billion unique characters.

D.Y.K.?

Adam West played Batman in the 1960s TV show, then provided his voice in the cartoons *The New Adventures of Batman* (1977) and *Super Friends* (1984–85). Twenty-nine years later, the actor – now perhaps equally well-known as *Family Guy*'s Mayor West – voiced a character based on himself in TT's *Lego Batman 3: Beyond Gotham* (2014).

Most villains in a Batman videogame

Alongside heroes such as Green Lantern and Martian Manhunter (top), *LEGO Batman 3: Beyond Gotham* boasts 56 of DC's darkest villains, including The Joker and Firefly (bottom). All can be unlocked by completing quests or missions, or finding character tokens.

Rarest PC achievement in *LEGO The Lord of the Rings*

The single-player-only achievement "Delved too greedily" requires more than 10,000,000,000 studs. As of 3 March 2015, this target had been hit by only 2.3% of Steam players. Xboxachievements.com says the trick is to "find and purchase Red Brick extras that will multiply the amount of studs you earn".

D.Y.K.?

LEGO Jurassic World, due out summer 2015 (to tie in with the blockbuster flick), lets you bust bricks and chase dinos through all four *Jurassic Park* movies, not just the new one.

Best-selling superhero game

As of 5 March 2015, *LEGO Batman: The Videogame*, released in 2008, had sold 13.1 million copies across the X360, Wii, DS, PS2, PS3, PSP and PC. Its music is by Danny Elfman, whose association with Batman began with his Grammy-winning soundtrack for Tim Burton's 1989 movie.

Fastest *LEGO Star Wars: The Video Game* any% completion

As posted to Twitch on 19 August 2014, Russian teen "JosephHTobinJr" took just 1 hr 13 min 42 sec to finish the first of TT Games' LEGO tie-ins. ("Any%" means to beat the game by any means.) Joseph also achieved the **fastest *LEGO Batman 2: DC Super Heroes* any% completion**: 3 hr 14 min 48 sec, as posted to YouTube on 30 June 2014.

Fastest completion of *LEGO Star Wars II: The Original Trilogy*

As posted to Twitch on 17 August 2014, US teenager "Poshact" blasted through the second *LEGO Star Wars* release in just 2 hr 25 min 33 sec.

Best-selling *Star Wars* videogame

LEGO Star Wars: The Complete Saga (2007) is by far, far away the best-selling *Star Wars* game. Developed by Traveller's Tales and combining the two earlier *LEGO Star Wars* games (covering Episodes I to VI), as of 5 March 2015 it had sold 14.73 million units across the Wii (5.51 million), DS (4.7 million), X360 (2.36 million) and PS3 (2.16 million).

First LEGO videogame made entirely out of bricks

The *LEGO® Movie Videogame*, released alongside the theatrical film of the same name in February 2014, was the first LEGO game in which everything in the game was constructed out of bricks, from buildings and furniture, to machines and vehicles. "We challenged ourselves to introduce a new element… giving players more authentic opportunities to interact with the world around them," said TT's Tom Stone.

Most prolific toy-based videogame series

Since LEGO entered the gaming scene in 1997 with Mindscape's *LEGO Island*, it had appeared in 62 games as of 6 March 2015. This includes the Bionicle franchise, entertainment licences, mobile games and sporting spin-offs.

Fastest completion of *LEGO Harry Potter*: Year 1

As posted to YouTube on 6 December 2014, Marius Losvik (Norway) sped through Year 1 of *LEGO Harry Potter* in 50 min 6 sec. He felt that he could have cut a further 15 sec off his time had it not been for a potions class.

LITTLEBIGPLANET

Summary: Despite becoming one of PlayStation's most recognizable franchises, the puzzle platform game *LittleBigPlanet* retains its quirky, home-made charm. Players use the in-game creation tools to make new content and share it in a vibrant online community.

Publisher: Sony
Developer: Media Molecule/ Various
Debut: 2008

Most player-created levels in a videogame

As of 22 April 2015, a staggering 9,271,916 *LittleBigPlanet* levels had been made by fans, along with 218,785 levels for the *LBP PS Vita*. With new levels appearing at a rate of 200 every hour – 5,000 a day – those figures can only rise.

Longest marathon playing *LBP2*

On 17–19 January 2011, David Dino, Lauren Guiliano and Sean Crowley (all USA) played *LBP2* for 50 hr 1 min in New York, USA. Their 272 levels played are the **most user-generated levels played in 24 hours**.

Fastest completion of *LittleBigPlanet 2*

Tad "RabidJellyfish" Cordle (USA) completed a single-segment run in 29 min 40 sec on 22 January 2014, using "The Overlord Glitch" to fool *LBP2* into thinking some levels had already been completed. The same gamer also achieved the **fastest completion of the original *LBP***, recording 29 min 39 sec on 19 January 2014.

Most "hearted" *LittleBigPlanet* level

Created by "DarknessBear", "Little Dead Space" takes gamers on a dark journey through the interior of the USG *Ishimura* from EA's survival-horror *Dead Space*. Since its publication in November 2008, the level had been played 41,039 times and "hearted" by a record 310,016 *LittleBigPlanet* players as of 23 April 2015.

8

Height in centimetres of the Sackpeople in *LittleBigPlanet*. Their rough hessian exterior hides a sweet secret centre, as they are stuffed with an unusual mixture of fluff and ice-cream.

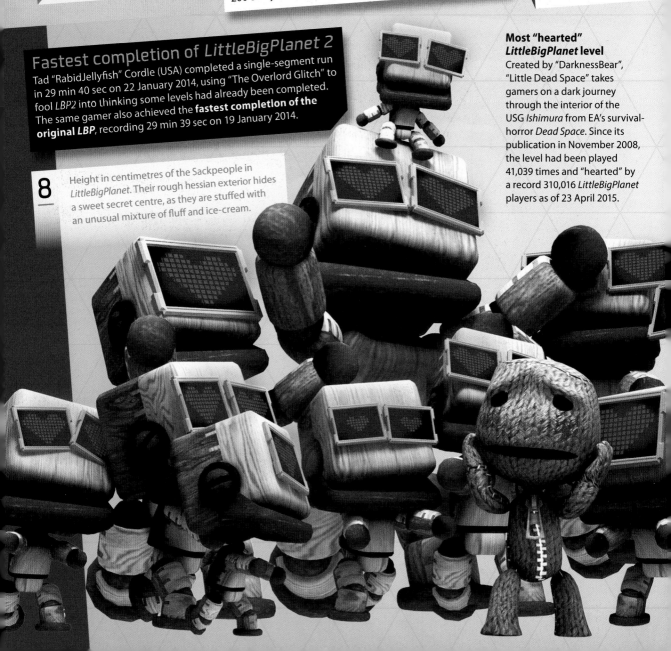

First public handheld platform beta test

LittleBigPlanet PS Vita invited players to join a beta test and emailed special codes to those who signed up to enable them to download the game. This allowed them access to a number of levels and the game's creative toolset.

Best-selling platform game for the PS Vita

As of 16 April 2015, *LBP PS Vita* had sold 1.08 million copies for the handheld console. This figure is even more impressive given that the game in second place, Ubisoft's *Rayman Origins* (2012), had sales of just 540,000. Sony's *Little Deviants* (2011) sits in third place, meanwhile, having shifted 290,000 copies.

Most downloadable platform game costumes

With more than 340 costume downloads for *LittleBigPlanet* – ranging from DC superheroes to the Muppets – there's no shortage of ways to personalize your Sackgirl (above) or Sackboy.

Close
Huh?
Close

First RPG remade in *LittleBigPlanet*

LittleBigPlanet diehard Jamie "LittleBigPlanet Show" Colliver spent two years recreating the classic JRPG *Final Fantasy VII* in *LittleBigPlanet 2*. He completed the quest on 18 November 2014, and there are now 113 videos on his YouTube channel that document its incredible making.

First browser-based level search in a game

Puzzle platformer *LBP2* allowed users to connect to the LBP.me website to find new community levels, which they could queue up to play the next time they connected their consoles to the PlayStation Network. The website allows users to check level statistics and even generate QR codes for their self-created levels.

Most critically acclaimed 3D platform games for PS3

Game	Year	Reviews	Rating
LittleBigPlanet	2008	77	94.75%
Journey	2012	54	92.56%
LittleBigPlanet 2	2011	70	92.04%
Ratchet & Clank Future: Tools of Destruction	2007	76	88.74%
Ratchet & Clank Future: A Crack in Time	2009	70	87.88%
Sonic Generations	2011	29	79.29%
Ratchet & Clank Future: Quest for Booty	2008	46	77.80%
Ratchet & Clank: Into the Nexus	2013	34	77.06%
de Blob 2	2011	39	75.13%
The Simpsons Game	2007	31	71.60%

Source: GameRankings as of 16 April 2015

D.Y.K.?

As of April 2015, players of *LittleBigPlanet 3* had used 105,661,120 layers for their levels – that's more than the distance from Miami to New York, USA.

Most BAFTA wins for a platform series

As of April 2015, Sackgirl, Sackboy and *LittleBigPlanet* had won four British Academy of Film and Television Arts awards. In 2009, the first game won the Artistic Achievement prize, while the PSP version took the Handheld award a year later. At the 2012 ceremony, *LittleBigPlanet 2* won both the Family and Game Innovation categories. This is no small feat for *LBP*, especially when you consider that Nintendo's all-conquering *Super Mario* platform franchise has won just two BAFTAs.

Best-selling platform game series for PS3

With a formidable 5.75 million copies of *LittleBigPlanet* and 3.32 million of *LittleBigPlanet 2* sold as of 16 April 2015, Sackboy's adventures have shifted even more copies on the PlayStation 3 than those of *Ratchet & Clank* and *Sonic the Hedgehog*.

Activision

Founded in October 1979 by a group of Atari programmers, Activision is one of the longest-running videogames publishers, and also the world's **first independent software developer and distributor**. The company has gained critical acclaim for titles such as *Guitar Hero*, helped bring about tech innovations with toys-to-life series *Skylanders* and smashed sales records with chart-busting hits such as *Call of Duty*. In July 2008, it joined forces with *World of Warcraft* publisher Vivendi Games, becoming Activision Blizzard.

94.75%

TOP 10 BEST-SELLING SERIES PUBLISHED BY ACTIVISION

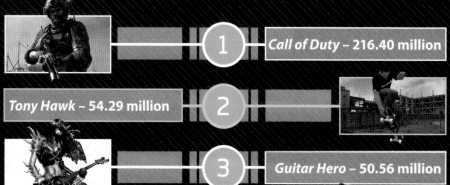

1 — *Call of Duty* – 216.40 million

Tony Hawk – 54.29 million — **2**

3 — *Guitar Hero* – 50.56 million

Spider-Man – 35.35 million — **4**

5 — *Skylanders* – 18.63 million

Star Wars – 14.17 million — **6**

7 — *Transformers* – 12.20 million

X-Men – 11.72 million — **8**

9 — *Destiny* – 10.17 million

True Crime – 6.43 million — **10**

Source: VGChartz as of 29 April 2015 (excludes Blizzard games)

GameRankings rating for *Tony Hawk's Pro Skater 2* (2000) on the PlayStation, making it the most critically acclaimed of all Activision games as of 29 April 2015.

4.5 million

Activision's first smash-hit game was the groundbreaking platformer *Pitfall!*, which was released in April 1982 and sold more than 4.5 million copies for the Atari 2600 – making it the console's best-selling title after *PAC-Man*.

$500 MILLION

Total value of stock sent out to retailers for the launch of *Destiny* on 9 September 2014.

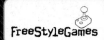

Activision Blizzard owned 13 games studios as of April 2015, including *Call of Duty* creator Infinity Ward and *Skylanders* team Toys For Bob.

WANT TO MAKE GAMES?

"Aspiring developers should engage in as many opportunities to develop their skills as possible. There have been many opportunities for young developers to learn via uni courses, YouTube videos and smaller developers starting up throughout the world. Game development is challenging work, but can also be incredibly rewarding."

Daniel Suarez, from CoD developer Sledgehammer Games

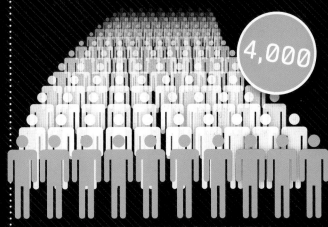

4,000

NUMBER OF PEOPLE CURRENTLY
EMPLOYED BY ACTIVISION

Q&A

Alex Ness, Chief of Staff at *Skylanders* developer Toys For Bob

What's it like to work as part of the *Skylanders* developer team?
It's actually a very surreal experience – in a good way. There are just so many creative people with a lot of ideas that really care about this franchise.

What *Skylanders* innovations are you most proud of?
Bringing toys to life in a videogame. Combining two things kids like – action figures and videogames – is a big part of what makes them like *Skylanders*. So while we've done a lot of really cool things, it's the initial innovation that made the whole thing possible.

Are you innovating anything new for future *Skylanders* titles?
We don't have anything we can officially announce at this point. But in the same way that *Skylanders: Spyro's Adventure* was innovative in bringing toys to life and, most recently, *Skylanders: Trap Team* effectively brought life to toys with the whole trapping mechanic, we have learned that we can't rest on our laurels; we've got to come up with something new and big and surprising for our fans.

MADDEN NFL

Summary: For over 25 years, *Madden NFL* has been bringing the physical intensity and spectacular athleticism of American football into living rooms. In-depth player analysis and changing ratings ensure that the series keeps evolving and remains one of the most realistic sports videogame series of all.

Publisher: EA Sports
Developer: Various
Debut: 1988

Highest-rated QB in *Madden NFL 15*

Based on stats measuring speed, play action, stamina, throwing power and accuracy, as of February 2015 Tom Brady of the New England Patriots was the No.1 quarterback, with an overall score of 99.

Most successful *Madden* player

Eric "Problem" Wright (USA) is widely considered to be the greatest *Madden* player ever. As of 20 March 2015, the all-conquering field king had won 18 *Madden* gaming titles and earned $380,000 (£255,773) from *Madden* competitions.

D.Y.K.?

An overall score of 97 made Seattle Seahawks' Marshawn Lynch the highest-rated running-back in *Madden NFL 15*.

Longest-running sports videogame series

Despite John Madden's broadcasting retirement in 2009, the series that bears his name shows no sign of slowing down. With 31 games released in 27 years as of 11 March 2015 – the **most videogames in an NFL franchise** – *Madden NFL* is the most enduring title in sports gaming. Since the series debuted in 1988, only one year has passed without a new *Madden* title: 1989.

First team on consecutive *Madden NFL* covers

To celebrate *Madden NFL*'s 25th anniversary edition, fans were polled to see which star should be on the cover. An incredible 40 million votes were cast – the **most votes for a videogame cover**. From a list of 60 players, Detroit Lions' former running-back Barry Sanders topped the poll and duly appeared on the front of 2013's *Madden NFL 25*. In doing so, he followed in the footsteps of another Detroit Lions player, wide receiver Calvin Johnson Jr, who had appeared on the cover of *Madden NFL 13* (2012).

Highest-ranked team in *Madden NFL 15*

Developer EA Tiburon regularly updates football players' scores, meaning they and their teams' ratings change as the season progresses. As of February 2015, the New England Patriots were the team to beat, with an impressive overall score of 92.

First female winner of the Madden Bowl

First held in 1995, the annual Madden Bowl takes place every Super Bowl weekend and features celebrities and athletes battling it out. At Madden Bowl XVII in February 2011, TV presenter and actress Maria Menounos became the first woman to lift the trophy.

PHIL SIMMS · JIM NANTZ

Fastest-selling NFL videogame

Released on 26 August 2006, *Madden NFL 07* was the first game in the franchise to be released for the PlayStation 3 and Wii consoles, and the last to appear on the Game Boy Advance. Hotly anticipated, it went on to sell an incredible two million copies in its first week of sale.

First American football videogame to use Kinect voice commands

As anyone who's ever visited a stadium knows, sports fans aren't shy when it comes to voicing opinions. But with the release of *Madden NFL 13* on 28 August 2012, gamers could do more than just argue with the calls – using their voice, they could call plays and change formations.

Most lines of commentary in an NFL videogame

Including play-by-play by Gus Johnson, colour commentary by Cris Collinsworth (both USA) and voiceovers by players, broadcasters and various actors, *Madden NFL 11* has a staggering 90,000 lines of commentary.

Highest margin of victory on *Madden NFL 09*

Serial gaming record-breaker and *Madden* ace Patrick Scott Patterson racked up a winning margin of a whopping 192 points during a game on *Madden NFL 09 All-Play* on the Wii, as verified on 24 June 2009.

Longest-serving commentator

The first *Madden* game might have hit the shelves in 1988, but it wasn't until the release of *Madden NFL 96* that the technology could support commentator John Madden's famous tones. He hung up his gaming microphone 12 years later, in 2008, after completing work on *Madden NFL 09*.

Most critically acclaimed American football games

Game	Publisher	Year	Ranking
NFL 2K1	Sega	2000	94.50%
Madden NFL 2002	Electronic Arts	2001	92.32%
Madden NFL 2004	Electronic Arts	2003	91.77%
NFL 2K	Sega	1999	91.53%
Madden NFL 2003	Electronic Arts	2002	91.20%
Madden NFL 2001	Electronic Arts	2000	90.78%
ESPN NFL 2K5	Sega/2K Sports	2004	90.52%
Madden NFL 2005	Electronic Arts	2004	90.33%
NFL Blitz	Midway	1998	90.13%
NFL 2K3	Sega	2002	89.79%

Source: GameRankings as of 1 April 2015

Tips 'n' Tricks

In *Madden NFL* – just like the actal NFL – special teams can play a crucial role in grinding out the win. Kick-off returns offer you the chance to score a devastating touchdown. When your receiver catches the ball, head straight down the middle of the field. Take advantage of all the blocks your team-mates can throw at the opposition before breaking to the outside, where there is more space. With a bit of luck and a lot of practice, you'll soon have your receiver dancing his way towards the endzone.

MARIO KART

Summary: Mixing the high-octane excitement of the racetrack with the crazy, unmistakeable world of Mario and co., *Mario Kart* is one of the most addictive and successful series in gaming. Racers dodge slippery banana peels and hurl Koopa shells at fellow drivers in a madcap dash for the chequered flag.

Publisher: Nintendo
Developer: Various
Debut: 1992

Best-selling racing series

With sales of 104.3 million across all iterations, *Mario Kart* has far outsold any other racing franchise, as of 8 April 2015. *Mario Kart Wii*, released in 2008, still sells strongly seven years later. With 35.15 million units shifted, it is the **best-selling racing game**.

Fastest lap of Airship Fortress in *Mario Kart DS*

On 26 July 2014, Swiss gamer Thomas Bolton dodged Bullet Bills and Rocky Wrenches as he hurtled around the Airship Fortress track in 34.1 sec. The **fastest lap of the Koopa Beach 2** track is 12.7 sec, by David Roldan (Spain) on 4 October 2014.

200 cc

Speedy new racing class added to *Mario Kart 8* in a free update, released on 23 April 2015. With 150 cc being the game's previous premium class, it's the **fastest mode for a *Mario Kart* game**.

First *Mario Kart* game with full anti-gravitational racing

Initially, the developers for 2014's *Mario Kart 8* considered attaching drills to the front of players' carts, allowing them to drill underground. But this idea was ditched in favour of anti-gravity racing. Although it had been glimpsed in the Rainbow Road course in *Mario Kart DS* (2005), this was the first time anti-grav racing had been used as a major gameplay feature.

D.Y.K.?

In *Mario Kart 8*, the plumber's famous facial hair has been fully animated, giving it a life of its own – his moustache can be seen twitching as he hurtles around the track.

Longest-running kart videogame series

Mario Kart 8 debuted in Japan on 29 May 2014, some 21 years 275 days after the original *Super Mario Kart* on 27 August 1992. The series evolves with every new release: *Mario Kart 8* used the Wii's HD capabilities to become the **first high-definition** *Mario Kart* **game**.

Highest-rated racing game on Nintendo DS

Mario Kart DS had a mighty GameRankings score of 91.43%, as of 30 March 2015. This places it way out in front of the second-placed handheld racing game, Codemasters' *Race Driver: Grid* (2008), which can boast an otherwise respectable score of 82.55%.

Best-selling handheld racing game

With worldwide sales of 23.11 million as of 31 March 2015, according to VGChartz, *Mario Kart DS* (2005) stands proudly at the top of the handheld racing podium. It is also the **first Nintendo-published game to feature competitive online play**. Earlier online Nintendo titles, such as *Animal Crossing* and *Phantasy Star Online Episode I & II*, had not offered players the opportunity to battle each other.

Fastest lap of Rainbow Road

Since *Super Mario Kart* was released by Nintendo on the SNES in August 1992, gamers have been trying to master its final, most challenging track – Rainbow Road. On 9 November 2014, Guillaume Leviach (France, inset) set a lap time of 16.53 sec on the NTSC edition of the game, beating the previous record by just 0.01 sec!

Most successful *Super Mario Kart* gamer

French racing whizz Guillaume Leviach (above) has racked up 18 "world-record" times on various tracks in the PAL version of *Super Mario Kart* on the SNES, and 11 "world-record" times in the NTSC version – making for a grand total of 29 records as of 28 February 2015.

Most *Super Mario Kart* World Championship trophies

The first annual *SMK* World Championship was held in 2002. Each year players compete across four modes of the 1992 SNES classic. As of 8 April 2015, 31-year-old Florent Lecoanet (France) was the overall winner, winning seven gold trophies.

Most viewed racing game fan film

Daredevil French prankster Rémi Gaillard certainly knows how to get noticed. Since uploading his *Mario Kart* homage to YouTube on 3 December 2008 – in which he drives along real-life roads dressed as the iconic plumber – he had received 63,083,695 views as of 27 April 2015.

Fastest *Super Mario Kart* time trial (female)

Leyla Hasso (UK) wasn't even born when *Super Mario Kart* was released on the SNES in 1992. But that hasn't stopped her setting the track alight. On 22 February 2014 – aged just 14 years 9 months – Leyla recorded a time of 51.87 sec on the PAL version of Vanilla Lake 2 at the Games Expo East Kent in Margate, UK.

Fastest completion of Mario Circuit 1 in *Super Mario Kart* (NTSC version)

On 23 November 2014, veteran *Mario Kart* racer Sami Çetin (UK) flew around the Mario Circuit 1 track and crossed the finishing line in just 55.97 sec.

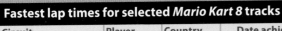

Fastest lap times for selected *Mario Kart 8* tracks

Circuit	Player	Country	Date achieved	Time
Bowser's Castle	"Kyser"	USA	26 February 2015	1 min 58.896 sec
Cloudtop Cruise	"Ray"	Canada	30 March 2015	1 min 58.487 sec
Dolphin Shoals	"Sinuous"	UK	19 December 2014	1 min 58.496 sec
Mario Circuit	"Chonko3"	Japan	15 April 2015	1 min 43.891 sec
Mario Kart Stadium	"Diogo"	France	4 February 2015	1 min 34.899 sec
Shy Guy Falls	"Danny"	Netherlands	11 April 2015	1 min 54.213 sec
Sunshine Airport	"Domenico"	Italy	13 March 2015	1 min 56.605 sec
Sweet Sweet Canyon	"Victor"	France	12 April 2015	1 min 48.384 sec
Twisted Mansion	"Tyler"	Canada	21 March 2015	1 min 54.756 sec
Water Park	"Domenico"	Italy	22 April 2015	1 min 40.365 sec

Source: Mario Kart World Records as of 27 April 2015

Fastest completion of the All-Cup Tour

Mario Kart Double Dash!! (2003) includes an All-Cup Tour in which players have to race on all 16 game tracks. On 26 December 2007, Benoît "TJazZ" Boudreau (Canada) took home the trophy with a total time of 29 min 7 sec.

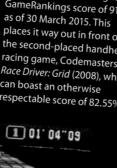

MASS EFFECT

D.Y.K.?

The Catalyst's voice in *Mass Effect 3* is, in fact, three different voices combined: leads Mark Meer and Jennifer Hale, and the boy Shepard meets in the game's first mission.

Fastest completion of ME3 ("Insanity" mode)

On 24 June 2013, French gamer "SpartanB218" uploaded a YouTube video in which he completed the game on its highest difficulty setting in 3 hr 48 min 48 sec.

The **fastest completion of Mass Effect 3 multiplayer match on "Platinum" difficulty** is 6 min 43 sec, achieved by the team of "Cricketer15", "d_nought", "dunvi" and "Payn3zz" on 13 May 2013.

1,800

Years of combined playing time by four-player co-operative *Mass Effect 3* matches on PS3 and Xbox 360 in two weeks from 2 August 2012 – the **most popular multiplayer mode in a console RPG**.

Summary: An acclaimed and hugely successful sci-fi action RPG series, *Mass Effect* follows Commander Shepard's attempts to save the galaxy from the ancient machine race of the Reapers. Gamers not only engage in blistering shoot-outs, but they can also start romances with their crew.

Publisher: Microsoft/EA
Developer: BioWare
Debut: 2007

First *Minecraft* mash-up texture pack

Minecraft's mash-up texture packs for its console edition began with *Mass Effect*. The downloadable add-on introduced 36 character skins from the sci-fi RPG, as well as transforming all of *Minecraft*'s blocks and items into their *Mass Effect* equivalent.

Most popular *ME3* squad member

It helps to have people – and aliens – that you trust by your side when you're saving the universe. Perhaps that's why, 24.1% of *ME3* players in 2013 chose to have the brave-yet-sensitive Liara T'Soni on their team, according to BioWare.

Fastest completion of *Mass Effect 2*

On 8 February 2014, gamer "LettersWords" (USA) completed the sci-fi sequel in a single-segment run of just 1 hr 32 min 28 sec. He did so on "Casual" difficulty, with DLC, and having previously completed the game.

The **fastest completion of *Mass Effect*** is 1 hr 40 min 5 sec, achieved on 2 February 2013 by a player mysteriously known only as "your name here".

First person named after a *Mass Effect* character

On 7 January 2014, Adam and Cheri Rose (USA) gave birth to a daughter called Tali'Zorah, named after a Quarian alien. BioWare celebrated the arrival by tweeting a photo of the baby, saying "Welcome to Earth, Tali'Zorah".

Highest rank on *Mass Effect 3* multiplayer

The N7 ranking is the total number of points a player has gained in *Mass Effect 3* multiplayer mode. The more points accrued, the higher the player's ranking. As of 21 January 2015, gamer "Idlehands88 7s" (USA) was ranked highest, with 100,345 points.

Most critically acclaimed RPG

Mass Effect 2 on Xbox 360 boasted a hugely impressive GameRankings rating of 95.77% from 75 reviews, as of 7 April 2015. This placed it ahead of *The Elder Scrolls V: Skyrim* in second place, with 95.15%. *Mass Effect 2* for the PC was in third place with a rating of 94.52%, underlining the title's incredible reputation.

Most prolific videogame voice actor

Steve Blum (USA) had made 354 credited videogame appearances as of 10 March 2015, including Grunt in *Mass Effect 2* and *3*. "On a game like *Mass Effect*, they really do go for quality," he told 411Mania. "We have to put some really solid chops into each line. And they take their time with us until we get it right."

Most prolific videogame voice actor (female)

As of 22 January 2015, the vocal talents of Jennifer Hale (Canada) can be heard in 168 games. One of her major roles is the female version of Commander Shepard in the *Mass Effect* series (right).

Most popular *Mass Effect* single-player character class

According to BioWare's own statistics, *Mass Effect* players love a straight shooter. In *Mass Effect 2*, more gamers played as a Soldier than all other classes put together, while the Engineer was the game's **least popular character class**. The trend continued in *Mass Effect 3*, with 43.7% of players opting for the Soldier rather than selecting a character class possessing the game's more unusual powers.

Most challenge points in *Mass Effect 3* multiplayer

Challenge points are earned by completing in-game tasks such as scoring with a particular weapon multiple times. As of 21 January 2015, gamer "Red Eileen" (British Virgin Islands) had 575,675 points. Earning these took 4,598 hr on the in-game clock, across more than 11,155 matches.

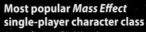

Most popular *Mass Effect* romance				
Character	Gender	Occupation	Appearances	Fan votes
Dr Liara T'Soni	Female	Asari scientist	3	29%
Tali'Zorah nar Rayya	Female	Quarian machinist	3	27%
Garrus Vakarian	Male	Turian agent	3	13%
Miranda Lawson	Female	Human Cerberus officer	2	9%
Kaidan Alenko	Male	Human Sentinel	3	6%
Jack	Female	Human criminal	2	=5%
Ashley Williams	Female	Human soldier	3	=5%
Samantha Traynor	Female	Human comm specialist	1	=2%
Thane Krios	Male	Drell assassin	2	=2%
Steve Cortez	Male	Human Alliance pilot	1	1%

Source: www.poll-maker.com as of 14 April 2015

First downloadable alternative ending

Some fans were disappointed by *Mass Effect 3*'s multiple-choice conclusion, so they launched the "Retake *Mass Effect*" campaign. BioWare's co-founder Dr Ray Muzyka (Canada) apologized and promised an "extended cut" to clarify the ending. This was issued in June 2012, with additional cutscenes to explore players' in-game decisions.

METAL GEAR

Summary: The brainchild of Hideo Kojima, the long-running *Metal Gear* series is the most successful and influential in the stealth genre. Many of its most popular outings focus on the silent-but-deadly talents of special forces operative Solid Snake.

Publisher: Konami
Developer: Konami/
Kojima Prod./Platinum
Debut: 1987

Most hidden ghosts in a game

Metal Gear Solid has 43 hard-to-find images, or "ghosts", hidden in the game. To view these ghosts – in fact, pictures of *Metal Gear Solid*'s producers – you need to take photos with the camera at certain specific spots, such as Sniper Wolf's dead body.

8

Number of different camouflages – including Spirit, Moss and Hornet Stripe – that can be won in *Metal Gear Solid 3: Snake Eater*. These are acquired by players defeating a boss with their bare fists or a tranquilizer gun.

First stealth game to use the Fox Engine

Built by Kojima Productions, the Fox Engine is designed to make it easier for the studio to develop games across different platforms. It made its full debut in 2013 with the release of *Pro Evolution Soccer 2014*, and was first used on a stealth game for *Metal Gear Solid V: Ground Zeroes*, released on 18 March 2014.

D.Y.K.?

In order to defeat the Psycho Mantis in *Metal Gear Solid* (1998), the player must break his "psychic connection" by unplugging the controller and reconnecting it into the second port on the console.

Best-selling stealth game

As of 8 April 2015, *Metal Gear Solid 2: Sons of Liberty* had sold 6.05 million copies on the PS2 alone, according to VGChartz. Hideo Kojima's series can boast total sales of 36.75 million, making *Metal Gear* also the **best-selling stealth series**.

Tips 'n' Tricks

Metal Gear Rising: Revengeance initially foxed players with its parrying system. In order to parry, you need to push the directional stick towards an attack and press the Light Attack button. Your enemy will glow red when it is preparing to mount an attack that can be parried, giving you a helpful warning. If an attack can't be parried, evasive manoeuvres include jumping, dodging and ninja running. Remember: practice makes perfect, so use the tutorials at the start of the game to hone your technique.

Longest cutscene in a game

A cutscene is a non-interactive film between game levels that helps to explain the story. *Metal Gear Solid 4: Guns of the Patriots* (2008) not only features a record-breaking 27-min cutscene but also an epic end sequence lasting 1 hr 9 min 4 sec – the **longest end sequence in a game**.

First stereoscopic stealth game

Metal Gear Ac!d² (2005) introduced the "Solid Eye", an add-on stereoscopic device for the PlayStation Portable. In reality, the gizmo is less impressive than it sounds – a folding cardboard box with specialized lenses that fit over the PSP's screen to create a 3D image.

Most bosses in a *Metal Gear* game

There are 11 major enemies in *Metal Gear 2: Solid Snake* – in order of appearance: Black Ninja, Running Man, Hind D, Red Blaster, Four Horsemen, Jungle Evil, Night Fright, Dr Drago Pettrovich Madnar, Metal Gear D, Gray Fox and Big Boss.

Longest marathon on a stealth game

On 6–8 August 2011, Ben Reeves (USA) played the *Metal Gear Solid* series for 48 hr in Minneapolis, Minnesota, USA.

Best-selling PSP strategy game

As of 8 April 2015, *Metal Gear Ac!d* had sold 870,000 copies, ahead of Sony's *Invizimals* in second place.

First interactive digital graphic novel for the PlayStation Portable

Released in the USA on 13 June 2006, *Metal Gear Solid: Digital Graphic Novel* was a digitized version of the *Metal Gear Solid* comic illustrated by revered Australian artist Ashley Wood. It featured original music and animation, and also allowed readers to zoom in and out using the analogue stick. Images could then be scanned and stored on to a database.

Fastest completion of *Metal Gear 2: Solid Snake*

A speed-runner known as "Jaguar King" (USA) completed the PS2 version on the "Easy" setting in a time of 51 min 9 sec on 17 August 2014. "Jaguar King" performed his run on the European PAL version of the game as it runs faster than any Japanese or US versions – an obvious advantage when it comes to speed-running.

Most critically acclaimed stealth game

As of 8 April 2015, *Metal Gear Solid 2: Sons of Liberty* had accrued a mighty rating of 95.09% on GameRankings.

Fastest completion of *Metal Gear Rising: Revengeance*

While most *Metal Gear* games involve stealth, *Metal Gear Rising* is a more action-orientated title starring the cyborg ninja Raiden. On 19 August 2013, gamer "General_Beatrix" completed *Revengeance* on the "NewGame+" mode on the "Hard" difficulty setting in a super-quick 50 min 44 sec.

Fastest single-segment completion of *Metal Gear*

Marko "Master-88" Vanhanen (Finland) completed the NES version of the original *Metal Gear* (1987) in just 27 min 57 sec on 15 June 2010. The **fastest completion of *Metal Gear Solid* on "Extreme" difficulty** is 1 hr 7 min 56 sec, recorded by "TheSlade" on 19 January 2014. But that's a lifetime compared with the **fastest single-segment completion of *MGS V: Ground Zeroes***. On 26 August 2014, a YouTube video showed "danielducruetU3" (Spain) completing the game's main mission in just 2 min 59 sec.

LONGEST JOURNEY IN MINECRAFT

In March 2011, Kurt J Mac (USA) set out on an epic quest to reach the fabled Far Lands – the area roughly 12,500 km (7,767 mi) from a player's initial spawn point, where technical issues in pre-version-1.8 releases caused strange anomalies in the terrain. Kurt has been documenting his journey on his YouTube channel "Far Lands or Bust!", using his quest to raise money for charity.

On 10 April 2015, Kurt discovered that he had walked 2,097,152 blocks (2,097.15 km; 1,303 mi). By this point, he was crossing a threshold that caused the game to become more glitchy. "There's a computational rounding error that will only get worse as I get further," he said. Incredibly, after three years of continuous travelling, Kurt was only 16.78% of the way towards his final destination.

FAR LANDS OR BUST!

"Having a unique theme or spin definitely helps you gain attention."

Kurt J Mac

820

Amount in dollars of Kurt's original charity target – which fans helped him reach in just five days. He has since gone on to raise $250,000 (£166,963) for the Child's Play charity.

LU[...]IN[...] IN THE OVERWORLD

BLOCKBUSTING SUCCESS

In a few short years, *Minecraft* has become an award-winning and record-breaking phenomenon, shattering sales records on its way to becoming the third-best-selling videogame of all time. It drives millions of gamers to distraction as they build their own blocky versions of the world, and it has elevated some of its fans on YouTube to global superstars.

There is almost no limit to what can be crafted in this unique sandbox game, and it has inspired a whole lot of record-breaking. Here, over the next 20 pages, you'll find enough Guinness World Records to fill a mineshaft, and you'll also get the chance to set some *Minecraft* records of your own.

MINECRAFT CHALLENGES

The graphics are blocky and there's practically no storyline… indeed, if you choose to, you can just wander around a randomly generating landscape bothering sheep and digging holes. But it doesn't take long to realize that this is the joy of Markus Persson's block-building and now blockbusting game.

The open-ended 3D world of *Minecraft* has tapped into something fundamentally human – not just in videogamers but in millions of people who would otherwise not consider themselves gamers. With the choice between two modes – Creative and Survival – you can decide what you want your *Minecraft* experience to be. Like LEGO®

before it, it's a pastime limited only by your imagination.

Here, we celebrate some of our favourite *Minecraft* record-breaking and give you the chance to attempt a few of your own. Get digging!

As a reader of this year's *Gamer's Edition*, you have the chance to get your hands on a brand-new Guinness World Records certificate for your *Minecraft* skills. Our gaming consultants have devised a series of 10 challenges that put your mining and crafting skills to the test, all of them against the clock. So, you think you're good at *Minecraft*? Then let's see!

Starting here, you'll find the basic guidelines for each challenge at the bottom of the page. These set out the rules that you must stick to when attempting your record. Be sure to follow these, or you risk being disqualified.

To make it all official, we'll need you to video-record your attempt and upload this as evidence. Make sure we can see the screen clearly! And you'll need a good digital stopwatch.

For the full guidelines and details of how to upload your evidence, visit the link below. Good luck!

guinnessworldrecords.com/minecraft

MINECRAFT CHALLENGES

1. Fastest time to dig to bedrock

Here's an easy enough record challenge to get you started: how quickly can you dig your way to bedrock – the lowest possible layer in *Minecraft*? To give you a head start, fill your hotbar with whatever you like.

1 To give everyone a fair and equal chance, we've chosen a seed for use with this challenge. To enter the seed, select "More World Options" when creating your world and type in this code:

GWR

The stopwatch must start as soon as you spawn in the newly created world.

2 Once you spawn in Creative mode, you can load your hotbar with whatever you want – except for TNT!

You must then switch to Survival mode by opening the console box and entering:

/gamemode s

You're now free to pick a spot and start digging (below).

Q+A: *MINECRAFT* – THINKING INSIDE THE XBOX

We spoke to Chris van der Kuyl (far left) and Paddy Burns (left) of 4J Studios, the company that developed *Minecraft* for consoles.

Do you think the emphasis on gameplay creativity carries genuine benefits for its players?

CHRIS: The creativity that *Minecraft* unleashes is why it's so successful. I don't think there's anything that we do as developers that the players aren't doing themselves inside the game. You only have to go on YouTube to see the imaginations of millions of people worldwide. We're stunned by it every day.

Have you got any ideas for new record challenges?

PADDY: Well, I've seen many people trying to do records like the most dynamite blocks that blow up. They put them up on YouTube and then immediately try to better them.

CHRIS: The possibilities for record-breaking are almost endless, really. What blows me away is when you find teams of people spending weeks or months on a single world. Some of the big YouTubers have now been building single worlds for years and they're still going. That's unprecedented in videogames. We released the console edition three years ago and it's still drawing in new people. Most games have shelf lives of six months. So that's amazing.

Do you think that *Minecraft* might inspire new generations of architects and designers?

PADDY: Well, it definitely makes kids think creatively. The design element is going to bring them on from a very early age. It opens their imaginations and gives them a tool to show what they can do.

CHRIS: In about 20 years time, you're going to see major cities such as London filled with block buildings. And that will all be *Minecraft*'s fault!

THE CHALLENGES

You'll find a mix of Creative and Survival mode challenges to test your *Minecraft* skills:

1. **Fastest time to dig to bedrock** (see bottom of the page)

2. **Tallest staircase built in one minute** (p.102)

3. **Fastest time to kill 10 Zombie Pigmen** (p.104)

4. **Longest minecart track built and ridden in three minutes** (p.106)

5. **Fastest time to craft all 10 *Minecraft* tools** (p.108)

6. **Fastest time to build an Iron Golem** (p.110)

7. **Most wood collected in three minutes** (p.112)

8. **Fastest time to make and eat three cakes** (p.114)

9. **Fastest time to build a house** (p.116)

10. **Fastest time to build a two-block piston door** (p.118)

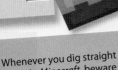

3 Whenever you dig straight down in *Minecraft*, beware of falling into a monster-filled cave system, an abandoned mineshaft or a lava cavern. Consider placing torches as you go so that you can see where you're going.

4 Bedrock is the indestructible lowest layer in *Minecraft*, but it's not an even layer of rock. You might hit bedrock at varying depths, depending on the landscape. As soon as you see it (right), stop the stopwatch.

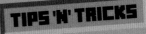
TIPS 'N' TRICKS

When loading up your hotbar, go for something strong, such as a Diamond Pick or Shovel.

Take advantage of the terrain: starting from the top of a mountain will mean you have more ground to cover. Finding cave systems that open out on to the surface could save you a lot of time if you're looking to get close to bedrock.

To avoid digging your way into an unexpected pool of lava, consider digging a hole that's two blocks wide, digging downwards in alternating steps to prevent a surprise drop to your death.

24 Number of *Simpsons* character skins introduced to *Minecraft* on 27 February 2015, including Homer, Marge, Bart, Lisa, Maggie, Principal Skinner, Willie, Otto, Milhouse, Mrs Krabappel, Ralph and Nelson.

Most popular videogame beta
Minecraft entered beta testing on 20 December 2010. Between then and its PC and Mac release on 18 November 2011, some 10 million gamers signed up to play. The nature of the content was hinted at by the developers, with enigmatic statements such as, "Throwing an egg has a chance of spawning a chicken."

D.Y.K.?
The distinctively textured and now iconic sword originated with a similar item in Markus Persson's unfinished pre-*Minecraft* RPG *Legend of the Chambered*.

BEST-SELLING GAME ON HOME COMPUTER FORMATS

Official Mojang figures, as of 17 March 2015, put *Minecraft*'s PC/Mac sales at 18,910,800. Will Wright, designer of its closest rival *The Sims* (11.24 million), wrote in *Time* magazine: "A lot of people are trying to figure out how to teach seven-year-olds to code, and it's a tricky thing to do. *Minecraft* is one of the clear landmarks along that path."

MINECRAFT CHALLENGES

2. Tallest staircase built in one minute
Mode: Creative
Your second challenge is to build a staircase as high as you can, using stair blocks crafted from any material you wish. You have one minute and the time starts from the instant you spawn. (And don't forget to film your attempt!)

1

The staircase must be free-standing – i.e., not built against the side of a hill or mountain – so find a clearing with no large structures nearby. The time starts when you spawn, so your hotbar will be empty at the beginning of the attempt. Your first task, therefore, will be to select the materials you want to use. For this record, you can build the staircase from any material you wish – but you have to craft the stairs first, not just use them straight from your inventory.

2
You must craft proper L-shaped stair blocks that change your elevation without needing to jump (which would save your energy if you were in Survival mode). Each stair block can be made from a different material if you so desire.

"'Indie games' wasn't even a term when I started..."

Markus "Notch" Persson, creator of *Minecraft*

BEST-SELLING INDIE GAME

Microsoft's 2014 acquisition of Mojang for $2.5 billion (£1.6 billion) put paid to the developer's indie credentials, but *Minecraft* had already sold 60 million copies. Its non-console sales alone are nearly twice the population of Sweden – homeland of Markus Persson (above).

MOST-PLAYED XBOX LIVE GAME

Minecraft had been played for 1.75 billion hr on Xbox Live as of May 2014. This equates to 199,772 years – nearly the same time that modern humans have been on Earth.

The *Xbox 360 Edition*, by Mojang and 4J, debuted on the platform in May 2012 and sold so speedily that, according to Markus Persson, it turned a profit within an hour.

As of 17 March 2015, this edition is the **best-selling game on Xbox Live Arcade**, shifting 1,152,725 copies. However, that's just a fraction of its overall sales. VGChartz, which counts physical sales, calculates a global tally of 7.08 million. Microsoft put the combined total at more than 12 million as of 4 April 2014, ranking it in Xbox's top five best-sellers.

"When we started talking about sales," Mojang's Daniel Kaplan said, "we would be super-happy to sell one million copies. That would have put us on par with *Battlefield 1943* and *Castle Crashers*, which are both awesome games."

BEST-SELLING IOS APP

As of 26 February 2015, *Minecraft: Pocket Edition* – designed specifically for mobile devices – had sold over 30 million copies. According to Apple, it secured the top spot as the best-selling paid app – not just game – of 2014 on both iPhone and iPad, despite having been released back in 2011.

Highest-grossing indie game

Between October 2010 and December 2011, *Minecraft* made $80.8 million (£52 million) before tax. In 2012, it took in $237.7 million (£154 million) pre-tax. Combined, that's a whopping $318.5 million (£206 million). "It's a bit strange," Persson marvelled to Forbes, "that I can create something once and keep getting paid."

Most concurrently played non-competitive PC game

It's not just sales and profits that mark popularity: Mojang figures reveal that on 9 January 2015, the number of users playing *Minecraft* simultaneously hit 1.4 million (and that excludes mobile and offline players).

TIPS 'N' TRICKS

3 Your staircase should run smoothly upwards without any gaps, although you can – if you wish – build horizontal landings. It should be possible to walk to the very top of the steps without needing to jump.

Remember, the record is based on the difference in elevation between the bottom and top of the staircase – i.e., the *height* of the staircase, not the number of blocks.

4 When your one minute is up, stop building but keep filming: we need to be able to see the newly built steps clearly as you walk down. To get an accurate measure of the height, we'll use your co-ordinates. Press **F3** (or **alt-F3** on a Mac) to bring up the "debug screen". Then look for the Y co-ordinates – this is your elevation. Note your elevation at the bottom of the stairs then at the top.

The difference between the two is the record value.

It's important that you video your attempt clearly so that our adjudicators can see that your staircase rises without a break. If you build straight up in a diagonal line, it will be easier to adjudicate, but it's up to you to find the most efficient design.

For every stair block you place (apart from the first one), you will need a supporting solid block to anchor the step above. The key to this record is finding your rhythm as you place the alternating stair blocks and solid blocks. Master this, and you could be a record-breaker!

LUL" U_T_ _

LONGEST *MINECRAFT* MARATHON

Whether you're taking on Creepers or foraging for material to build your dream home, time in *Minecraft* can fly by. But Martin Fornleitner of Vienna, Austria, took marathon gaming to the next level. On 19–20 August 2011, he played *Minecraft* on a Sony Xperia Play handset for 24 hr 10 min – equating to 72.5 in-game days. Despite numerous attempts to beat it, his record still stood as of 27 March 2015.

Most common block in *Minecraft*

As air is neither solid nor indeed visible, it's easy to forget that it counts as a block in *Minecraft* terms. What's more, this eminently forgettable element is the most common block in the game. Air occupies every space not already filled by another block, and even spreads to adjacent areas. In fact, the only place you won't find air is down in the Void – although, thanks to the mysteries of *Minecraft*, you won't suffocate if you end up there. In the alpha/beta 1.3 release, players could count air blocks in their inventory.

FASTEST NO-GLITCH COMPLETION

Utilizing a predetermined world seed (known as an Any% Set Seed), "Funderful1000" (Canada) defeated the Ender Dragon in 9 min 40 sec, as seen on a video uploaded to YouTube on 21 March 2015.

Most wins in *Minecraft's* Survival mode

The introduction of the Ender Dragon gave *Minecraft* players a new goal to aim for – completing the game. While some players vie to reach the end credits as quickly as possible, others try to outdo the rest with their quantity of wins. As of 3 March 2015, *Minecraft* player "Gravey4rd" had killed the Ender Dragon a whopping 4,502 times. That means that more than half of "Gravey4rd"'s 7,545 games have ended in victory – an impressive success rate by anyone's standards.

FARTHEST DISTANCE RIDDEN ON A PIG IN *MINECRAFT*

If you don't fancy tackling *Minecraft's* vast terrain on foot, you could always follow the example of L J Pegross (USA). As of 3 March 2015, this enterprising player had travelled a hoof-blistering 667.03 km (414.47 mi) on the back of a pig, beating the previous record by 536 km (333 mi).

FASTEST COMPLETION WITH GLITCHES

Game glitches such as item duplication help speed-runners finish *Minecraft* even more quickly. A video uploaded to YouTube on 28 April 2015 showed "joshgaming4" sprinting through the game in just 4 min 7 sec.

MINECRAFT CHALLENGES

3. Fastest time to kill 10 Zombie Pigmen

Mode: Survival

These neutral mobs don't pose a danger to you until you attack them, and this record challenges you to attack them to death, so expect a bit of resistance. First, though, to reach these rotting undead pig-people, you'll need to build a portal to the Nether…

 1 Before you start the stopwatch, you can fill the eight slots in your hotbar with whatever you want in Creative mode. (The minimum will be 14 x obsidian and 1 x flint and steel to build a portal.) Choose carefully, as you won't be able to add to your hotbar once the challenge is underway. In the example below, we've selected a diamond sword and armour, five steaks (to provide health) and the blocks needed to build the portal.

 2 With your hotbar filled, you must now switch to Survival mode. You do this by opening the console box and entering

/gamemode s

3 When you're ready, start the stopwatch. Your first task is to build a Nether Portal from 14 blocks of obsidian (left). The portal doesn't require corners, but you must include them for this record. Activate the Nether by striking the flint and steel inside the frame – you'll know it's worked when the purple vortex appears (right).

BRILLIANT BLOCKS

RAREST BLOCK

The dragon egg appears above the End Portal once players have defeated the Ender Dragon and won the game's final battle. With only one egg spawned per game, it is the ultimate *Minecraft* trophy.

RAREST ORE BLOCK

With an average of 0.2 blocks spawning per *Minecraft* world chunk (which comprises some 65,356 blocks), emerald ore is pretty hard to find. Thankfully, it has limited in-game use.

STRONGEST MINEABLE BLOCK

With a Hardness rating of 50 and a Blast Resistance rating of 6,000, obsidian is the perfect material for players looking to reinforce their houses. But you'll need a diamond pickaxe to mine it.

STRONGEST BLOCK

Bedrock makes up the lowest layer of each *Minecraft* world. It has a Hardness rating of -1 and a Blast Resistance rating of 18,000,000, making it impervious to TNT.

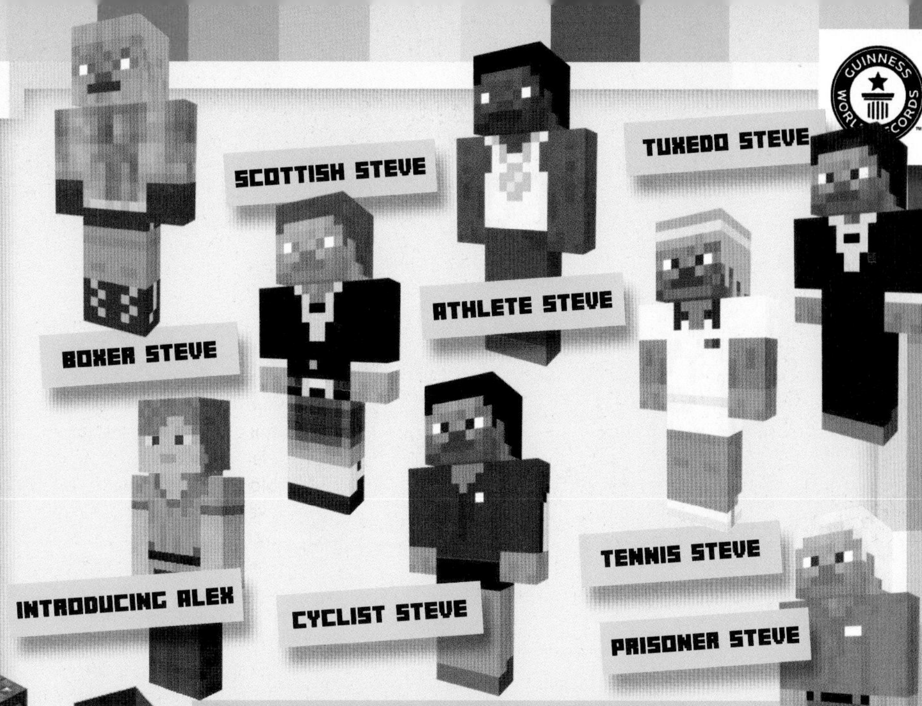

SCOTTISH STEVE

TUXEDO STEVE

ATHLETE STEVE

BOXER STEVE

INTRODUCING ALEX

CYCLIST STEVE

TENNIS STEVE

PRISONER STEVE

INTRODUCING STEVE AND ALEX

Minecraft's default player mode is one of the game's most recognizable characters, and was referred to as "Steve" during the early stages of development. With the 1.8 update in 2014, a female variant of the main character, known as "Alex", was added to the *Minecraft* world – although technically both characters should be referred to as "Steve?" and "Alex?"

Fastest time to build 100 Snow Golems in *Minecraft* (Creative mode) Comprising two stacked snow blocks – and with a pumpkin or jack-o'-lantern for a head – Snow Golems hold the distinction of being *Minecraft*'s **first player-built mobs**. On 17 April 2015, gamer Ashley Surcombe (UK) built 100 Snow Golems in just 1 min 46.246 sec in

Cheltenham, Gloucestershire, UK. She achieved her record time by crafting the Snow Golems' bodies first, before flying overhead and dropping pumpkins on top of each one. Better known by her YouTube name of AshleyMarieeGaming, Ashley posts *Minecraft* videos to her fans, and as of 28 April 2015 had 533,141 subscribers and 31,044,371 video views.

4 The Nether is *Minecraft*'s equivalent of Hell. Watch out for the health-depleting fires and the rivers of lava. (If you die down here, you'll respawn in the Overworld but you're likely to lose your inventory items. If this happens, the attempt must be abandoned.) If you're carrying armour, now's the time to get it on!

5 Hunt down those Zombie Pigmen and start the slaughter. They become more aggressive as you attack, so watch out – they can gang up on you! The time stops once you've killed your 10th Pigman.

TIPS 'N' TRICKS

You can use any weapon(s) you want for this challenge, and there are plenty of ways to kill a Pigman, so get creative! You can take your sword to them, obviously, but consider a bow and arrow, damage potions and even cacti. The key to success is dispatching the Pigmen as quickly as possible. They do fight back, so you need to get the right balance of weapons to armour and food in your hotbar – remember: you start off in Creative mode, but you'll be fighting in Survival mode, so you will not be invincible.

MO _ _ ULE

Rarest *Minecraft* title screen

As of 3 March 2015, there are 359 possible title splash texts in the PC version of *Minecraft*, ranging from "Ride the pig!" to the *Star Fox*-inspired "Does barrel rolls!" However, there's also a 0.01% chance that the title itself will change on the menu screen, rearranging the letters to spell "Minceraft".

FIRST BOSS MOB IN *MINECRAFT*

Unlike *Minecraft*'s normal mobs, boss mobs feature advanced attack patterns and are designed to challenge even the most skilled players. The Ender Dragon made its debut on 11 November 2011. In order to reach the dragon's home world, players must collect 12 Ender Pearls from defeated Endermen and craft them into Eyes of Ender.

FIRST ANIMAL MOB IN *MINECRAFT*

Today's *Minecraft* is filled with animal mobs, but it wasn't until 22 August 2009 that the pig appeared in *Minecraft* release *0.24_05*. Since then pigs have undergone several revisions, notably correcting their earliest cross-eyed versions.

Rarest biome

Biomes are distinct types of terrain, ranging from snowy hills and arid desert planes to lush forests and marshy swampland. The rarest biome in *Minecraft* is known as Jungle Edge M, which is a sub-type of the already-rare Jungle biome. To make this type uniquely special, Jungle Edge M must also contain mountainous terrain, which is largely uncommon at the edge of a biome's area.

STRONGEST MOB IN *MINECRAFT*

Unsurprisingly, the toughest mob in *Minecraft* is one of the game's two boss mobs. Despite its formidable speed and imposing appearance, the Ender Dragon has to settle for second place behind the Wither – a floating three-headed terror whose HP of 300 is 100 higher than the dragon.

Largest playable area in an open-world game

For much of *Minecraft*'s existence, its map size has, technically, been limitless. As of its 1.8 ("Bountiful Update") release for PC on 2 September 2014, however, land is no longer generated beyond 30 million blocks from a player's starting position. This gives the *Minecraft* world a finite playing surface area of 3.6 billion km² (2.2 billion sq mi). As such, each *Minecraft* map is approximately seven times larger than planet Earth.

D.Y.K.?

Strange but true: *Minecraft*'s villager mobs will only fall in love and create baby villagers if there is at least one door present in the village.

SMALLEST MOB IN *MINECRAFT*

The silverfish is a diminutive critter that made its in-game debut on 9 September 2011. Silverfish are so small that they don't reach the top of half-block-high slabs – but they are still twice as hardy as *Minecraft* chickens.

MINECRAFT CHALLENGES

4. Longest minecart track built and ridden in three minutes

Mode: Creative

Minecarts have multiple uses, whether you're moving resources, building a roller-coaster or just looking to move around faster. This record tests your ability to build a minecart track – and also to ride it – in a three-minute window.

1 The time for this record starts as soon as you spawn. Your task is to build a track using minecart rails. You've got three minutes, but in this time you've got to lay the tracks and – importantly – ride the entire length of the track inside a minecart!

2 You can lay the track on a structure built from scratch (such as this stone ramp, left) or make the most of the terrain by laying the track down a mountainside (below). You will be judged on the number of connected track pieces you lay, so design carefully!

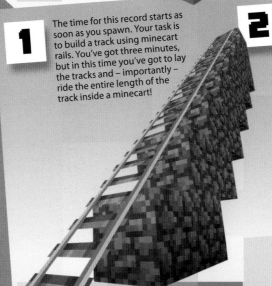

FIRST HOSTILE MOB IN MINECRAFT

Enemies, or hostile mobs as they're known in-game, didn't make their debut until 14 August 2009. The first hostile mob to appear was the zombie, which arrived alongside skeletons in the game's 0.24_02 release. As fast as humans, they were a nasty surprise...

Highest biome

Although it's possible to create incredibly tall, mountainous biomes using *Minecraft*'s "Amplified" world generator, there's one natural biome that dwarfs all others.

WEAKEST MOB IN MINECRAFT

The chicken has only 4 Health Points to call its own – two fewer than the bat, four fewer than the sheep and six fewer than the rabbit! By comparison, the mighty boss mob Wither has 300 HP. Let's hope they don't meet.

BLAZE

GUARDIAN

WITCH

RABBIT

MOOSHROOM

ENDERMAN

VILLAGER

FLASH MOBS

Minecraft wouldn't be the same without mobs – the passive, neutral, hostile and boss creatures that roam the game's expansive world. Named after a classic computer term denoting their "mobile" nature, mobs have been part of the *Minecraft* experience since the game's early stages. When mobs are killed, they often drop items that can be useful resources.

The Savannah M biome (and its near relative, the Savannah Plateau M) features giant mountains and steep cliffs that jut out from the surrounding terrain, frequently passing through the cloud layer and often reaching the game's maximum height limit. Altitudes of y=200 and above make Savannah M higher even than the mountainous terrain of the Extreme Hills biome.

FASTEST MOB IN MINECRAFT

As of 27 March 2015, no mobs can move faster than the spider. Not only can they move almost as fast as the player character, but they can also scuttle up walls and through blocks, making them hard to shake off.

TIPS 'N' TRICKS

Holding down the "W" on your keyboard adds a little forward momentum when you're in your minecart – this gets you down a ramp quicker or nudges you forward on a level stretch of track.

To ensure that your minecart comes to a complete stop before the three minutes are up, make sure there's a definite end to the rails. If you're still coasting after three minutes, you will be disqualified.

Be wary of placing a block at the end of the track, as you might bounce back and end up travelling in the wrong direction!

4 Keep an eye on the time – the last part of the record requires you to place a minecart (from the inventory) at the very start of your track and ride it to the end. You MUST reach the end of your track before the three minutes are up: if you're still moving along the track during the three minutes, your attempt will be invalid. The time stops once your cart comes to rest (so think about how this might influence the design of your track).

3 Consider the option to build down as well as up. If you think it will give you a competitive edge, you can dig down and run the track into your newly dug hole. You can even lay the track down a mountain then into a hole. Again, it's up to you to decide how best to use your three minutes.

13

Age of the founding member of "ChiseledBrick", one of the teams of building experts who came forward to help with the construction of the Walt Disney World Resort in *Minecraft*.

FIRST PLAYER-BUILT STRUCTURE

When *Minecraft's* public alpha version was released on 17 May 2009, users were quick to catch on to the game's architectural possibilities. It took TIGSource forum user "muku" just 49 min to post an image of a bridge he or she had made in *Minecraft* consisting of nine stone blocks linking one raised area with another.

LARGEST REAL-WORLD THEME PARK RECREATED IN *MINECRAFT*

Covering an area of 110.3 km² (43 sq mi), the Walt Disney World Resort in Bay Lake, Florida, USA, is one of the largest entertainment complexes in the world. As of 3 February 2015, the MCMagic server had recreated five of the resort's six theme and water parks. Every ride and show is present, and costumed "cast members" are on hand to help out.

D.Y.K.?

Over 150 different building blocks can be found in *Minecraft* – from dirt and clay to obsidian, which is used to create a portal to the hell-like Nether dimension.

MINECRAFT CHALLENGES

5. Fastest time to craft all 10 *Minecraft* tools

Mode: Creative

You won't get very far in *Minecraft* without your tools! This record challenges you to build the 10 tools on the right (in any order you like) in Creative mode. Start the stopwatch with an empty crafting grid – the time stops when you place the 10th tool into your inventory. Simple, really! It's just a matter of speed…

IRON PICKAXE

You can hack your way through everything but bedrock and obsidian with an iron pickaxe.

3 x iron ingots
2 x sticks

STONE SHOVEL

Dig through clay, dirt, gravel, sand and snow (and make snowballs) with a cobblestone shovel.

1 x cobblestone
2 x sticks

FISHING ROD

It's not just useful for catching raw fish – a rod can hook land creatures and small objects.

3 x sticks
2 x string

FLINT AND STEEL

Need to start a fire? Use flint and steel to light a spark – just be careful: those flames can spread like, well, wildfire!

1 x iron ingot
1 x flint

FIRST DOCUMENTED TOWER BUILT

Fifty-three minutes after *Minecraft*'s public alpha version release on 17 May 2009, TIGSource forum user "increpare" built the first four-walled structure in the game, offering a glimpse of the creative opportunities that would help make the game a global phenomenon.

First pixel art made in *Minecraft*

With its images created from individual squares of colour, pixel art is a natural fit for the blocky world of *Minecraft*. Two-and-a-half hours after the game's alpha version release on 17 May 2009, TIGSource forum user "jwaap" posted a pixel art recreation of Nintendo's Mario.

First *Minecraft* mash-up texture pack

On 4 September 2013, Mojang released a *Minecraft* add-on that introduced 36 character skins and environments from the successful sci-fi RPG *Mass Effect* (see p.94).

Most popular texture pack for *Minecraft*

The "LB Photo Realism Pack 256x256 Version 10.0.0", by "Scuttles", is designed to make the natural environments in the *Minecraft* world more realistic. As of 17 March 2015, it had been downloaded 2,195,836 times from fansite Planet Minecraft.

First full-scale-modelled country in a videogame

In April 2014, the Danish Geodata Agency published a 1:1 scale recreation of Denmark in *Minecraft*, based on their own geodata. The map allows players to explore every inch of the country, which measures

FIRST ATTEMPT TO RECREATE AN ENTIRE REAL-WORLD MUSEUM

In September 2014, the British Museum in London, UK, launched a project to recreate its entire building and interior – complete with all of its exhibits – in *Minecraft*. Through its own website, the British Museum sends gamers challenges that contribute to the building's construction. As of 27 March 2015, the epic project was still ongoing.

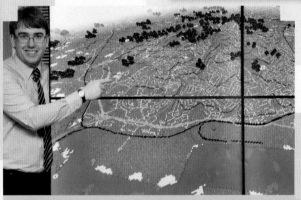

LARGEST REAL-WORLD PLACE RECREATED IN *MINECRAFT*

On 23 September 2014, the Ordnance Survey (OS) released an updated map of mainland Britain and its surrounding islands called "GB Minecraft 2". Based on the OS's own geographical data, the map represents some 224,000 km^2 (86,500 sq mi) and required 83 billion blocks, with each block representing a ground area of 25 m^2 (269 sq ft).

43,000 km^2 (16,602 sq mi). On 7 May 2014, cyber vandals managed to smuggle dynamite into the country and blew up a small area of the project. Thankfully, the damage was soon repaired by other players.

First exhibition of real-world art in *Minecraft*

On 21 November 2014, the Tate Modern gallery in London, UK, announced plans to build an exhibition in *Minecraft*. As of 2 February 2015, two paintings – *The Pool of London* (1906) by André Derain, and Christopher Nevinson's *Soul of the Soulless City* (1920) – had been recreated in-game and were available for download from the Tate Modern's website.

LEAD

Fancy yourself as a *Minecraft* Indiana Jones? You'll need to fashion yourself a slimy, mob-snaring lasso/whip.

4 x string
1 x slimeball

SHEARS

Use shears to strip leaves from trees, shred a cobweb and trim the wool from a living sheep (you get three times more if you don't kill it!).

2 x iron ingots

CLOCK

Tell the time using the position of the Sun or Moon with a clock (remember, it won't work in the Nether or the End).

4 x gold ingots
1 x redstone

COMPASS

Similar to the clock but crafted from iron instead of gold, the compass points you back to your last spawn point.

4 x iron ingots
1 x redstone

IRON HOE

You'll need a hoe to make your first steps towards farming in *Minecraft*, allowing you to till dirt and grass into farmland.

2 x iron ingots
2 x sticks

DIAMOND AXE

Feeling flush? Get wood-chopping faster with a glitzy diamond pickaxe.

3 x diamonds
2 x sticks

LARGEST *MINECRAFT* CATHEDRAL

Minecraft's ever-ambitious community is no stranger to spectacular builds, and "GNRfrancis"'s creative project Epic Cathedral certainly lives up to its name. Uploaded to YouTube on 30 October 2012, this gargantuan edifice – replete with elegant spires, stained-glass windows and buttresses – is made from a staggering 2,082,348 blocks, and took GNRfrancis more than a year to complete.

Longest *Minecraft* tunnel
On 3 August 2013, Australian *Minecraft* player Lachlan Etherton headed underground and dug a tunnel measuring 10,502 blocks (equating to 10,502 m or 34,455 ft). Etherton's tunnel took him 50 min to dig, 20 min to light by hand with torches, and a further 10 min to record a video corroborating his efforts.

FIRST WORKING COMPUTER CIRCUIT BUILT IN *MINECRAFT*

Minecraft players have produced some impressive feats of engineering using the power-transmitting block redstone. On 28 September 2010, "theinternetftw" uploaded a video of a working 16-bit Arithmetic Logic Unit (ALU) in the game, earning the approval of Notch himself.

Tallest possible structure in *Minecraft*
Although *Minecraft* is designed to allow as much creative freedom as possible, there are some restrictions. Structures cannot exceed 256 blocks in height – owing to the fact that each world is made of "chunks" measuring 16 x 16 x 256 blocks. However, in order to build that high, construction must begin immediately above each world's bedrock layer. In other words, mega-builders will need to go down before they can go up...

MINECRAFT CHALLENGES

6. Fastest time to build an Iron Golem

Mode: Creative

Vine-covered Iron Golems are non-hostile mobs that spawn in big villages, but you can make one of your own. We challenge you to build one in the fastest time – but from scratch! So yes, you'll need to build a furnace and smelt the iron from ore. Ready? Steady? Go-lem!

1 An Iron Golem is built from a pumpkin on top of a T-shape of iron blocks. Although you're in Creative mode, with this record you will need to craft the iron blocks from raw iron ore.

2 Before you start the stopwatch, you must pre-load your hotbar with the following blocks:

64 x stone, 64 x coal, 1 x pumpkin, 36 x iron ore, 4 x wood

When you're ready to go, give a loud, clear signal ("Go!") and start the timer.

3 You'll need to do some crafting, so your first step will be to make a crafting table. To do this, turn your wood blocks into planks.

4 Next, you'll need to build a furnace (because you'll need to smelt iron into iron ingots before you can make iron blocks). For one furnace, you'll need eight cobblestones arranged in a square pattern (left). There are enough stone blocks in your hotbar to make eight furnaces, but it's up to you to decide how many you think will be sufficient.

BIGGEST SMALLEST HOUSE IN MINECRAFT

On 30 November 2013, "DRRcreations" uploaded his mega-version of "GTFOCreepers'" smallest house in *Minecraft* (see below) to YouTube. Expanded to a ratio of 1 block:1 pixel, the super-sized house is a towering 64 blocks tall, as opposed to the original's four.

Smallest house in *Minecraft*

Big doesn't have to mean beautiful in the gargantuan world of *Minecraft*. Builder "GTFOCreepers" (see above) went in completely the opposite direction, building a tiny house that took up a mere six blocks (four blocks high, with two additional blocks to the side). It may be diminutive, but it is also fully functional, as it features all of the basic amenities required for the game's Survival mode – including a bed, a furnace, crafting box and storage chest.

And, owing to its three surrounding doors, players can take shelter inside from hostile mobs.

Longest straight minecart track in *Minecraft*

Inevitably, mining plays a major role in the game, particularly in Survival mode where the ability to shift large quantities of resources is key to success. And the most efficient way to do this is by using carts and rails.

On 6 June 2012, Planet Minecraft user "Arcadeportal32" set about fashioning an ambitious 2,414 km (1,500 mi) of railroad at a ratio of 1 block:1 metre. It was called "The Railroad =Of= Notch", in honour of Markus Persson. As of 25 March 2015, the project remained unfinished, but at 200,000 blocks (200 km; 124 mi) it was more than long enough for "Arcadeportal32" to claim the record.

FIRST PLAYABLE GUITAR IN *MINECRAFT*

On 27 September 2013, *Minecraft* player "disco" used a complex series of redstone circuits to create a mile-long (1.6-km) guitar. Once a user has kickstarted a strum loop of their choice, it's possible to switch chords and perform music by moving between 10 available chord plates.

Longest bridge in *Minecraft*

On 9 August 2014, Canadian *Minecraft* gamer "Pie Hole" tried to tame the landscape (and make transportation around the world a little less fraught) by building a single-block-width wooden bridge that stretched for 26,011 blocks – which equates to 26.01 km (16 mi) in real-world distance.

LONGEST MINECRAFT ROLLER-COASTER TRIP

Thrill-seekers should take a look at this ride built by Czech Planet Minecraft user "Gaermine". Packed with sharp twists and hair-raising drops, it thunders above the clouds on a 50-min journey that makes this the longest roller-coaster trip in the game, as of 24 March 2015.

255

Number of "layers" in *Minecraft*, which measure altitude within the game. Sea level is layer 62, clouds appear at layer 127, and layer 255 marks the uppermost edge of the game environment.

5 With your furnace(s) built, you can start smelting the 36 iron ore blocks into the ingots you need. To smelt the ore, you need a fuel – in this case, coal. You have 64 pieces of coal to play with, so get smelting!

6 You need four iron blocks to make your golem, and each block is made up of nine iron ingots (so you'll need to smelt 36 ingots in total).

7 With your iron blocks made, arrange them into the T-shape shown below.

8 The final ingredient is the pumpkin. Drop this on top of the iron structure you've just made and your mob will magically come to life. *Voilà*, you've built your Iron Golem. All that's left for you to do is shout "Stop!" and stop that stopwatch.

T 'N' L T

73,669

Total number of views that Ragnur Le Barbare's *Minecraft* recreation of the *Battlestar Galactica* had earned on the Planet Minecraft website, as of 28 April 2015. It had also been downloaded an amazing 16,715 times and received 744 diamonds – Planet Minecraft's much sought-after form of "likes". And if Ragnur continues to work on the ship's interior (of which there are tantalizing glimpses in his update logs), then his creation's popularity will surely continue to grow.

LARGEST *MINECRAFT* SPACECRAFT

Minecraft user Ragnur Le Barbare's gargantuan recreation of the titular starship from the popular sci-fi series *Battlestar Galactica* took over four-and-a-half months to build and measures a whopping 1,400 x 500 x 200 blocks. If that's not mind-boggling enough for you, the entire build consists of more than 5,043,664 blocks… and Le Barbare also embarked on a selection of interiors for the ship.

MINECRAFT IN THE MIDDLE

A Middle-Earth server initiated on 16 October 2010 by user "q220" is an ambitious, community-based attempt to recreate J R R Tolkien's world in its entirety. It features some of fantasy's most famous locations, including The Shire, Rivendell, Helm's Deep and Mordor.

Largest original fantasy city completed in *Minecraft*

Minecraft builders aren't afraid of putting in long hours. Check out Adamantis, a beautiful project by "jamdelaney1", who spent three months building the sprawling city with lofty spires, sweeping staircases, palatial courtyards and intricate detail – a solo project that used more than 60 million blocks. Much of the city is built from ice, obliging explorers to download a special mod beforehand to prevent its stunning, torch-illuminated streets from melting straight into the ground.

LARGEST ORIGINAL FICTIONAL WORLD

Players on the Aerna server are crafting the mother of all original fictional *Minecraft* worlds. Work on Aerna is ongoing – but, as of 4 February 2015, the 84-GB project measured 102,400 x 51,200 blocks. Spanning multiple continents, it covered 5,242.88 km^2 (slightly over 2,000 sq mi), with impressively detailed landmarks and sprawling towns.

MINECRAFT CHALLENGES

7. Most wood collected in three minutes

Mode: Survival

Harvesting trees is pretty much the first objective for anyone in Survival mode, and this record challenges how quickly you can hack them down. You can use your hands on their own or fashion yourself an axe – it's up to you – but you've only got three minutes…

1

This record is about chopping down trees and collecting as much wood as you can. It starts from the moment you spawn in Survival mode. Trees are common in most biomes, but to ensure fairness, use this seed:

gwrhome

Here, you'll find yourself surrounded by trees. There are six main species – oak, dark oak, birch, spruce, acacia and jungle – but it doesn't matter which you chop down.

2

WOODEN AXE

You've got three minutes, so you might want to consider building a wooden axe to speed up your chopping. Of course, this takes time so might not be your best option…

POLICE PUBLIC CALL BOX

THE *MINECRAFT* TARDIS THAT IS BIGGER ON THE INSIDE

Minecraft has a unique take on the laws of physics, but YouTube user "HiFolksImAdam" has excelled with his in-game re-creation of Doctor Who's beloved *TARDIS*. Using crafty technical know-how – involving the ability to clone and paste certain portions of the world map on demand – "HiFolksImAdam" created a version of the blue box that's considerably bigger on the inside than its exterior would suggest.

The Time Lord *officially* came to the world of *Minecraft* for the first time in October 2014, with the release of *Doctor Who Skins Volume I* on Xbox Live. The full version featured several iterations of the Doctor, some of his most popular companions and iconic enemies such as Zygons and Daleks.

Highest-rated movie-based *Minecraft* add-on

Minecraft fans clearly like their old-school sci-fi, because the highest-rated Xbox Live add-on based on a film series, as of 19 March 2015, is the *Star Wars Classic Skin Pack*. User ratings place this and other *Star Wars* skins far ahead of franchises such as *Guardians of the Galaxy*, *The Avengers* and *Spider-Man*.

Most common *Minecraft* bug

First raised on mojang.com on 24 October 2012 and unresolved as of 8 May 2015, the most persistent issue is the evidently infuriating "Mobs visually sinking through solid blocks". However, it has been speculated that this glitch is due to internet connection speeds rather than a flaw in the game itself.

MINECRAFT: 'WARTS 'N' ALL

Harry Potter's alma mater Hogwarts is one of the most recognizable places in modern fiction, and the ambitious PotterCraft project sought to build the entire school, including the Great Hall, the common rooms, the Chamber of Secrets and even the Room of Requirement. Sadly, the server is no longer active, but PotterCraft remains one of the most ambitious fan projects undertaken in *Minecraft*.

LARGEST RECREATION OF AN EXISTING FICTIONAL WORLD

George R R Martin's *A Song of Ice and Fire* fantasy series has spawned HBO's *Game of Thrones* and a *Minecraft* project to replicate its setting, Westeros. As of 4 February 2015, the WesterosCraft project had mapped out around 806.5 km² (311.4 sq mi), using approximately 22,000 x 59,000 blocks.

3,631

Kickstarter backers who had pledged a total of $210,297 (£130,705) towards *Minecraft: The Story of Mojang* when funding closed in 2011. The documentary was released the following year. In 2014, however, Mojang put a stop to a campaign for a fan-made feature film. Notch tweeted: "We don't allow [...] kickstarters based on our ip without any deals in place. :/"

D.Y.K.?

The resurgence of interest in archery might not be just down to Katniss Everdeen using a bow in the *Hunger Games* series – the weapon, crafted from wooden sticks, is also popular in *Minecraft*. The Super Cheats site suggests watching out in case a skeleton mislays one: "there is a very, very rare chance that the bow that they drop will be an enchanted one".

Ultimately, the metric for this record is the number of logs you gather of any species. You don't have to chop down the entire tree (right) – you can hack out a single block (above) if you so choose – it's up to you.

4 If you opt to make an axe, the wood you use for the work bench and the axe will *not* count towards your final total – it's only the wood blocks in your inventory that counts.

5 Don't forget to collect the wood blocks as you go – if it's not collected, it doesn't count towards the record.

UNLI_ _N_TI_

2,622 MINECRAFT PLAYERS TOGETHER!

FIRST MINECRAFT MULTIPLAYER SERVER

On 31 May 2009, Markus "Notch" Persson released a four-minute video of himself and several friends leaping around in the game and building structures together, all logged into his own private server.

First *Minecraft*-related forum post

On 17 May 2009, Notch posted a message on the TIGSource forum announcing the release of *Minecraft*'s initial public alpha version. Within minutes, other users had posted images and videos of their creations (see pp.108–09) and suggested new features. *Minecraft*'s vibrant online community was born.

MOST CONCURRENT PLAYERS ON A SINGLE *MINECRAFT* SERVER

Minecraft's mixture of building and survival challenges might be a popular co-operative pursuit but, surprisingly, its server-based multiplayer component was never intended to be used by large numbers of people at once. Yet on 1 August 2011, YouTube channel Yogscast managed to squeeze 2,622 players on to a single *Minecraft* server.

MINECRAFT CHALLENGES

8. Fastest time to make and eat three cakes

Mode: Creative

Feeling hungry? This record will really fill you up! It's a *Minecraft* twist on the classic Guinness World Records gluttony record… except this time you've got to make the cakes *and* eat them! Baking is a piece of cake – what's challenging here is that you're cooking against the clock…

1 This record requires you to make and eat three cakes as fast as you can, but you must eat each cake in its entirety (all six slices) before you start on the next one.

Luckily, you'll be in Creative mode for this, so there's no need to find milk, wheat, sugar and so on.

The recipe (left) will fill your whole crafting grid. For each cake, you will need the following:

3 x milk

2 x sugar

1 x egg

3 x wheat

2 The time starts as soon as you spawn, so your first task is to gather your ingredients. Then get baking. (Are those cherries on top? Where did they come from?!)

First online appearance of the name *Minecraft*

Inspired by the webcomic *The Order of the Stick*, Notch initially intended to call his creation *Minecraft: Order of the Stone*. But eventually he dropped the subtitle and announced the shorter name on 14 May 2009, just prior to the game's alpha release.

FIRST MINECRAFT SERVER WITH BITCOIN ECONOMY

In *Minecraft* server BitQuest, transactions require emeralds – which can be mined using an iron or diamond pickaxe, crafted using a block of emerald, or smelted using emerald ore. Each emerald is worth a fraction of a bitcoin in-game, and can be used to purchase goods such as blocks.

MOST POPULAR MINECRAFT FAN ART

DeviantArt user "Djohaal" made this digitally produced image of a striking *Minecraft* landscape complete with hills, water, underground lava and a small stone tower. As of 29 January 2015, it had been viewed 375,442 times and downloaded 582,105 times, making it the most popular piece of *Minecraft* fan art on the website.

Most popular *Minecraft* forum

Much of the building game's stratospheric success can be attributed to the passion of its online fanbase. The *Minecraft* community has produced millions of forum posts, generated billions of YouTube video views and shared countless in-game creations.

Featuring community-generated content on almost every conceivable *Minecraft* topic – including mods and maps, survival tips and advice on making the most of creative mode – Minecraft Forum had 3,473,458 registered users as of 30 January 2015. It had played host to more than two million threads and a mind-blowing 26 million posts.

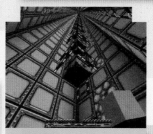

MOST-DOWNLOADED MINECRAFT PROJECT

With 1,248,878 downloads as of 29 January 2015, "The Dropper" by "Bigre" plunges players into a series of dizzying free-falls, in which they must avoid different shapes and structures to reach the level floor intact.

First online *Minecraft* video

Perhaps unsurprisingly, it was creator Markus Persson who posted YouTube's first *Minecraft* video, on 13 May 2009. The game was at such an early stage that Persson had yet to decide upon a name for his creation, and the video's block-based action was simply referred to as "Cave game tech test".

Most popular *Minecraft* server network

On 28 January 2015, an amazing 34,434 gamers played *Minecraft* concurrently on the Mineplex server network. Mineplex's MMO-style experience is made possible by its use of multiple servers, which communicate simultaneously to keep the game from grinding to a halt.

3 To eat your cake, you need to place it in front of you on the ground – you can't eat it from your hotbar like other foodstuffs. You have to right-click on it six times to devour each delicious – and thankfully calorie-free – slice. (Just be careful not to destroy the block underneath the cake, as this causes it to disappear forever.) Once it's eaten, you can get crafting the next cake. The time stops when the third cake is fully consumed.

REAL MINECRAFT CAKE TO EAT

If all this talk of cake is making you peckish, why not bake a genuine *Minecraft*-inspired cake of your own? Just make a simple sponge or chocolate cake and cover it with white and red icing. Just don't make and eat three back to back – that would be greedy!

TIPS 'N' TRICKS

It's worth knowing where to look for your cake ingredients. Eggs can be found anywhere there are groups of chickens. You can find wheat in farms or plant your own. Sugar is refined from sugar cane – the tall, stalk-like plant seen along the edges of water. For milk you need three buckets, each made of three iron ingots. Once you have these, you just need a cow. Using the bucket on the cow will fill it with fresh milk.

MOST VIEWED *MINECRAFT*-BASED CHANNEL ON YOUTUBE

Despite the huge amount of *Minecraft* content on YouTube, when it comes to video views one channel obliterates all the competition: "BlueXephos", home of Yogscast's Lewis & Simon. Thanks to the duo's infectious *Minecraft*-related comedy antics, as of 20 March 2015 it had amassed a staggering 3,008,460,349 views across 3,609 videos.

Oldest fan-made *Minecraft* video on YouTube

On 17 May 2009 – the day on which the game formerly known as *Minecraft: Order of the Stone* debuted in its abbreviated form – TIGSource user "Evil-Ville" posted the **first fan-made *Minecraft* video on YouTube**. This clip, which demonstrated Evil-Ville's castle-building prowess, is sadly no longer available. Instead, the longest-surviving fan video on YouTube is the simply titled "minecraft" by "jwaap". This minute-long tour of a rudimentary map and bridge-like structure appeared online on the same day, shortly after Evil-Ville's inaugural effort.

MOST WATCHED GAMING VIDEO

"Revenge – A Minecraft Parody of Usher's DJ Got Us Fallin' in Love" by "CaptainSparklez" isn't just the **most watched *Minecraft* video**. Its 156,076,698 views as of 20 March 2015 also makes it the most watched YouTube video for any videogame. All together now: "Baby tonig the creeper's trying to steal your stuff again…"

Highest-earning *Minecraft* contributor to YouTube

As of February 2015, YouTube stats expert Social Blade estimated that the highest-earning YouTuber focusing on *Minecraft* is "PopularMMOs", with annual earnings ranging between $750,900 (£495,343) and $12 million (£7.9 million) – which works out at a mean average annual income of $6.37 million (£4.2 million).

The "PopularMMOs" stream features unusual *Minecraft* missions and fun in-game mods, and had amassed an astonishing 2.4 billion views and 4,255,285 subscribers as of 3 May 2015.

MOST SUBSCRIBED *MINECRAFT* CHANNEL ON YOUTUBE

As of 20 March 2015, the "Sky Does Minecraft" channel had secured an incredible 10,907,974 subscribers. Its most popular offering is "New World – A Minecraft Parody of Coldplay's Paradise", which had racked up 55,237,329 views. "Sky" is a pseudonym of Adam Wahlberg, who previously played *RuneScape* on his "Jin the Demon" channel.

Most videos in YouTube's *Minecraft* songs top 10

Thanks to his all-conquering Usher parody "Revenge" (see above), "CaptainSparklez" (USA) is far and away the most successful musical *Minecraft* parodist on YouTube. As of 23 March 2015, CaptainSparklez could count five entries in the most-viewed *Minecraft* songs top 10. His parodies of Usher's "DJ Got Us Fallin' in Love", Taio Cruz's "Dynamite", Coldplay's "Viva la Vida", Justin Timberlake's "Take Back the Night" and PSY's "Gangnam Style" have totalled 448,552,576 views.

MINECRAFT CHALLENGES

9. Fastest time to build a house

Mode: Survival

Shelter is one of your basic needs in life, and that's no less true when you're in *Minecraft*. This challenge involves building a basic, secure home – the kind that you might build on a first night in Survival mode. The record is based on how fast you can complete it.

 1

The home you need to build for this record should cover a minimum area of 4 x 4 blocks, but you can build it as big as you want. The walls can also be made of anything you want, but remember that this challenge is in Survival mode. You'll be judged on how fast you can build it, so choose wisely! Oh, and you must use this seed:

gwrhome

The time starts as soon as you spawn, so you'll need to harvest all the materials you need as quickly as you can.

 2

When placing the first layer of blocks, leave a gap for the door. Another requirement for a house is at least one window, so be sure to make room for it while building your second layer.

8,491,514

Number of subscribers to "CaptainSparklez"'s YouTube channel, as of 23 March 2015. His popular *Minecraft* parodies made his only the fifth solo-gaming channel to reach 1 billion views.

First *Minecraft* "Let's Play" video

On 21 May 2009 – a mere four days after *Minecraft*'s initial public release – YouTube user "The Carlz0r" posted the very first "Let's Play"-style video dedicated to Notch's game, explaining how to build a fortress from stone and wood.

FIRST *MINECRAFT* YOUTUBE SERIES

YouTuber "paulsoaresjr" uploaded the first episode of his popular "Minecraft Tutorials" on 29 July 2010, less than a month after the game entered its alpha stage. "How to Survive Your First Night" began a "How to Survive and Thrive" series that totalled seven seasons and 89 episodes by its dragon-battling conclusion three years later.

MOST WATCHED OFFICIAL *MINECRAFT* VIDEO

Mojang's YouTube channel "TeamMojang" features the most popular official video (and second-most-viewed *Minecraft* video overall): "Official *Minecraft* Trailer", uploaded 18 days after the game's release in late 2011 and viewed 112,607,362 times as of 20 March 2015.

LONGEST-RUNNING *MINECRAFT* VIDEO SERIES

Founder of the MindCrack community of content creators, "GuudeBoulderfist" (aka Jason) launched his "Minecraft MindCrack" series on 19 October 2010. As of 8 April 2015, his YouTube channel had amassed 458,102 subscribers, while "Minecraft MindCrack" had racked up five seasons and 224 episodes and was still going strong.

Most watched live-action fan film based on *Minecraft*

Posted to YouTube on 17 February 2011 by gamer "CorridorDigital", "Minecraft: The Last Minecart" ditches the usual animated insanity of most *Minecraft* videos and tells a live-action post-apocalyptic tale set in Mojang's block-building world. With zombies roaming the Earth, heroes Niko and Sam must craft the ultimate weapon if they are to escape on the last minecart.

As a result of its winning blend of real-life actors, action-packed battles and *Minecraft*-inspired special effects, the film had been viewed 29,518,687 times as of 23 March 2015.

3 Next, you need a roof over your head. To qualify for the record, you need to craft stair blocks to create a sloping roof. We've used wood in the picture below (and note that the blocks between the stairs should be the same material as the steps).

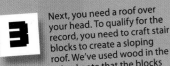

4 The only thing missing now is a door (six wood planks). The door needs to open inwards – not outwards – so you'll need to place it from *outside* your house to make it flush with the wall. As soon as the door is placed, stop the clock. Then walk around the house to show us it's finished.

TIPS 'N' TRICKS

Most players spend their first *Minecraft* night in less luxurious quarters than even the tiny home shown here. Your first day is crucial for gathering resources, so you might not have time for building. Any enclosed space with torches for light will keep away zombies – it might not be glamorous, but a hole in the ground or a blocked-in cave will do. You can always spend the night mining for resources as long as you have made some basic tools. The luxuries of a log cabin with space for a bed and somewhere to hang a painting can come later.

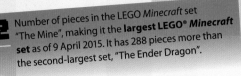

922 Number of pieces in the LEGO *Minecraft* set "The Mine", making it the **largest LEGO® Minecraft set** as of 9 April 2015. It has 288 pieces more than the second-largest set, "The Ender Dragon".

First *Minecraft*-controlled Christmas tree

On 16 December 2014, Ryan Carter (Canada) took *Minecraft*'s real-world applications to bizarre new heights. By logging on to a dedicated server created especially for the festive season, *Minecraft* players could not only turn on an in-game Christmas tree but also light up a real-life tree in the corner of Ryan's own

FIRST OFFICIAL MINECRAFT CONVENTION

Coinciding with the official 1.0 release of *Minecraft*, the first "MineCon" event was held at the Mandalay Bay resort in Las Vegas, USA, on 18 November 2011. It featured panels, contests, community events and exhibits centred on the building game.

FIRST LEGO SET BASED ON A VIDEOGAME

On 1 June 2012, Mojang and LEGO joined forces to release the official 480-piece LEGO *Minecraft* "Micro World – The Forest" set. The set's design featured a section of the game's Overworld, alongside main character Steve and an iconic Creeper. It proved so popular that more LEGO *Minecraft* sets followed, from "The Cave" and "The Farm" to "The End".

First official *Minecraft* gathering

On 31 August 2010, *Minecraft* players descended at the behest of Notch upon a damp park in Bellevue, Washington, USA, for what would be the first official real-world gathering of the game's fans. Although not a convention in the traditional sense, Notch dubbed the informal meet-up "MinecraftCon 2010" – a moniker that would inspire the first proper *Minecraft* convention the following year (see box, top right). Around 50 people braved the torrential rain for MinecraftCon 2010, including one hardy soul who turned up in a fully functional cardboard Creeper suit.

FIRST MINECRAFT-INSPIRED REAL-WORLD ART EXHIBITION

On 30 August 2013, the V&A Museum in London, UK, hosted an exhibition featuring life-size *Minecraft* models, animated projections and workshops. Pieces included a clay-sculpted "Book of Nether", a work inspired by Raphael's *Sistine Madonna* (above) and a stained-glass window by artist Greg Aronowitz depicting an idyllic *Minecraft* farmyard scene.

MINECRAFT CHALLENGES

10. Fastest time to build a two-block piston door

Mode: Creative

Your final challenge is the most technical yet, harnessing the almost-magical properties of redstone. Against the clock, you need to build a covered doorway – with piston-operated glass doors – connected by a redstone circuit to a switch.

1

Time starts as soon as you spawn in Creative mode. You can build the elements for this challenge in any order you want, but first up will probably be the doorway. Use four sticky pistons to create two pillars (four blocks apart). Pistons are blocks that can push other blocks out of the way, and sticky pistons (right) can pull as well as push, so make sure they're both facing the correct direction.

2

Next up are the doors, which must be two pairs of glass blocks. These are literally stuck to the sticky pistons, so that when the pistons are finally operated, the glass panels will slide closed as the pistons are activated. The doorway must also be covered, so enclose everything in a frame of solid blocks of your choice (right).

D.Y.K.?

/gamemode ARTPOP

Still don't believe that *Minecraft* is a bona fide cultural phenomenon? Then take a look at the surprising places it can make an appearance.
In gaming, *Borderlands 2* has a secret cave stuffed with *Minecraft* blocks and Creepers, while *The Elder Scrolls V: Skyrim* players can scale the Throat of the World mountain to retrieve the elusive "Notched Pickaxe". Elsewhere, the music video for Lady Gaga's 2014 single "G.U.Y." features a *Minecraft*-inspired online virtual wedding (inset), while one episode of the TV show *South Park* sees Stan's parents learning how to play the game in order to crack the security question that unlocks the family's cable box – "How do you tame a horse in *Minecraft*?"

FIRST COMPULSORY VIDEOGAME IN A SWEDISH SCHOOL

It was revealed on 9 January 2013 that the Viktor Rydberg secondary school in Stockholm, Sweden, had introduced compulsory *Minecraft* lessons to its 13-year-old students. The lessons were designed to introduce concepts of world-building, engineering, electricity grids and water-supply networks, and were delivered to some 180 pupils.

D.Y.K.?

On 28 June 2013, *Minecraft* was one of seven classic titles added to a videogame exhibition held at the Museum of Modern Art in New York, USA.

Most downloaded *Minecraft* skin

Skins change the way your character looks, and can vary from superheroes and famous celebrities to objects such as gumball machines – like most things in the game, the possibilities are endless. As of 23 March 2015, the "Ironman" skin by "YoursCrafter" had been downloaded 103,168 times from Planet Minecraft.

living room. The real-life tree actually responded quicker to the in-game switch than its virtual counterpart, which encountered a slight delay as the redstone picked up the signal. The server also featured switches for blue, green and red LEDs, enabling players to adjust the light display around Ryan's tree.

LARGEST LEGO MINECRAFT DIORAMA

On 27–30 November 2014, visitors to the Brick 2014 exhibition at ExCeL, London, UK, were invited to contribute to a diorama using LEGO *Minecraft* bricks built on 16-stud-wide square boards. Assembled into one piece by LEGO co-creation manager Julie Broberg and her team, the final cityscape measured 17.13 m² (184 sq ft).

3 Now it's time to crack out the redstone dust. Lay a line of this powerful powder so that it creates a circuit connecting both sides of your doorway. Redstone provides current to *Minecraft* blocks, triggering activatable blocks such as pistons and powered rails. For a piston to work, a block adjacent to it must be powered; this can include air blocks.

4 Finally, trail a little more redstone away from your doorway and add the final component: the switch. When activated, the switch will power your circuit. The time stops as soon as you flick the switch and the glass doors slide closed. Ah, the magic of redstone in action!

TIPS 'N' TRICKS

Redstone is a remarkably versatile block that, in its dust form, truly opens up a whole new dimension of *Minecraft*. Not only does it transmit power and bring your blocks to life, it can also be used to brew potions, craft clocks and compasses, and even form circuit boards, calculators and complex computers. You can get your hands on this enchanted stuff by smelting redstone ore, or alternatively try attacking a witch or looting a jungle temple.

Metacritic

When it comes to knowing what's hot and what's not in gaming, Metacritic is an invaluable resource. Based in San Francisco, USA, its enthusiastic team aggregates review scores from the most reputable critics across the globe, spanning not just videogames but also music, TV and film. Along with GameRankings, it's an invaluable tool for quantifying the most (and least) critically acclaimed releases. So if you're unsure whether the new *Halo*, *Uncharted* or *Dragon Age* expansion will be up to scratch, log in and let Metacritic settle the scores…

1

2

3

4

5

6

7

8

Although figures can fluctuate throughout the year, as of April 2015 Metacritic enjoyed an average of 10 million unique visitors a month

93% As we went to press, the highest aggregated score for a new original title released in 2015 was awarded to From Software's terrifying but well-crafted action RPG *Bloodborne*. "A visionary work by a visionary artist," claimed Digitally Downloaded, in just one of the horror epic's 58 reviews.

350,000

The number of different videogames in Metacritic's fast-swelling database, as of 20 March 2015. The site monitors 140 different review sites to pull together a final aggregate score – meaning that Metacritic has taken into account well over a million reviews in all.

87%

THE MOST GENEROUS REVIEWER
Now-defunct website Absolute PlayStation produced an average score of 87% across 98 reviews – higher than any other critic who had reviewed more than 20 games, as of April 2015.

FOUNDED 2001

Metacritic's seed was first sown in 1999, when the internet was still in its infancy. "I founded Metacritic with my friend and law school classmate Jason Dietz and my sister Julie Roberts," says co-founder and games editor Marc Doyle (see below).

Q&A

**MARC DOYLE
Metacritic co-founder and gaming editor**

How do you see Metacritic growing?
We're working on some updates, including new design elements, and adding features that will make the site even easier to use and a better tool to help users decide how best to spend their free time.

Do you play videogames yourself?
Yes, I do. It's not my practice to discuss the particular games I'm playing at any given time, but I spent an inordinate amount of time with *Quest for the Rings* (Magnavox Odyssey) and Intellivision's *Baseball* when I was in elementary school, and I logged far too many hours playing *NHL '94* during my gap year between college and grad school. These are certainly among my favourite games.

Any tips for someone who might want to work for you?
My content staff does uniformly excellent work, and I feel fortunate to say that most of our team has been working for Metacritic for many years. As such, openings don't surface regularly. But my advice for publications who might want their outlets to be tracked by Metacritic is to focus on the highest quality of writing and analysis in their reviews, and to review a broad variety of games.

metacritic.com
We Deal With Criticism®

NO.1 METACRITIC GAMES BY PLATFORM

The Legend of
Zelda: Ocarina
of Time

RELEASED: 23 November 1998
CRITIC REVIEWS: 22
99

SoulCalibur

RELEASED: 8 September 1999
CRITIC REVIEWS: 24
98

Tony Hawk's
Pro Skater 2

RELEASED: 20 September 2000
CRITIC REVIEWS: 19
98

Tony Hawk's
Pro Skater 3

RELEASED: 28 October 2001
CRITIC REVIEWS: 34
97

Halo:
Combat Evolved

RELEASED: 14 November 2001
CRITIC REVIEWS: 68
97

Metroid Prime

RELEASED: 17 November 2002
CRITIC REVIEWS: 70
97

Super Mario Galaxy

RELEASED: 12 November 2007
CRITIC REVIEWS: 73
97

God of War:
Chains of Olympus

RELEASED: 4 March 2008
CRITIC REVIEWS: 79
91

Grand Theft Auto IV

RELEASED: 29 April 2008
CRITIC REVIEWS: 86
98

Grand Theft Auto IV

RELEASED: 29 April 2008
CRITIC REVIEWS: 64
98

Grand Theft Auto:
Chinatown Wars

RELEASED: 17 March 2009
CRITIC REVIEWS: 85
93

World of Goo HD

RELEASED: 16 December 2010
CRITIC REVIEWS: 11
96

The Legend of Zelda:
Ocarina of Time 3D

RELEASED: 19 June 2011
CRITIC REVIEWS: 85
94

Persona 4 Golden

RELEASED: 20 November 2012
CRITIC REVIEWS: 61
93

Super Mario
3D World

RELEASED: 22 November 2013
CRITIC REVIEWS: 83
93

Grand Theft Auto V

RELEASED: 18 November 2014
CRITIC REVIEWS: 14
97

Grand Theft Auto V

RELEASED: 18 November 2014
CRITIC REVIEWS: 66
97

Grand Theft Auto V

RELEASED: 14 April 2015
CRITIC REVIEWS: 37
97

All figures correct as of 24 April 2015; games in order of release

MORTAL KOMBAT

Most numbered entries in a fighting series

While it may not have as many titles within its franchise as *Street Fighter* or *The King of Fighters*, *Mortal Kombat* has gone through more numbered iterations than any other fighting series. The 10th "main" instalment, *Mortal Kombat X*, was released on 14 April 2015. By contrast, the next *Street Fighter* game, due in 2016, will only be numbered "V".

4

Number of people who worked on the first *Mortal Kombat*: Ed Boon (programmer), John Tobias and John Vogel (graphics), and Dan Forden (audio).

Summary: The most notorious of all fighting series, *Mortal Kombat* has enthralled fans for 20+ years with its outlandish finishing moves and otherworldly characters. While it may not be as technically minded as *Tekken* or *Street Fighter*, it enjoys a thrilling style all of its own.

Publisher: Midway Games/ Warner Bros.
Developer: Midway Games/ NetherRealm Studios
Debut: 1992

MATURE 17+
M
CONTENT RATED BY
ESRB

First game to result in a software ratings board

The Entertainment Software Rating Board (ESRB) was set up in 1994 in response to public outcry to *Mortal Kombat*. The ESRB assigns age ratings to videogames in North America and Canada.

Fastest completion of *Mortal Kombat Mythologies: Sub-Zero*

Mortal Kombat Mythologies: Sub-Zero was a platformer set before the first game. Alex "AquaTiger" Nichols completed an eight-segment run on the PlayStation version in 50 min 32 sec on 11 December 2005.

Most viewed fan film based on a fighting videogame

Uploaded on 14 September 2014, "MORTAL KOMBAT ELEVATOR PRANK!" by popular YouTuber Yousef Saleh Erakat, aka "fouseyTUBE" (USA), had been viewed 37,929,219 times as of 27 March 2015. The comedy viral featured its maker "terrifying" elevator users while dressed as Sub-Zero. A follow-up had 12,198,609 views as of the same date.

Fastest Mortal Kombat match

On 3 December 2014, series fan "jEga jEga" pummelled his way through a two-round "expert level" match in 2011's *Mortal Kombat* in 34 sec. "jEga jEga" was fighting as Nightwolf against the four-armed Sheeva.

Fastest single-segment, "Very Hard" completion of *Ultimate Mortal Kombat 3*

Playing as cyber-ninja Smoke, Nick Matthews (USA) completed the arcade version of the 1995 classic in an incredible 8 min 28 sec at the Galloping Ghost Arcade in Brookfield, Illinois, USA – without losing a single round of combat.

First horror movie icon in a fighting game

Although most *MK* stars are a little creepy, 1980s movie ghoul Freddy Krueger added extra scares as a downloadable character in 2011's *Mortal Kombat*. Following suit, fellow Eighties villain Jason Voorhees (of *Friday the 13th*) is a DLC star in *Mortal Kombat X* (2015).

Highest-earning Mortal Kombat tournament player

Although a minor title on the eSports circuit, *Mortal Kombat* retains a dedicated circle of pro tournament players. The highest-earning *Mortal Kombat* player is Giuseppe "REO" Grosso (USA), who competed in 13 tournaments for *Mortal Kombat* (2011) – the ninth main iteration of the series. As of 8 April 2015, he had earned $21,236.60 (£14,219.30), winning three titles and four runner-up accolades.

Longest online winning streak in Mortal Kombat

Xbox Live user "WaTaDaaah" (Germany) had enjoyed an unbroken streak of 384 online wins in 2011's *Mortal Kombat* as of 23 June 2014.

Most live-action spin-offs based on a videogame

Across two feature films, the TV series *Mortal Kombat: Conquest* (1998–99) and two seasons of web series *Mortal Kombat: Legacy* (2011–), the cult fighting series had spawned 44 live-action episodes and films as of 8 April 2015.

Oldest character in a fighting game

In 2008, *Mortal Kombat* teamed up with DC Comics for the crossover beat-'em-up videogame *Mortal Kombat vs DC Universe*. The game's colourful cast included Superman, who had debuted 70 years earlier in *Action Comics No.1* in 1938.

Most character appearances in the *Mortal Kombat* series

Name	Description	Playable appearances	NPC cameos
Sub-Zero	Ice-firing superhuman	13	0
Liu Kang	Ex-Shaolin monk	=12	1
Jax	Special forces hero	=12	0
Scorpion	Undead ninja	=12	0
Raiden	Thunder god	=11	2
Sonya Blade	Special forces heroine	=11	2
Noob Saibot	Mysterious ninja	=10	0
Kitana	Deadly princess	=10	0
Reptile	Reptilian humanoid	=10	0
Shang Tsung	Evil sorcerer	9	1

Data correct as of 8 April 2015

Longest-serving developer of a fighting game

Since creating *Mortal Kombat* in 1992, programmer Ed Boon (USA) has worked across the series for the last 23 years. Not only the director of 2015's *Mortal Kombat X*, Boon also delighted fans by again providing Scorpion's signature lines, making him still the **longest-serving videogame voice actor**.

123

⚽ NBA 2K

Most three-pointers scored in one minute on *NBA 2K14*

On 25 June 2014, Tristen Geren from Fredericksburg in Texas, USA, scored six three-pointers in 60 sec. The proud holder of 16 current records as of 10 April 2015, Tristen is also a keen basketball fan who lists his *NBA 2K* achievements as his favourites.

On 6 June 2014, he made the **most basketball free throws on *NBA 2K14* in one minute**, with 15. He followed that up on 1 July 2014 with the **most consecutive basketball free throws on *NBA 2K9*** – 114. Tristen also shares the record for the **most basketball free throws scored on *NBA 2K9* in one minute** with Phoenix Legend Goad (USA) – 18, on 20 January 2014. His advice to would-be record-breakers inspired by his success? "Find your forte, practise and be patient."

2 PENN
9 MOTIEJUNAS
4 GRONA

LLIES

"Every time you succeed,
you succeed for the gaming
community as a whole..."

Tristen Geren

NBA 2K

Best-selling basketball videogame franchise

The *NBA 2K* series has played all its basketball game rivals off the courts. According to VGChartz, as of 12 March 2015 the franchise had sold a staggering 43 million copies. Developed by Visual Concepts, the game was originally published by Sega but has since moved to 2K Sports.

23

Jersey number of Michael Jordan for the majority of his career. Seven years after his retirement in 2003, Jordan could be seen once more in his iconic Chicago Bulls jersey as the cover star of *NBA 2K11*.

D Y.K.?

Music megastar Pharrell Williams was brought in to "curate" the soundtrack for *NBA 2K15*, and he selected tracks from artists as diverse as Lorde and The Black Keys.

Summary:
Boasting a groundbreaking fusion of sports gaming and an RPG-like career mode, this hugely successful franchise has had b-ball fans sinking three-pointers and slam-dunking from their sofas since *NBA 2K* debuted in November 1999.

Publisher: Sega/2K Sports
Developer: Visual Concepts
Debut: 1999

Best-selling *NBA 2K* videogame

Launched in October 2012, *NBA 2K13* is the most successful instalment in the series, with 5.8 million copies sold as of 12 March 2015, according to VGChartz. The critical response has been equally enthusiastic, with the game achieving an average review score of 90% on Metacritic.

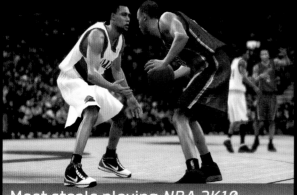

Most steals playing *NBA 2K10*

Stealing the ball from the opposition requires speed, lightning-quick reflexes and precision timing. At the NBA Jam Session in Dallas, Texas, USA, gamer Wesley Parker (USA) managed seven steals during a four-minute game (one minute per quarter) on 10 February 2010.

Most appearances by a basketball player on a videogame cover

Shooting guard Allen Iverson was an 11-time NBA All-Star who twice won the All-Star MVP award, in 2001 and 2005. He also appeared on the front of *NBA 2K* games for five consecutive years, from 1999 to 2003.

Most points in the first half of *NBA 2K10*

On 12 February 2010, Cody Redrick and Brandon McJunlain (both USA) ran up 17 points in one half of a four-minute game of *NBA 2K10* at the NBA Jam Session in Dallas, Texas, USA.

Most assists playing *NBA 2K11*

Bara[...]akovi (USA) managed an impressive 23 assists at the 2K Sports booth during the NBA All-Star Jam Session in Los Angeles, California, USA, on 18 February 2011.

Most critically acclaimed NBA videogame

As of 12 March 2015, *NBA 2K1* and *NBA 2K2* were the top-ranked NBA games on Metacritic, with scores of 93%.

Most points as Michael Jordan on *NBA 2K11*

Burtland Dixon (USA) managed to score 51 points with the former Chicago Bulls and Washington Wizards legend during a single game at the 2K Sports booth at the NBA All-Star Jam Session in Los Angeles, California, USA, on 18 February 2011. At the same event, Chico Kora (USA) set the record for **most points scored as Kobe Bryant on *NBA 2K10***, with an MVP-meriting 29.

First *NBA 2K* cover star to win the NBA Finals in the same season

In 2006, the cover star of *NBA 2K6*, Shaquille O'Neal (USA), enjoyed on-court success as his team, the Miami Heat, went on to win the NBA Finals.

Most points on *NBA 2K11*

On 20 February 2011, K'Lon Williams (USA) scored 23 points in one game at the *NBA 2K11* booth during the NBA All-Star Jam Session in Los Angeles, California, USA. Dwayne Travis (USA) scored 14 three-pointers in one game at the same event – the **most three-pointers playing *NBA 2K11***.

Highest-rated active player in *NBA 2K15*

With a rating of 98 out of 100, LeBron James of the Cleveland Cavaliers is the highest-rated player still active on the court as of 11 March 2015. But even "King James" has to take second place behind retired basketball superstar Michael Jordan, whose rating of 99 makes him the **highest-rated player in *NBA 2K15***.

First winner of Major League Gaming's *NBA 2K15* season

Competitive gaming organization Major League Gaming holds regular *NBA 2K* tournaments that mimic the format of the real-life NBA. Gamer "That Crossover[BL]™" emerged from the inaugural *NBA 2K15* season triumphant.

Longest-running basketball game

The biggest rivalry in basketball gaming is between *NBA 2K* and EA Sport's *NBA Live*. Although *NBA 2K* has been running since 1999, with 16 titles as of March 2015, the first of *NBA Live's* 18 titles appeared five years earlier (above). A third rival, *NCAA March Madness*, ran from 1998 to 2009.

Top-rated active athletes in *NBA 2K15*			
Name	Position	Team	Rating
LeBron James	Small forward	Cleveland Cavaliers	98
Kevin Durant	Small forward	Oklahoma City Thunder	95
Chris Paul	Point guard	Los Angeles Clippers	91
Tim Duncan	Power forward	San Antonio Spurs	90
Carmelo Anthony	Small forward	New York Knicks	=89
Kobe Bryant	Shooting guard	Los Angeles Lakers	=89
Kevin Love	Power forward	Cleveland Cavaliers	=89
Paul George	Small forward	Indiana Pacers	=89
Blake Griffin	Power forward	Los Angeles Clippers	=89
Stephen Curry	Point guard	Golden State Warriors	=89

Source: NBA 2K Facebook as of 12 March 2015

10

Number of years without car horns in *NfS* games – between 2002's *Need for Speed: Hot Pursuit 2* and 2012's *Need for Speed: Most Wanted*, beeping wasn't an option.

Summary: *Need for Speed* might be more than 20 years old, but the stalwart racing series keeps moving with the times – changing developers, adding new platforms and augmenting the adrenaline-pumping racing with car customization and even the occasional police pursuit.

Publisher: EA
Developer: Various
Debut: 1994

Longest marathon on *Need for Speed*

On 31 May–1 June 2013, Florian Fleissner (left) and Kenny Drews (right) played *Need for Speed: Most Wanted* for exactly 33 hr at City Center Langenhagen in Hannover-Langenhagen, Germany. Keen fans of the racing series since its first title in 1994, Kenny and Florian decided to break the record after seeing a Facebook announcement of an *NfS* competition. Their favourite aspects of the game are its track diversity and the option to customize cars.

Most drivers sponsored by a gaming publisher

Electronic Arts sponsored seven drivers across the Formula Drift, Time Attack and FIA GT3 motor-racing formats under the name "Team Need for Speed" (since disbanded). The team also sponsored drivers in marquee single-event races such as the 24 Hours of Le Mans and the Nürburgring 24-Hour.

Best-selling driving game series

As of 28 April 2015, *Need for Speed* had shifted 96.43 million units – more than any other non-kart racing franchise.

The **best-selling *Need for Speed* game** is 2004's *Need for Speed: Underground 2*, with sales of 10.95 million according to VGChartz.

Most prolific racing game series

Need for Speed has spawned 26 titles since debuting in 1994. It has delved into MMO territory twice, with 2001's *Motor City Online* and 2010's *Need for Speed: World*. Its most recent outing, *Need for Speed: No Limits* (2015), was its **first *NfS* game exclusive to mobile platforms**.

Most critically acclaimed racing game for PlayStation 3

For many, *Need for Speed: Hot Pursuit* (2010) represents the series' zenith on seventh-generation consoles, blending high-speed racing with a fun cops-and-robbers mechanic. And the critics seem to agree – *Hot Pursuit* had earned a rival-beating Metacritic score of 89% as of 20 April 2015.

Highest-grossing film based on a racing game

Released on 12 March 2014, the *Need for Speed* film follows an ex-convict street-racer as he embarks upon a dangerous cross-country race. Starring Aaron Paul from the TV series *Breaking Bad* and Dominic Cooper, the film had grossed a mighty $203,277,636 (£135,759,000) as of 20 April 2015.

Highest score on *Need for Speed: World*

"TIMEATT4CK" (Portugal) had racked up 1,039,028 points in the MMOR as of 15 May 2015, using a total of 42 cars.

Fastest completion of the "Beachfront" circuit in *Need for Speed: World*

French racer "IIAXELMRXII" drove a Mitsubishi Eclipse around the circuit in a time of 2 min 3.984 sec – a record, as of 20 April 2015.

Most platforms for a racing videogame series

As of April 2015, *Need for Speed* games had appeared on 21 different platforms across its 21-year history.

Fastest recorded speed for a car in a driving game

A video uploaded to YouTube by Fernando Moretti on 4 May 2007 shows a Ford GT reaching a nitro-assisted top speed of 682 km/h (423.7 mph).

Most developers of a racing game series

As of 14 May 2015, 20 different development studios had worked on *Need for Speed* iterations, from original creators Pioneer Productions to Ghost Games and Criterion Games, the collaborators behind 2013's *Need for Speed: Rivals*.

Fastest completion of the "Welcome to Palmont" circuit in *Need for Speed: World*

On 9 May 2015, Russian gamer "ACRYSE" shot around the track in a McLaren F1 Elite in only 59.45 sec.

Gamer "GIGAXER0" (Finland) achieved the **fastest completion of the "Lyons & Hwy" circuit in *Need for Speed: World***: 1 min 21.815 sec in May 2014, also in the McLaren F1 Elite.

Fastest "Grand Tour Hot Pursuit Event" time in *Need for Speed: Rivals*

On 9 December 2014, gamer "RwanVLG-974" uploaded a video to YouTube showing him or her completing the epic circuit in 7 min 43.65 sec.

Most advanced cockpit in a racing videogame

For 2009's *Need for Speed: Shift*, developer Slightly Mad Studios was determined to make the driving experience look as real as possible. It modelled the interiors so that each cockpit featured a functional dash as well as a driver model that reacted to the g-forces created by cornering and accelerating.

Tips 'n' Tricks

If you fall foul of the law in *Need for Speed: Rivals*, it can spell real trouble. Try to lose the cops by heading down small, twisting roads or making them follow you over a jump – they can struggle to land safely, giving you some breathing space and a chance to make your escape. Pursuit Tech options can also help, especially the super-charging Turbo or Shockwave, which can push other cars into walls or over cliffs. Alternatively, you can just lie low until the heat wears off – heading inside a Hideout will lose the cops.

PAC MAN

#9 US *Billboard* chart position reached by Jerry Buckner and Gary Garcia's "PAC-Man Fever" in 1982. Featuring original sound effects from the game, it sold more than 2.5 million copies, making it the **most popular PAC-Man song**.

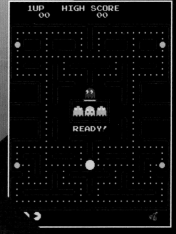

```
1UP        HIGH SCORE
   00            00

            READY!
```

Most recognized videogame character

PAC-Man, according to a poll by the Davie-Brown Index, is the best-known of all videogame characters, recognized by 94% of American consumers. Mario came a close second with 93%, while others with notable brand recognition included Lara Croft, Donkey Kong, Sonic the Hedgehog and Link from *The Legend of Zelda*.

Summary: It's hard to imagine a world without this spook-dodging, pellet-munching yellow fellow. Following the success of the arcade original, several spin-offs were released, of which *Ms. PAC-Man* proved rather more enduring than *Baby PAC-Man*, *Professor PAC-Man* and *Jr. PAC-Man*.

Publisher: Namco/
Bally Midway
Developer: Namco
Debut: 1980

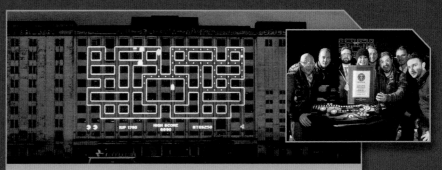

Largest architectural projection-mapped videogame

Architectural projection-mapping is the process of modifying a projection to fit the features of the surface it is displayed upon. On 18 November 2013, a *PAC-Man* game was projected on to the Millennium Mills building at ExCeL London, UK, by *The Gadget Show* (UK), at a size of 2,218.65 m² (23,881 sq ft).

Most successful coin-operated arcade game

Between 1981 and 1987, more than 293,000 *PAC-Man* machines were installed in arcades around the world, and Namco estimates that the game has been played more than 10 billion times in its 35-year history. The **biggest-selling US-made arcade machine** is *Ms. PAC-Man* – which, as of 1988, had sold 125,000 machines. However, the **highest-grossing arcade game** remains the original *PAC-Man*, which – from its launch in 1980 until 1999 – earned $3.5 billion (£2.16 billion).

First perfect completion

Legendary arcader Billy Mitchell of Florida, USA, achieved the first "perfect" *PAC-Man* game: he scored the maximum 3,333,360 points on 3 July 1999.

The **fastest perfect completion** is 3 hr 28 min 49 sec by David Race (USA) on 22 June 2013.

Most critically acclaimed *PAC-Man*

The arcade classic has lived on into the modern era, right through to titles for the seventh-generation Xbox 360 and PlayStation 3. The highest-rated of these on GameRankings is 2010's *PAC-Man Championship Edition DX* – the PS3 version of which, as of 2 March 2015, held a score of 91.06%.

First animated TV series based on a videogame

A *PAC-Man* animated series, produced by Hanna-Barbera, debuted on 25 September 1982 and ran for two seasons.

The **first *PAC-Man* game based on a TV show** was 2013's *PAC-Man and the Ghostly Adventures*, a tie-in with the TV show that launched four months earlier on 15 June 2013.

Costliest *PAC-Man* game

In May 2010, Google celebrated *PAC-Man*'s 30th anniversary with an interactive logo based on the arcade original. During the two days it was online, users played the game for nearly 500 million hours. Based on an average office worker's pay, it cost businesses an estimated £85 million ($122 million) in lost productivity.

Most players supported on a *PAC-Man* arcade game

Enabling up to four-way play, the *PAC-Man Battle Royale* cabinet was released in January 2011. Requiring at least two players, the more adversarial variant graduated from the arcade to the Xbox, PS3 and PC in 2014.

First playable female in a videogame

According to its creator, Toru Iwatani, the original *PAC-Man* was designed to appeal to women. The year after its launch, a sequel arrived in the form of *Ms. PAC-Man* (1982), complete with a hair bow, blusher and lipstick.

Most viewed video based on *PAC-Man*

In April 2009, prankster Rémi Gaillard (France) uploaded a video of himself, dressed in a PAC-Man costume, being chased through a supermarket and golf course by cohorts dressed as ghosts. As of 26 March 2015, it had notched up 49,214,865 views on YouTube.

Largest life-sized PAC-Man maze

About the size of a basketball court, the largest PAC-Man maze measured 580.86 m² (6,252.3 sq ft) and was created by Energy BBDO and Mosaic (both USA) in Los Angeles, California, USA, on 7 January 2015. The massive maze featured in a TV advert for Bud Light, shown during the 2015 Super Bowl. At least 45 cameras were used to capture the live human gameplay and 457 m (1,500 ft) of continuous, linear lighting was used to outline the top of the maze alone.

POKÉMON

Summary: Since its Game Boy debut in 1996, *Pokémon* has spawned dozens of chart-topping titles, including puzzle games and digital pet games. In the main series of RPGs, players train their Pokémon creatures before engaging them in turn-based battles with other Pokémon.

Publisher: Nintendo
Developer: Various
Debut: 1996

Best-selling JRPG series

The *Pokémon* series has sold a staggering 242 million units worldwide since 1996 – although this success can be partly attributed to publisher Nintendo's habit of selling multiple versions of the same games. With the November 2014 release of *Pokémon Omega Ruby* and *Alpha Sapphire* for 3DS (the latter pictured right and below) – featuring all-new characters such as Aarune, Lisia and Zinnia – its domination of the Japanese RPG market looks set to continue.

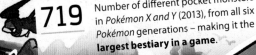

719 Number of different pocket monsters in *Pokémon X and Y* (2013), from all six *Pokémon* generations – making it the **largest bestiary in a game.**

Heaviest Pokémon
Weighing in at 950 kg (2,094 lb), "Ground-type Legendary" Groudon causes volcanoes to erupt when it awakens!

First Pokémon
Designed by artist Ken Sugimori, rhino-like Rhydon was the first ever character and appeared in the original 1996 RPG.

First videogame on the cover of *Time* magazine

The cover of America's prestigious *Time* magazine is usually reserved for presidents and Hollywood stars, but in November 1999 that honour was given to Pokémon – although the accompanying article warned that "Pokémania" might be addictive and lead to children fighting over cards.

Best-selling 3DS game

As of 5 March 2015, *Pokémon X and Y* (2013) was the best-selling Nintendo 3DS game, with 12.67 million sales worldwide according to VGChartz. This is nearly 5 million more than the next-highest-selling *Pokémon* game, 2014's *Pokémon Omega Ruby/Alpha Sapphire*.

Fastest-selling game on Nintendo DS

Boasting 156 new franchise characters, 2010's *Pokémon Black/White Version* was hotly anticipated by fans of the JRPG series. In its first two weeks on sale, it shifted 3,438,399 units. The game had already become the **most pre-ordered DS game**, having racked up 1.08 million pre-orders in Japan alone from 31 July to 22 August 2010.

D.Y.K.?

To celebrate the release of 2014's *Pokémon the Movie: XY*, a pop-up café in Tokyo, Japan, sold Pokémon-themed meals made to resemble Pikachu!

Most World Championship Pokémon titles

On 11 August 2012, 19-year-old Ray Rizzo defeated rival Wolfe Glick (both USA) in the *Pokémon* World Championship final – taking the title for a third consecutive time. Following his victory, Ray featured in *Pokémon Black/White Version 2* (2012) via a downloadable update.

Best-selling *Pokémon* games

Game	Platform	Year	Global Sales
Pokémon Red/Green/Blue	Game Boy	1996	31.37 million
Pokémon Gold/Silver	Game Boy	1999	23.10 million
Pokémon Diamond/Pearl	Nintendo DS	2006	18.21 million
Pokémon Ruby/Sapphire	Game Boy Advance	2002	15.85 million
Pokémon Black/White	Nintendo DS	2010	15.06 million
Pokémon Yellow: Special Pikachu Edition	Game Boy	1998	14.64 million
Pokémon X/Y	Nintendo 3DS	2013	12.67 million
Pokémon Heart Gold/Soul Silver	Nintendo DS	2009	11.71 million
Pokémon FireRed/LeafGreen	Game Boy Advance	2004	10.49 million
Pokémon Omega Ruby/Alpha Sapphire	Nintendo 3DS	2014	7.90 million

Source: VGChartz as of 11 March 2015

Most film spin-offs from a game series

Pokémon has inspired 18 feature-length animated films. The first *Pokémon* film, released in 1998, was a chart-topping sensation. Its worldwide earnings of $163,644,662 (£101,200,000) make it the **highest-grossing animated movie based on a videogame**.

Best-selling game for Game Boy Advance

Pokémon Ruby/Sapphire Version (2002) had sold 15.85 million copies as of 5 March 2015, according to VGChartz.

First fish to play a videogame

US college students Catherine Moresco and Patrick Facheris programmed a hack of the original *Pokémon* to respond to the movements of their dorm-room fish. As of 12 March 2015, a total of 5,206,382 Twitch users had watched Grayson "playing" the game.

First official theme park based on a videogame

Pokémon was the first gaming series to get its own theme park. The "PokéPark" was opened on 18 March 2005 in Nagoya, Japan. Attractions included Mudkip's Big Splash and the Pichu Brothers' Rascal Railway. The park closed in September 2005.

Largest collection of videogame memorabilia

As of 5 March 2015, Lisa Courtney (UK) could boast a Pokémon collection comprising at least 14,410 individual items.

Least popular Pokémon

Poor old Luvdisc! The heart-shaped water type came top of a 2014 poll of 500,000 people by the website Dorkly to find the least-loved pocket monster.

Smallest Pokémon

Bug-like Joltik is a mere 10 cm (4 in) in height, making it the tiniest pocket monster alongside the equally teeny Flabébé.

Fastest Pokémon

Third-generation Pokémon Deoxys has a scorching base speed of 180 points. Its name is a play on DNA – or deoxyribonucleic acid.

Classic Rivalries

Gamers love nothing more than a fiercely fought rivalry – especially when it involves some of their favourite virtual characters. Whether you prefer Mario to Sonic, or favour Lara over Drake, here are how the facts and figures stack up.

Debut: PlayStation (1994) – 104.24 million

Best-seller: PlayStation 2 – 157.68 million

PS4 sales: 21.1 million
Highest-rated Sony exclusive on PS4:
The Last of Us Remastered (2014) – 95.7%

Highest-rated: *FIFA Soccer 12* (2011) – 90.65% (PS3)

Series sales: 146.13 million

• *FIFA's* fantasy mode Ultimate Team is its most popular. From *FIFA 09* to *FIFA 14*, EA recorded 21,849,017 Ultimate Team players.

XBOX PLAYSTATION

FIFA  PES

Debut: Xbox (2001) – 24.65 million

Best-seller: Xbox 360 – 84.7 million

Xbox One sales: 12.02 million
Highest-rated Microsoft exclusive on Xbox One: *Ori and the Blind Forest* (2015) – 89.13%

Highest-rated: *World Soccer Winning Eleven 7 International* (2004) – 92.97% (PS2)

Series sales: 65.97 million

• PES League is one of the world's largest virtual sports tournaments. In 2015, some 4,000 gamers took part, with the 32 best players set to compete in the final in Germany.

Highest-rated: *Uncharted 2: Among Thieves* (2009) – 96.43% (PS3)

Series sales: 19.5 million

• Across his *Uncharted* travels, Drake's discoveries include the golden sarcophagus of El Dorado, a "yeti" and the lost city of Shambhala.

1996

2007

LARA CROFT VS NATHAN DRAKE

• Since pioneering a new breed of gaming heroine, Lara has made discoveries including Thor's Hammer and a *T. rex*. Forbes has estimated her net worth at $1 billion (£670 million).

The *Tomb Raider* vs *Uncharted* battle rumbles on. *Rise of the Tomb Raider* (due end 2015) and *Uncharted 4: A Thief's End* (2016) are two of the most anticipated titles currently in development.

Highest-rated: *Tomb Raider* (1996) – 90.02% (PS)

Series sales: 36.88 million

Highest-rated: *Super Mario Galaxy* (2007) – 97.64% (Wii)

Series sales: 533.31 million

• Proving that appearances can be deceptive, Mario has fronted 19 sports games – the **most sports videogames based on a platform series**.

MARIO **VS** SONIC

Sonic's gaming debut was decidedly sneakier than Mario's – he was a swinging car freshener in 1991 arcade racer Rad Mobile.

• YouTube video "Game Theory: How Fast is Sonic? DEBUNKED | Gnoggin" estimated Sonic's top speed to be around 5,235.77 mph (8,426.16 km/h)!

Mario debuted in Donkey Kong (1981) under his initial guise of "Jumpman". He then played the bad guy for one time only in the 1982 sequel Donkey Kong Jr.

Highest-rated: *Sonic Adventure* (1999) – 86.51% (Dreamcast)

Series sales: 110.04 million

• Since its release in March 2015, more than 2 billion minutes of *Battlefield: Hardline* had been played online as of 8 April 2015.

Highest-rated: *Call of Duty 4: Modern Warfare* (2007) – 94.16% (Xbox 360)

Series sales: 216.4 million

The 2013 YouTube video "Battlefield vs Call of Duty Rap Battle!" by "jackfrags" sums up the rivalry between these military FPS giants perfectly. As of 28 April 2015, it had been viewed 10,029,196 times.

2002

2003

BATTLEFIELD **VS** CALL OF DUTY

Highest-rated: *Battlefield 2* (2005) – 90.07% (PC)

Series sales: 42.28 million

• As of 7 April 2015, 2.5 billion Exo Zombies had been slayed in *Call of Duty: Advanced Warfare's* gruesomely popular multiplayer mode.

Source: All sales figures from VGChartz. All critical ratings from GameRankings.

PRO EVOLUTION SOCCER

98 Overall rating of fierce rivals Cristiano Ronaldo (Portugal) and "Leo" Messi (Argentina) in the *PES 2015* player rankings – making them jointly the **best-ranked players in *PES 2015*.**

> "The most realistic football title there is"

PES 2015 cover star Mario Götze (Germany)

D.Y.K.?

Owing to licensing issues, only one team from the English Premier League appears under its actual name in *PES 2015* – Manchester United. The rest of the teams all appear under cunningly designed aliases.

Summary: Peeeeeep! From the first whistle, *Pro Evolution Soccer* offers players all the passion and excitement of the "beautiful game" – great goals, thunderous tackles, and skilful tricks and dribbles. *PES*'s gaming rivalry with *FIFA* is as competitive as anything seen on the pitch.

Publisher: Konami
Developer: Konami
Debut: 2001

Fastest goal in *PES 2015*

Having won the Golden Boot at the FIFA World Cup in Brazil and signed for global giants Real Madrid, Colombian superstar James Rodríguez (above) must have enjoyed his 2014. Yet his exploits didn't end there: controlled by gamer "Afro Gwada", James managed to score for Real Madrid against Barcelona with just 35 sec on the game clock during a *PES* match on 4 October 2014. This works out at just 4 sec in real time, and was achieved by lobbing the opposition goalkeeper straight from kick-off.

First videogame to use the Fox Engine

PES 2014 and *Metal Gear Solid V: Ground Zeroes* were among the first games to be made with Kojima Productions' new Fox Engine. But while *Metal Gear's* Solid Snake was meant to be the face of the Fox Engine, it was *PES 2014* that was released first, landing in the UK on 20 September 2013, six months before *Ground Zeroes*.

First 3D soccer videogame

Launched in Japan on 25 March 2011, *PES 2011 3D* (aka *Winning Eleven 3D Soccer*) was the first soccer videogame to be playable in stereoscopic 3D.

Most successful pesleague.com player

Since the official *PES* League became a global competition in 2011, Ettore "Ettorito" Giannuzzi, aka "VietKong90321" (Italy), has been crowned World Champion in 2011 and runner-up in 2014. He also won the first UEFA Youth League in 2014.

Highest margin of victory in a *Pro Evolution Soccer* game

Spanish gamer Francisco Javier Muros Ponce (inset) posted a video on 2 November 2014 in which he defeated the computer opponent on *PES 2011* for PS3. Playing as Spain against Qatar, Muros put 119 goals past the opposition in two 30-min halves. In fact, the goal blitz was so fierce that it broke the game's goal counter!

Most cover appearances on soccer games series

Argentina's Lionel Messi was the cover star of *PES 2009*, *PES 2010* and *PES 2011* before transferring to EA Sports' *FIFA* game. Having since featured on the cover of 2012's *FIFA Street* and *FIFA 13*, *14* and *15*, Messi can now boast a total of seven soccer cover appearances to his name.

Largest stadium to host a *PES* League World Final

Konami's annual *PES* League World Championships is hosted in the hospitality suite of a major football stadium each year. On 14 September 2012, the 2012 *PES* League World Final was contested at the Santiago Bernabéu Stadium, home to Spanish side Real Madrid, which boasts a full-stadium capacity of 81,044.

Longest game marathon on a *Pro Evolution Soccer* game

On 18–20 November 2011, Portuguese gamers Marco Ramos and Efraim Ie played *Pro Evolution Soccer 2012* for 38 hr 49 min 13 sec at the Alegro Alfragide shopping mall in Lisbon, Portugal. The marathon match-ups were sponsored by the game's developers and publishers, Konami.

Most watched *PES* fan video

Uploaded to YouTube by Luciano Nuñez, "Tiro Libre Cristiano Ronaldo 40mts – PES 2011 PC" shows the Portuguese wizard scoring a long-range free-kick for Real Madrid against Barcelona. By 31 March 2015, it had been viewed 4,259,644 times.

Highest-ranked player at the *PES* Virtual UEFA Champions League

As of 25 March 2015, gamer "Restartlindo" (Brazil) sat proudly at the top of the global rankings from 474,300 players. He won 1,879 of his 2,164 games, racking up 1,326 points; see the top 10 in the table below.

Highest-ranked *PES* Virtual UEFA Champions League players

Player	Country	Played	Won	Points
"Restartlindo"	Brazil	2,164	1,879	1,326
"BETISS90"	Spain	1,442	1,313	1,306
"CuervosPes2013"	Argentina	1,884	1,664	1,299
"alexalguacil_8"	Spain	1,682	1,492	1,295
"rojodavid"	Colombia	1,548	1,338	1,293
"usmakabyle"	France	1,339	1,216	1,293
"franracchi"	Argentina	1,413	1,280	1,277
"MARCIANOESKRLATA"	Colombia	1,543	1,326	1,277
"bad_boy_g_2011"	UK	432	293	1,274
"ghalbim_pes"	Brazil	1,095	1,025	1,269

Source: PES Virtual UEFA Champions League as of 25 March 2015

D.Y.K.?

The *PES* Shop in *Pro Evolution Soccer 6* (2006) offered gamers the chance to do more than alter their players' hairstyles – it let them buy ostriches or dinosaurs for their team to ride! And if gamers ever became bored of traditional soccer kits, they could also buy penguin costumes for their stars to wear...

✦ RESIDENT EVIL

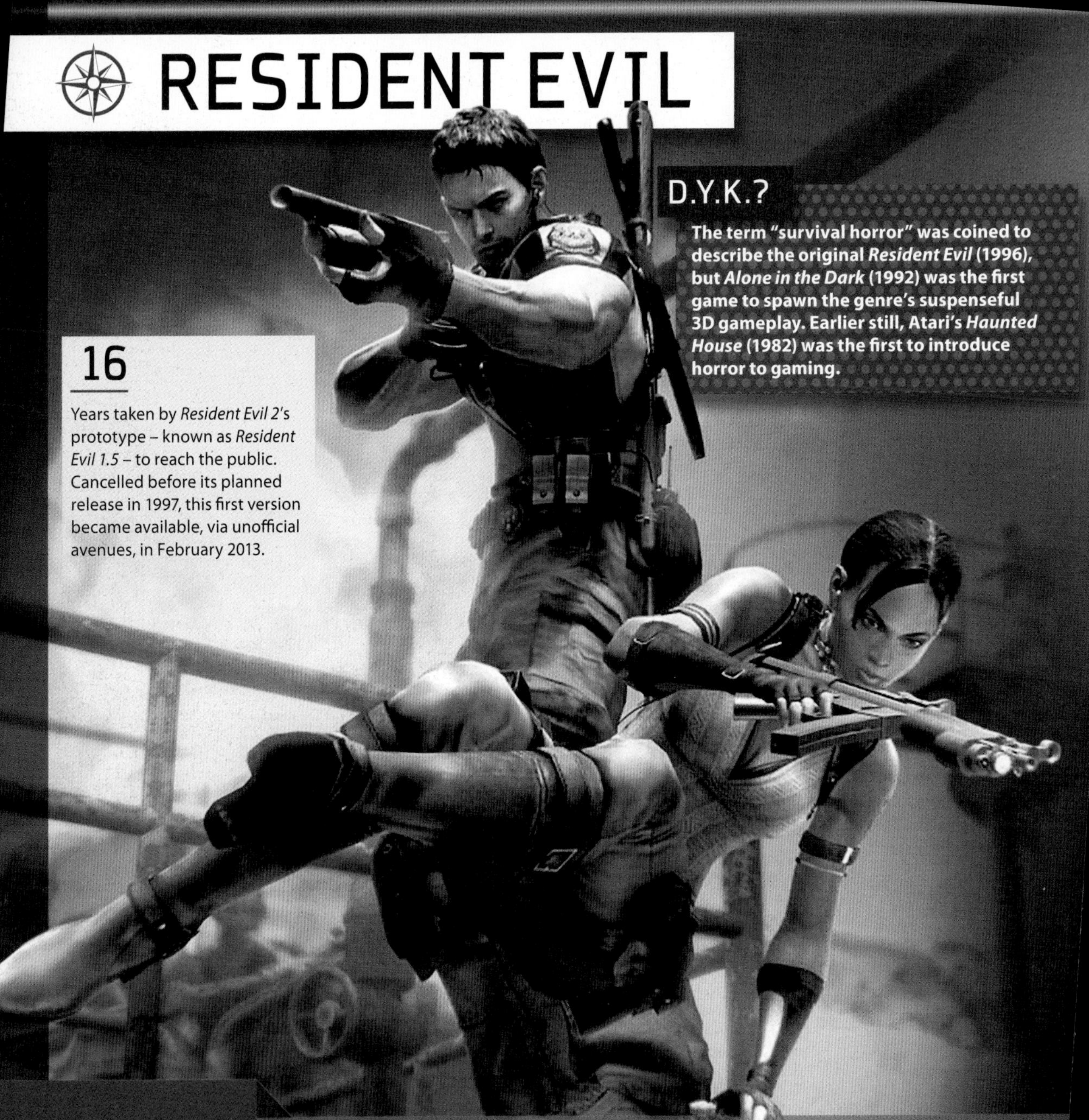

The term "survival horror" was coined to describe the original *Resident Evil* (1996), but *Alone in the Dark* (1992) was the first game to spawn the genre's suspenseful 3D gameplay. Earlier still, Atari's *Haunted House* (1982) was the first to introduce horror to gaming.

16

Years taken by *Resident Evil 2*'s prototype – known as *Resident Evil 1.5* – to reach the public. Cancelled before its planned release in 1997, this first version became available, via unofficial avenues, in February 2013.

Summary: A misleading title hasn't prevented *Resident Evil* from becoming a monster. Its name refers to evil lurking in a mansion in which the first game was set, but to which the series has never returned. Its Japanese name, *Biohazard*, is more representative of the zombie carnage that defines the franchise, but *Resident Evil* remains a wicked winner.

Publisher: Capcom
Developer: Capcom
Debut: 1996

Best-selling survival horror series

When it comes to virtual horror thrills, Capcom's pioneering *Resident Evil* is way ahead of the horde. As of 29 April 2015, the zombie-bating series had sold 58.24 million games across approximately 25 sequels, remakes and spin-offs. The fifth main instalment, *Resident Evil 5*, is also the **best-selling survival horror game (multi-platform)**. Released in 2009, it whisked off players to an African setting to investigate strange events. As of the same date, it had sold 8.55 million units for PS3, Xbox 360 and PC.

Best-selling "Mature"-rated game on 3DS

Described as containing "intense violence, blood and gore, sexual content and/or strong language", *Resident Evil: Revelations* had achieved global sales of 830,000 as of 23 March 2015. This makes it the best-selling 3DS game to carry a US "Mature" ESRB rating.

Most successful live-action movie series based on a videogame

As of January 2015, *Resident Evil* films had grossed $915.9 million (£596.8 million).

The third film, *Resident Evil: Extinction* (2007), marked the **first live-action movie trilogy based on a videogame**, while the five films form the **most live-action movie adaptations of a game series**.

The **most internationally successful Canadian movie** is *Resident Evil: Afterlife* (2010), grossing $296 million (£189.5 million).

Worst videogame dialogue

"Here's a lockpick – it might be handy if you, the master of unlocking, take it with you" was voted the worst game dialogue ever by US magazine *Electronic Gaming Monthly* in 2002. The line appears near the start of the first *Resident Evil* game.

Longest survival horror gaming marathon

Minneapolis gamer Tim Turi (USA) played *Resident Evil* games for 27 hr 8 min on 6–7 August 2011.

Most main character death animations

Resident Evil 4 includes at least 47 ways for protagonist Leon S Kennedy to meet his maker.

Greatest aggregate time playing *Resident Evil 6*

According to residentevil.net, as of 3 March 2015, gamer "Brutaldactyl" had spent a total of 4,453 hr 4 min 13 sec playing *Resident Evil 6* on the Xbox 360. The **greatest aggregate time on *RE6* for the PlayStation 3** is by "sslazio1989": 4,145 hr 45 min 40 sec. And the **greatest time on *RE6* for PC** is by "nadin": 2,336 hr 7 min 17 sec.

Most misspelt 3DS boxes distributed

Ninety-thousand copies of 2012's *Resident Evil: Revelations* were shipped with the title misspelt as "Revelaitons" on the box.

Most variations of a survival horror game

The first *Resident Evil* has seen four remakes: 1997's Director's Cut (itself updated as 1998's Dual Shock Version to incorporate rumble feedback), 2002's GameCube version, 2006's *Deadly Silence*, enhanced for Nintendo DS, and the *Resident Evil HD Remaster*, released in January 2015 for Xbox One, PS4 and PC.

Fastest completion of the original *Resident Evil*

"PopovAmiral" (France) took just 1 hr 2 min 30 sec to finish 1996's *Resident Evil*. He played the PlayStation version on a PS2 and uploaded a video to YouTube on 16 October 2013.

The **fastest completion of *Resident Evil 4* (Load Game) on the Xbox 360**, using "New Game +" mode, is 1 hr 31 min 29 sec by Robert Brandl (Germany) on 20 August 2013.

First episodic *Resident Evil* game

Revelling in nerve-shredding cliffhangers, *Resident Evil: Revelations 2* was originally available across four downloadable episodes. The first of these was issued globally in February 2015, with subsequent parts following weekly. A "complete season" download and retail version was also released in March 2015, featuring additional content.

Most playable female in *Resident Evil*

The series' overall **most playable character** is Chris Redfield, with 13 appearances to date. However, *Resident Evil* is also known for its strong female characters. Anti-bioterrorism agent Jill Valentine can boast 10 playable appearances: the 1996 original and its 2002, 2006 and 2015 remakes; *Resident Evil 3: Nemesis*; *Resident Evil: The Umbrella Chronicles*; *Resident Evil 5* and its Gold Edition; *Resident Evil: The Mercenaries 3D*; and *Resident Evil: Revelations*.

SAINTS ROW

Fastest completion of *Saints Row IV*

On 10 November 2014, German gamer "Baqonator" flew through the PC version of *Saints Row IV* in 4 hr 11 min 20 sec. This smashed the previous record of 4 hr 22 min 5 sec set by Matt "BLiTZ" Siegfried. However, Siegfried's record was especially impressive in that it was set four days after the game came out, on 24 August 2013.

71

Number of floors in the Phillips Building, making it the tallest building in Stilwater. First appearing in *Saints Row 2*, it serves as an HQ for the Ultor Corporation.

D.Y.K.?

Saints Row: Gat out of Hell reveals that 3rd Street Saints Dex and Troy are in Hell, making Johnny Gat (pictured above) the longest-surviving member of the original gang.

Summary: An open-world action-adventure with its foot on the throttle and its tongue firmly in its cheek, *Saints Row* gets crazier with every new instalment. Gamers find themselves facing off against a host of bad guys including street gangs, aliens and even the Devil himself…

Most vehicles stolen in one minute on *Saints Row: The Third*

On 6 August 2013, Scottish gamer Nathan Buchan posted a video in which he stole a grand total of 11 different vehicles, including a patrol car and a motorcycle, in 60 seconds of larcenous mayhem.

Publisher: THQ/Deep Silver
Developer: Volition
Debut: 2006

Highest insurance fraud in *Saints Row IV*

The "Insurance Fraud" activity encourages players to injure themselves in order to make fraudulent insurance claims. On 13 January 2014, "PrestigeIsKey" earned $2,790,836 (£1,841,020) from a single, very painful incident in *Saints Row IV*.

Longest car-surfing in *Saints Row: The Third*

"GreatDazeTazer" managed to car-surf along the roads of Steelport for a death-defying 3 min 23 sec on 1 April 2012. His tip for a successful car surf? To "tap, tap, tap-a-roo!", which is a quote from the golfing movie character Happy Gilmore.

Longest stunt jump in *Saints Row: The Third*

On 28 February 2012, Jacob Burcar (USA) drove a fully upgraded Emu car off a ramp, leaping 5,028 m (16,496 ft) before crash-landing into the ocean. In order to give his car additional boost, he attached satchel charges to the back of it, and these were then detonated.

Most dangerous armchair in a game

Expansion pack *Saints Row: Gat out of Hell* (2015) introduced the Armchair-a-geddon: an upholstered mobile war machine with twin chain guns mounted into the armrests. To celebrate the game's release, a real-life replica was built and filmed driving around the streets of London, UK.

Fastest completion of *Saints Row: Gat out of Hell*

Despite making some "major mistakes", USA gamer "redemption99" redeemed himself by polishing off the latest series addition, *Saints Row: Gat out of Hell*, in just 44 min 34 sec. He completed this devil-trumping feat on 19 February 2015, as shown in a video he uploaded to Twitch.tv.

Fastest completion of *Saints Row 2*

Dedicated gamer Dave "FoxAndRavens" Kindel (USA) went from Steelport jail-breaker to kingpin in just 5 hr 3 min 52 sec on 10 January 2015.

The **fastest completion of *Saints Row: The Third*** was by Hungarian gamer "Ditto", who managed to finish the game in 3 hr 46 min 27 sec on 3 May 2014.

First supernatural *Saints Row* game

It may have started out as a gritty open-world crime game in the mould of *GTA*, but *Saints Row* has evolved into something seriously "out there". Following *Saints Row IV*'s introduction of aliens, the 2015 expansion pack *Saints Row: Gat out of Hell* featured demons and angels, players flying on feathery wings and William Shakespeare as a demon DJ.

Most expensive videogame package

Priced at exactly $1 million (£580,000) and limited to just one, the "Super Dangerous Wad Wad Edition" of 2013's *Saints Row IV* is only available to gamers with extremely deep pockets. Alongside an edition of the game itself, the package also includes a shiny Lamborghini Gallardo car, a seven-night stay in Dubai, plastic surgery, a personal shopper (and spending spree), a "hostage rescue" experience and other prize goodies. As of 1 April 2015, this extravagant bundle was still yet to attract a buyer.

Tips 'n' Tricks

Saints Row IV players have to acquire superpowers if they hope to defeat alien tyrant Emperor Zinyak. One of the most important superpowers is telekinesis, which allows players to move objects using their minds only. When you acquire it, make sure you take part in a TV challenge, hosted by Professor Genki, involving the telekinetic propulsion of objects through rings. It's a great way to get to grips with your new power, which you can then turn upon the alien invasion force.

Most expensive weapons in *Saints Row: The Third*

Name	Weapon type	Cost in "cash"
Woodsman	Chainsaw	=100,000
Cyber Blaster	Submachine gun	=100,000
Nocturne	Sword	50,000
McManus 2015	Sniper rifle	25,000
S3X Hammer	Shotgun	=20,000
Viper Laser Rifle	Rifle	=20,000
Annihilator	Rocket launcher	15,000
AR-55	Assault rifle	=10,000
AS3 Ultimax	Police shotgun	=10,000
Grave Digger	Shotgun	=10,000

Source: Saints Row Wiki as of 24 March 2015

SILENT HILL

Most critically acclaimed *Silent Hill* game

According to GameRankings, *Silent Hill 2* (2001) is the pick of the survival horror franchise. As of 13 March 2015, it boasted a rating of 85.82%, higher than the series' other instalments and spin-offs. The spine-chilling game follows hero James Sunderland as he searches Silent Hill trying to uncover the truth about his deceased wife.

> "A lot of thinking has to go into the game design when dealing with psychological horror..."
>
> **Masashi Tsuboyama, Chief Designer** on *Silent Hill 4: The Room*

2208330

Phone number for Konami customer support, which players of *Silent Hill: Shattered Memories* can call on their in-game mobile. But don't expect them to save you!

Summary: One of the most iconic games in the survival horror genre, *Silent Hill* has evolved over the years in order to keep its fans on their toes. But one thing hasn't changed – whether it's Pyramid Head or Asphyxia, the monsters of Silent Hill are the stuff of nightmares...

Publisher: Konami
Developer: Konami
Debut: 1999

Q&A

SAM BARLOW wrote *Silent Hill: Shattered Memories.* His new mystery, *Her Story,* is centred on police interview footage.

What were you most proud of in *Shattered Memories*?
We made a game that was personal with an emotional core that told a story about real people in a contemporary world.

***Her Story* is a crime story based around a police interview. Was it a departure from *Silent Hill*?**
I've always wanted to tackle the crime genre – in fact, *SH: SM* was originally pitched as a psychological detective story. I'd used the psychiatric interview to help frame *SH: SM* and I was drawn to the police interview in *Her Story* for similar reasons. There's a structure to it, a set of rules. It's storytelling gold.

Was *Her Story* inspired by social media and YouTube?
That was very important. I love games that use text prompts and input. Now that everyone uses Google, text prompt has become second nature. At the same time, video has had its second wind thanks to streaming and mobile. We see the news first through grainy YouTube videos.

Downpour is 1 hr 37 min 19 sec, achieved by "blaze8876" on the Xbox 360 on 20 May 2013.

First 3D survival horror game for a console system

Silent Hill: Downpour (2012) was the first survival horror game to support a stereoscopic 3D gameplay mode. This mode can only be viewed on special 3D-enabled television sets.

Most popular fan-made *Silent Hill* video

"*P.T.* (*Silent Hills*) Demo Full Playthrough + Ending THIS GAME WILL BLOW YOUR MIND!" by social media legend "PewDiePie" had been viewed 6,733,105 times on YouTube as of 12 March 2015. It was uploaded on 19 August 2014.

First multiplayer mode in a *Silent Hill* game

Silent Hill: Book of Memories (2012) was the first game in the franchise to introduce

Fastest completion of *Silent Hill 2*

The creepy sequel held no fear for Russian gamer Andrew "Bigmanjapan" Bondarenko, who breezed through it in just 44 min 18 sec on 1 December 2014. He completed his speed-run playing the PC version of the game.

Fastest completion of *Silent Hill 4: The Room*

On 21 March 2015, speed-runner "AnEternalEnigma" of Georgia, USA, completed the Xbox version in just 57 min 21 sec. Meanwhile, the **fastest completion of *Silent Hill:***

Largest collection of *Silent Hill* memorabilia

Super-fan Whitney Chavis (USA) has been amassing *Silent Hill*-related objects since 1999. As of 24 July 2014, her collection numbered some 342 different items – and included everything from posters, flyers and T-shirts to signed promo notebooks, towels and plastic bags.

multiplayer gameplay. The 10th game in the series, *Book of Memories* was also the **first survival horror for PlayStation Vita**. Gamers using Sony's handheld console could now team up online to solve puzzles and battle the horrifying monsters that lurk in the game's fiendish top-down isometric dungeons.

First demo to win "game of the year" awards

Despite its brevity, "playable teaser" *P.T.* became the first

demo to be recognized with significant end-of-year gongs. Polygon.com featured it in its "Best Games of 2014" list, Giantbomb.com awarded it "Best Horror Game", and visitors to Bloody-disgusting.com voted it "Scariest Game of 2014". *P.T.* was directed by *Metal Gear* creator Hideo Kojima and movie director Guillermo del Toro, both of whom were expected to collaborate on the series sequel *Silent Hills*. However, as of April 2015, that game's future seemed uncertain.

First "playable teaser" for a console

Released by the non-existent game studio 7780s Studio on 12 August 2014 as a free PS4-exclusive download, *P.T.* was a short first-person survival horror. Upon completion, it revealed itself to be a teaser for the as-yet-unreleased game *Silent Hills*. *P.T.* proved a success in its own right, and had been downloaded 1,589,643 times as of 16 March 2015.

Fastest completion of *Silent Hill*

On 22 October 2004, speed-runner Brandon "Ekudeht" Armstrong completed the original game in 35 min 29 sec. He played on normal settings and didn't use glitches to speed his progress.

D.Y.K.?

Following its release in 2004, rumours began to circulate that *Silent Hill 4: The Room* had started life as another game altogether – perhaps because this new instalment was so different to the rest of the franchise. However, as its developers later explained, this wasn't the case: they had always intended a change to the gameplay mechanics of *Silent Hill 4* in order to keep the series fresh.

THE SIMS

Most sophisticated use of emotions as a game mechanic

Previous *Sims* games charted characters' moods, but 2014's *The Sims 4* made emotions entirely central to gameplay. As part of a sophisticated new system, sims were prone to 31 different emotions (including superlatives), ranging from dazed and embarrassed to inspired and energized. These were dynamically affected by in-game interaction and events. Extreme emotions could even prove fatal...

8

Number of different shades of eyebrow colour to choose from when creating your character in *The Sims 4*. There are also 13 eye colours and 18 different skin tones.

Summary: Real life getting you down? Head on over to the virtual world of *The Sims*, a sandbox life-simulation game. Created by Will Wright, the franchise has become a global institution, earning its publisher Electronic Arts more than $1 billion (£672 million).

Publisher: Electronic Arts
Developer: Maxis/ The Sims Studio
Debut: 2000

Longest-running city-building series

When *SimCity* was released in February 1989, it offered gamers the opportunity to build sprawling cities from the ground up, braving earthquakes and nuclear meltdowns along the way. There had been four major sequels as of 26 March 2015, most recently 2013's *SimCity*.

D.Y.K.?

SimCity was inspired by creator Will Wright's work on shoot-'em-up *Raid on Bungeling Bay* (1984), in particular the sophisticated map features he designed.

Longest-running social simulation series

Games focusing on human interaction stretch back to 1985's *Little Computer People*, but no series has lasted longer than *The Sims* (2000–). Evolving iterations have encouraged gamers to practise social interaction and simulate various professions.

First official music video in Simlish

Although a number of artists contributed vocals to the *Sims 2: Seasons* soundtrack, Lily Allen's Simlish rendition of her hit single "Smile" was the first honoured with an official video crafted by EA. It was released in March 2007.

Best-selling *Sims* game on Nintendo consoles

Featuring cute cartoon-style graphics, *MySims* was aimed at younger gamers and proved that the series was appealing to all ages. Based on figures compiled by Edge Online, the 2007 spin-off sold 3.72 million copies for the Nintendo Wii and DS in its first six months of sale.

Most downloads of user-generated content for a simulation game

Set 25 years before the original game, *The Sims 3* (2009) can claim an incredible 250 million downloads of user-generated content (UGC). Aficionados of the game have created a comprehensive range of mods for the game, including individual characters, houses and stories.

First game to use the SmartSim Engine

The Sims 4 employed a completely new game engine – the SmartSim Engine – to power both the game's emotion mechanics and its online Gallery functionality, which allows players to share their creations with fellow *Sims* fans.

Most prolific simulator game series

Since the release of 1989's *SimCity*, the hugely successful *Sims* series – based around the *Sims* and *SimCity* franchises – has become the most prolific in the genre, with at least 142 games bearing some variation of the name as of 31 January 2015.

Most critically acclaimed virtual life-simulation game

The Sims 2 (2004) transferred the series into a full 3D environment, while introducing six distinct life stages and an aspiration system for characters. As of 26 March 2013, it had scored 90.76% on GameRankings – just ahead of the original *The Sims*, with its overall ranking of 89.74%.

Best-selling PC game series

With its various sequels and expansion packs, *The Sims* series can lay claim to total sales of 50.86 million, more than any other series on the same platform.

When the original game was released in 2000, publisher Electronic Arts projected sales of just 160,000 units – so it's fair to say that the game has exceeded their wildest expectations. In fact, *The Sims* had shifted 11.24 million copies as of 26 March 2015 according to VGChartz, making it the **best-selling *The Sims* game** – far out in front of *The Sims 3*, with 7.72 million sales.

Most viewed fan video based on *The Sims*

Uploaded by Amanda Haug on 24 March 2007, a music video featuring footage of *The Sims 2* set to a soundtrack of the pop band Aqua's 1997 hit "Barbie Girl" had amassed a total of 24,648,647 views on YouTube as of 26 March 2015.

Most popular custom-made worlds in *The Sims 3*			
World	**Description**	**Creator**	**Votes**
Beach City	Beachfront city	"rflong7"	133
Mayfield Springs	Lively town near a mountain	"Ryph"	120
Alpine County	Large US metropolis	"Western077"	74
Vice City	*Grand Theft Auto* crossover	Fresh Prince Creations	55
St Claire	Peninsula with sea views	"Awesims"	51
Mesa Grande	Small rural town	"aaronrogers8i3"	50
Alpine County – Populated	Large US metropolis	"Western077"	47
Palm Shadows	Tropical island paradise	"Cink Sims"	38
Legacy Island 3	Medium-sized island	"rflong7"	34
Los Aniegos	Sprawling city	"Coasterboi"	=30
Strange Town	Small desert town	"aaronrogers8i3"	=30

Source: sims3createaworld.com as of 9 April 2015

Best-selling videogame toy line

According to publisher Activision, as of February 2015 *Skylanders* had sold a staggering 240 million toys, out-selling established brands such as *Star Wars* and *Transformers* for three years in a row. Activision announced that the franchise had made a whopping $3 billion (£1.9 billion) since its inception.

Largest *Skylanders* collection

Verified on 27 January 2015, the largest collection of *Skylanders* memorabilia consists of 4,100 unique items and is owned by Christopher Desaliza of Pace in Florida, USA. Christopher's collection includes *Skylanders* figurines, trading cards, stickers, covers, lanyards and posters.

10,971

Total end-to-end length in miles of *Skylanders* toys bought as of February 2015. In other words, if you laid down every single purchased toy in a row, they would stretch all the way from London, UK, to Sydney, Australia.

Summary: To play *Skylanders*, gamers place character figures on the "Portal of Power" peripheral, turning their toys into in-game heroes. This innovative toys-to-life series has become a sensation, with its toy line taking on, and out-selling, previously untouchable franchises.

Publisher: Activision
Developer: Toys For Bob
Debut: 2011

First interactive gaming toy line for consoles

The groundbreaking *Skylanders: Spyro's Adventure* (2011) used the "Portal of Power" to connect players' toys to an online gaming world. Such has been its success, major rivals have emerged including Disney's *Infinity* range, Nintendo's amiibo figures and the forthcoming *LEGO® Dimensions*.

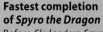

Highest-altitude freefall videogame session

As part of the European launch of *Skylanders: Trap Team* on 10 October 2014, publisher Activision hired a group of daredevil skydivers, dubbed the "Skytrappers", to play the game in freefall from an altitude of 12,500 ft (3,810 m).

Fastest completion of *Spyro the Dragon*

Before *Skylanders*, Spyro was the star of his own 3D platform games. On 1 November 2012, Jefferson "Surreal" Cline completed a single-segment run of Spyro's debut game in 44 min 8 sec. Matt "Crash41596" Leblanc achieved the **fastest completion of *Spyro 2: Ripto's Rage!*** in a single-segment run of 29 min 23 sec on 2 December 2011.

Most viewed *Skylanders* video

On 1 October 2012, Activision uploaded to YouTube a TV trailer for *Skylanders: Giants* entitled "Tall Tales", introducing fans to new, super-sized characters. As of 13 April 2015, it had been viewed 13,727,096 times.

D.Y.K.?

According to developer Toys For Bob, only one *Skylanders* character has made it to the prototype stage without making the final game – the unfortunate Tarclops.

Rarest *Skylanders* figures

At E3 2011, Activision created 600 specially packaged figures to promote the launch of *Skylanders: Spyro's Adventure*. Lucky recipients could choose between a Spyro, Gill Grunt or Trigger Happy character.

Highest health for a *Skylanders* Giant character

With his giant hammer and catchphrase "It's Crush Hour!", Earth Giant Crusher is one of the most imposing figures in *Skylanders*. His health score of 470 is the highest of the Giants, 10 more than Thumpback in second place.

Most playable characters in an action RPG

Released in October 2014, *Skylanders Trap Team* has more than 300 playable characters. This total includes the 244 characters from the previous games (of which 31 were from *Swap Force*), as well as the Legendary variants (which come with different skills and stats). *Trap Team*'s 71 new characters include 28 Trap Masters.

Largest Skylander

Carved from polystyrene by the UK-based Sculpture Studios, the "life-sized" statue Tree Rex appears at exhibitions and events around the world. It stands 315 cm (10 ft 4 in) high, and is an exact replica of the Skylander Giant with the flashing eyes.

Most viewed fan film based on *Skylanders*

In his YouTube channels "EvanTubeHD" and "EvanTubeRAW", nine-year-old critic Evan reviews toys and videogames such as *Skylanders*. "Toys "R" Us Shopping (Episode 2)" – in which Evan visits the toy shop to pick a present for a friend's birthday – had earned 7,220,206 views as of 13 April 2015.

Tips 'n' Tricks

The Kaos Mode in *Skylanders: Trap Team* provides the ultimate test of your fighting skills, pitting you against wave after wave of enemies. Keep an eye out for the Mystery Box of Doom, which drops randomly into arenas. If enemies can break it open, a larger and more dangerous opponent will appear, so do everything you can to take them out before the box can reveal its contents.

Most critically acclaimed 3D platformers for the Xbox 360

Game	Publisher	Year	Rating
Skylanders: Swap Force	Activision	2013	84.68%
Skylanders: Giants	Activision	2012	81.58%
Skylanders: Spyro's Adventure	Activision	2011	80.95%
Marble Blast Ultra	GarageGames	2006	80.86%
Banjo-Kazooie: Nuts & Bolts	Microsoft Game Studios	2008	80.66%
de Blob 2	THQ	2011	78.90%
Sonic Generations	Sega	2011	78.67%
Banjo-Tooie	Microsoft Game Studios	2009	77.00%
The Maw	Microsoft Game Studios	2009	76.06%
Kung Fu Panda	Activision	2008	75.97%

Source: GameRankings as of 14 April 2015

SONIC

Summary: One of the most recognizable and beloved characters in gaming, Sega's spiky blue hedgehog has been careering around screens and gobbling up golden rings for nearly 25 years. With every new release, the *Sonic* universe expands, offering a host of extra playable characters.

Publisher: Sega
Developer: Various
Debut: 1991

Fastest completion of *Sonic the Hedgehog 3 & Knuckles*

Playing as Knuckles the Echidna, Adrian "HDL" Perez completed a single-segment run in 22 min 40 sec on 11 December 2013. His run made use of glitches and tactical deaths to increase the speed of his progress on the combined game for the Sega Mega Drive/Genesis.

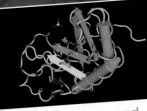

First gene named after a videogame

First detected in fruit flies, the hedgehog genes (hh) gained their name after embryos with the mutated genes acquired spiky, hedgehog-like projections. In 1993, biologist Dr Robert Riddle named one gene "Sonic hedgehog" (or Shh) after the Sega hero.

D.Y.K.?

Designer Naoto Ohshima's prototypes of Sonic were dubbed "Mr Needlemouse" – a literal translation of "hedgehog" in Japanese.

Fastest completion of *Sonic: Lost World*

The 21st release in the *Sonic* series, *Lost World* sees the "Blue Blur" taking on Doctor Eggman and the Deadly Six. On 6 August 2014, gamer "DarkspinesSonic" (aka Carlos Johnson) set an any-percentage speed-run record for the game on the Wii U, completing it in just 1 hr 1 min 47 sec.

15

Sonic's age in years – making him younger than the game series in which he appears. The heroic hedgehog celebrates his birthday on 23 June, the release date of the original *Sonic the Hedgehog* way back in 1991.

Longest-running comic based on a videogame

Archie Comics' *Sonic the Hedgehog* first appeared in July 1993. In January 2015, its 268th edition rolled off the presses. Spin-offs include *Sonic Boom* and *Sonic Universe*, which was first published in 2009 and had reached issue #72 by February 2015.

Most expensive *Sonic the Hedgehog* game
In December 2011, a rare copy of *Sonic the Hedgehog* for the Sega Master System appeared on eBay. It was one of the European PAL versions of the game Sega had shipped over for the US market, complete with a US barcode sticker on the back. This was enough to spark a bidding war among collectors, with the game eventually selling for $981.33 (£636).

Highest score on *Sonic the Hedgehog*
On 15 May 2011, Michael Sroka (USA) scored 812,140 points on the original game. The **highest score on *Sonic the Hedgehog 2*** is an incredible 3,261,620 points, achieved by Eric Schafer (USA) on 20 May 2012.

Most chart-topping games for Sega platforms

As of 13 April 2015, *Sonic* games sit proudly at the top of the charts for four different Sega platforms: Genesis/Mega Drive (*Sonic the Hedgehog 2*, with 6.03 million sales), Dreamcast (*Sonic Adventure*, 2.42 million), Sega CD (*Sonic CD*, 1.5 million) and the Game Gear (*Sonic the Hedgehog 2*, 400,000).

Fastest completion of *Sonic Generations*

On 20 January 2014, gamer "Frokenok" (Greece) completed a single-segment speed-run on the PC version of the 2011 game in just 58 min 11 sec.

Fastest completion of *Sonic the Hedgehog*

Australian gamer Mike "mike89" McKenzie completed Sonic's debut platform title in just 11 min 8 sec on 29 June 2009. This was a single-segment run carried out on the Sega Game Gear version of the game.

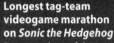

Best-selling *Sonic* videogame

During the 1990s, when Sega and Nintendo were arch-rivals, few could have predicted that one day they would unite. *Mario & Sonic at the Olympic Games* (2007) saw eight characters from both worlds competing in sporting events from the Beijing Olympics. It had achieved 13.06 million sales as of 22 April 2015.

Longest tag-team videogame marathon on *Sonic the Hedgehog*

Four members of the US-based gaming collective "Respawn Point" played *Sonic* videogames for seven days from 28 December 2011 to 4 January 2012, in a live-streamed record attempt.

Fastest Skeleton Run in *Mario & Sonic at the Olympic Winter Games* (Wii)

On 16 February 2014, Shawn Alvarez (USA) completed the Skeleton Run in 65.05 sec in Burlington, Wisconsin, USA.

Most critically acclaimed *Sonic* games

Game	Year	Platform	Rating
Sonic Adventure	1998	Dreamcast	86.51%
Sonic Advance 2	2002	Game Boy Advance	85.65%
Sonic Advance	2001	Game Boy Advance	83.32%
Sonic Adventure 2	2001	Dreamcast	83.26%
Sonic Rush	2005	DS	83.23%
Sonic & All-Stars Racing Transformed	2012	X360	82.88%
Sonic's Ultimate Genesis Collection	2009	X360	81.64%
Sonic Advance 3	2004	Game Boy Advance	81.37%
Sonic's Ultimate Genesis Collection	2009	PS3	81.13%
Sonic Rush Adventure	2007	DS	80.15%

Source: GameRankings as of 13 April 2015

Tips 'n' Tricks

As *Sonic* veterans will know, collecting golden rings is the key to success in the game – and 2013's *Sonic: Lost World* is no different. Rings can be found in the tall grass of the Windy Hill courses and inside crystals in the Desert Ruins zone. Smashing semi-transparent boulders will also help up your count. Remember that five Red Star Rings are hidden away on each level, and you'll need to collect them in order to get a 100% completion score. So keep your eyes peeled.

Evolution of Spaceships

Spaceships have been a cornerstone of videogaming since the beginning. We take a look back at over 50 years of fighter craft, battle cruisers and interstellar titans...

1962

The Needle and The Wedge • Spacewar! (Steve Russell et al)
Despite having less detail than a cave painting, *Spacewar!* was both the **first videogame shooter** and the **first videogame to feature a spaceship**. It was developed for the PDP-1 computer.

1979

Arrow Ship • Asteroids (Atari)
Just before the 1980s ushered in a new era of gaming, Atari released *Asteroids* – the **first videogame to use real-world physics**. The player controlled a triangular spaceship armed with asteroid-busting lasers.

Vic Viper • Gradius (Konami)
Gradius is not only a timeless shoot-'em-up, it also gave the *Vic Viper* its maiden voyage. At least nine variations of this pioneering spacecraft are known to exist.

1985

TCS Tiger's Claw • Wing Commander (Origin Systems)
This strike carrier has appeared in more *Wing Commander* media than any other spaceship.

1993

Arwing • Star Fox (Nintendo EAD, 1993)
The *X-wing*-like *Arwing* moved at a speed of 4.2 Mach (3,197 mph) in atmosphere and introduced "barrel-rolling".

1990

1995

Epoch • Chrono Trigger (Square)
While it looks like a typical spaceship, the *Epoch* also functions as a time machine, enabling its crew to travel across the fourth dimension. The earliest point in time that the crew can fly back to is 65 million years BC.

1998

SD Lucifer • Descent: FreeSpace – The Great War (Volition)
This massive super-destroyer hounded players throughout the original *FreeSpace*. It was only by luring it into subspace that it could finally be destroyed.

Terran Battlecruiser • StarCraft (Blizzard)
The *Battlecruiser* may not be the biggest fish in virtual space, but it was the only non-hero unit in the original *StarCraft* capable of surviving a direct nuclear strike.

1997

Navy Super Titan • Colony Wars (Psygnosis)
Taking its cue from *Star Wars*, the final boss in *Colony Wars* was like an even bigger *Star Destroyer*. To beat it, you had to destroy its shields, then hit it with artillery.

Kushan Mothership • Homeworld (Relic Entertainment)
The Kushan *Mothership* is an interstellar arc that housed the remnants of a stranded civilization. Its mission was to find them a new homeworld.

1999

Von Braun • System Shock 2 (Irrational Games)
The *Von Braun* was like a haunted house in space. It had 1.8 billion scientific and security systems – the **most systems in a videogame spaceship**.

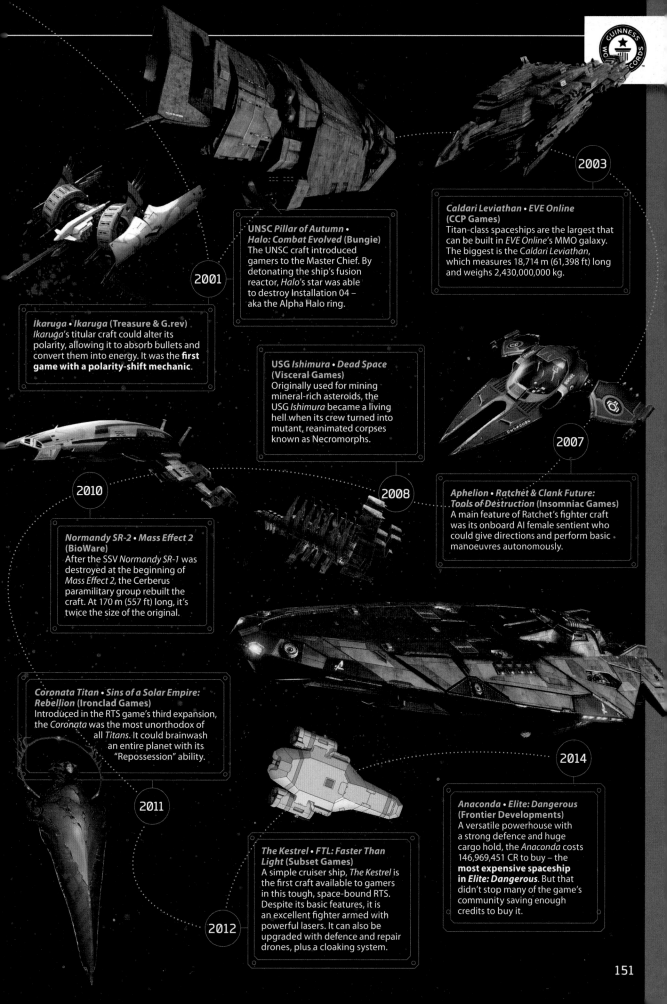

2003

Caldari Leviathan • EVE Online (CCP Games)
Titan-class spaceships are the largest that can be built in *EVE Online*'s MMO galaxy. The biggest is the *Caldari Leviathan*, which measures 18,714 m (61,398 ft) long and weighs 2,430,000,000 kg.

2001

UNSC *Pillar of Autumn* • *Halo: Combat Evolved* (Bungie)
The UNSC craft introduced gamers to the Master Chief. By detonating the ship's fusion reactor, *Halo*'s star was able to destroy Installation 04 – aka the Alpha Halo ring.

***Ikaruga* • *Ikaruga* (Treasure & G.rev)**
Ikaruga's titular craft could alter its polarity, allowing it to absorb bullets and convert them into energy. It was the **first game with a polarity-shift mechanic**.

USG *Ishimura* • *Dead Space* (Visceral Games)
Originally used for mining mineral-rich asteroids, the USG *Ishimura* became a living hell when its crew turned into mutant, reanimated corpses known as Necromorphs.

2007

2010

2008

***Aphelion* • *Ratchet & Clank Future: Tools of Destruction* (Insomniac Games)**
A main feature of Ratchet's fighter craft was its onboard AI female sentient who could give directions and perform basic manoeuvres autonomously.

***Normandy SR-2* • *Mass Effect 2* (BioWare)**
After the SSV *Normandy SR-1* was destroyed at the beginning of *Mass Effect 2*, the Cerberus paramilitary group rebuilt the craft. At 170 m (557 ft) long, it's twice the size of the original.

***Coronata* Titan • *Sins of a Solar Empire: Rebellion* (Ironclad Games)**
Introduced in the RTS game's third expansion, the *Coronata* was the most unorthodox of all *Titans*. It could brainwash an entire planet with its "Repossession" ability.

2014

2011

***The Kestrel* • *FTL: Faster Than Light* (Subset Games)**
A simple cruiser ship, *The Kestrel* is the first craft available to gamers in this tough, space-bound RTS. Despite its basic features, it is an excellent fighter armed with powerful lasers. It can also be upgraded with defence and repair drones, plus a cloaking system.

***Anaconda* • *Elite: Dangerous* (Frontier Developments)**
A versatile powerhouse with a strong defence and huge cargo hold, the *Anaconda* costs 146,969,451 CR to buy – the **most expensive spaceship in *Elite: Dangerous***. But that didn't stop many of the game's community saving enough credits to buy it.

2012

151

STREET FIGHTER

Longest-running playable female in a fighting game series

Ex-Interpol agent Chun-Li ("Beautiful Spring" in Mandarin Chinese) has 24 years of combat action under her belt. Debuting in *Street Fighter II* (1991), she has appeared in every *Street Fighter* sequel and crossover title since. The **first female player character in a fighting game** was Lan-Fang in *Yie Ar Kung-Fu II*, released by Konami in 1986.

63

Number of playable characters in the main *Street Fighter* series as of 2 March 2015. The franchise has come a long way since the original game, in which players only had the choice of two characters – best friends Ryu and Ken.

Summary: *Street Fighter* is the hard-hitting granddaddy of fighting games. Since heroes Ryu and Ken first appeared in the arcades back in the late 1980s, the series has gone on to become one of the biggest-selling franchises in the world, with a dizzying array of sequels and spin-offs.

Publisher: Capcom
Developer: Capcom
Debut: 1987

Most prolific fighting game series

Street Fighter has amassed an incredible 126 different titles in the series (soon to be 127, with the 2016 release of *Street Fighter V*). Along the way, characters such as Ryu, Ken and Chun-Li have faced off against rivals from 13 other franchises including the X-Men, Marvel Comics and *Tekken*, also making it the **most prolific crossover fighting game**.

Highest earnings in a fighting game tournament

The grand finals of the 25th anniversary *Street Fighter* international tournament were held in California, USA, on 8 December 2012. Korean gamer "Infiltration" (Lee Sun-woo) went home with $76,300 (£47,568).

Longest combo performed in *Super Street Fighter IV: Arcade Edition*

Turkish gamer "ErDeM2206" published a YouTube video on 24 March 2014 featuring a skull-cracking 219-hit combo. He achieved this in the 2012 patch's "Training" mode by playing Chun-Li with a full super metre against a cornered Dee Jay. If this combo was performed in a tournament, the damage would come to a staggering 857 points.

Highest score on *Super Street Fighter IV* arcade mode

On 5 December 2010, Rob "Desk" Seymour earned 2,587,000 points on the PS3 version of *Super Street Fighter IV*, more than doubling the previous record. He used high-scoring combos to pile on the points and deliberately lost one round per fight to allow the maximum scoring opportunities across all three rounds in a bout.

Longest winning streak on *Street Fighter IV*

Playing as Sagat, Ryan Hart (UK) remained unbeaten for 169 matches of *Street Fighter IV* playing against human opponents at GAME in Hull, UK, on 27 March 2010.

Highest score in *X-Men vs. Street Fighter*

Clarence Leung (USA) racked up 2,098,100 points on 16 March 1999. The game (in which Wolverine and co take on the Street Fighters) was played under tournament conditions, with maximum difficulty settings and damage, and no continues.

First use of parrying in a *Street Fighter* game

Parrying, a subtle form of blocking designed to unbalance an opponent in order to draw him into a counter-strike, is a key element of martial arts. It is distinguished from blocking by the way it can be adapted, mid-move, to form the basis for retaliatory strikes. The earliest use of parrying in this series can be seen in the 1997 release of *Street Fighter III*.

Most viewed competitive videogame match

As of 2 March 2015, 4,804,793 fight fans had viewed the match between Daigo "The Beast" Umehara (Japan) and Justin Wong (USA) from the 2004 EVO competition in *Street Fighter III: 3rd Strike*. The bout was notable for Umehara's stunning last-ditch series of parries before a counter-attack combo sealed the win.

First fighting videogame to feature stereoscopic 3D

When *Super Street Fighter IV: 3D Edition* launched alongside the Nintendo 3DS on 26 February 2011, it utilized stereoscopic 3D technology to add depth to the super combos.

Largest collection of *Street Fighter* memorabilia

As of 7 January 2015, the *Street Fighter* collection of Clarence Lim of Ontario, Canada, stood at 2,723 individual objects.

Most critically acclaimed fighting game on a seventh-generation console

Released on 12 February 2009, *Street Fighter IV* on PS3 had achieved a GameRankings score of 93.64% as of 12 March 2015, delivering a knockout blow to all of its bare-knuckle brawling competitors. Hadouken!

Most popular tournament character in *Ultra Street Fighter IV*

According to rankings data on fighting game enthusiast site Shoryuken, one-eyed giant and tiger-uppercutting *muay thai* expert Sagat had been selected as a main-choice character in 77 *Ultra Street Fighter IV* tournaments, as of 2 March 2015.

SUPER MARIO BROS.

Summary: After 35 years of frenetic platform, racing and puzzle action, the multi-million-selling plumber with the bushy moustache remains the most iconic figure in gaming. And with *Mario Maker* set for a September 2015 release, gamers will be able to create their very own levels.

First *Mario* game for Apple hardware

When, in March 2015, Nintendo announced that its characters would be coming to mobile platforms, gamers were surprised: for m█ console generations, Mario and co. had only appeared on Nintendo hardware. But this has not always been the case: before the NES launched in the USA in 1986, Nintendo allowed its games to be ported to various platforms. In 1984, Atari even released a version of *Mario Bros.* for the Apple II computer.

Fastest completion of level 1-1 on *Super Mario 3D Land*

Tristen Geren (USA, pictured) sprinted through the opening level in just 31 sec on 22 June 2013, equalling the record set by Adrian Keung (China) on 6 November 2012. Tristen also holds the record for the **highest score on Sort or 'Splode in *New Super Mario Bros.*** – 337 points, set on 17 January 2013.

Publisher: Nintendo
Developer: Nintendo
Debut: 1983

125

Weeks spent in the *Billboard* ringtone chart by "Ground Theme", the iconic soundtrack to *Super Mario Bros.* composed by Koji Kondo. The familiar ditty has also been performed in concert by live orchestras.

D.Y.K.?

Super Mario 3D World's Cat Suit has been described by IGN as the "most powerful skill-based Mario power-up in history". It lets you cling to surfaces and dive-bomb enemies.

Most prolific party videogame series

Mario Party players compete on a board game crammed with mini-games, using a multiplayer mode that accommodates up to eight players. As of 22 April 2015, the series had 14 titles. The most recent game, *Mario Party 10* (2015) for the Wii U, was the first to support Nintendo amiibo figures.

Most viewed online game walkthrough

A DS guide uploaded by gamer "cesaritox09" on 8 June 2009, "New Super Mario Bros Walkthrough Part 22" had been viewed 30,221,835 times as of 3 May 2015.

Best-selling Wii U game

New Super Mario Bros. U had sold 4.70 million copies as of 17 April 2015, ahead of *Mario Kart 8* in second place with 4.38 million.

Highest score on Super Mario Bros.

On 8 January 2015, Andrew Gardikis (USA) scored a mighty 1,435,100 points. This was more than enough to beat the long-standing record of 1,237,450 points set by Jessica Goldsmith back in 2011.

Fastest single-segment completion of *Super Mario Bros. 3*

Making full use of a Tanooki suit, warp gates and a skip glitch on level 7-1 that takes the player to the end of the game, "MitchFlowerPower" completed the NES version in a startling 3 min 8 sec on 9 February 2015.

Fastest completion of *Super Mario Bros.*

On 27 June 2014, speed-runner "Blubber" whipped through the 1985 NES classic in 4 min 57.69 sec, executing every jump with near-faultless precision. The **fastest completion of Super Mario World** for the SNES is 9 min 47 sec, recorded by gamer "GreenDeathFlavor" (USA) on 23 January 2015.

Fastest completion of *Super Paper Mario*

A platform RPG for the Wii, *Super Paper Mario* allows players to switch between 2D and 3D gameplay. On 14 December 2014, "Gamerob" (Canada) worked his way through to the end of the game in a super-speedy time of 4 hr 24 min 40 sec.

First *Super Mario* game released for a non-Nintendo system

Super Mario Bros. Special (1986) was the first Nintendo-licenced follow-up to the NES smash hit. It was released on the NEC-PC8801 and Sharp X1 Japanese PCs months before *Super Mario Bros.: The Lost Levels*, and two years before *Super Mario Bros. 2*.

First movie based on a videogame

Feature-length anime *Super Mario Bros.: The Great Mission to Rescue Princess Peach!* was released in Japan in 1986, seven years before 1993's live-action flop *Super Mario Bros.*

Highest score on *Mario Bros.* (arcade)

Before the NES hit the US and made the plump plumber a global superstar, Mario was already a smash in the arcades. Steve Kleisath (USA) holds the highest score on the arcade *Mario Bros.*, with 5,424,920 points on 10 January 2015.

Best-selling *Mario* games

Game	Platform	Year	Global sales
Super Mario Bros.	NES	1985	40.24 million
Mario Kart Wii	Wii	2008	35.17 million
New Super Mario Bros.	DS	2006	29.67 million
New Super Mario Bros. Wii	Wii	2009	27.97 million
Mario Kart DS	DS	2005	23.13 million
Super Mario World	SNES	1990	20.61 million
Super Mario Land	Game Boy	1989	18.14 million
Super Mario Bros. 3	NES	1988	17.28 million
Super Mario 64	N64	1996	11.89 million
Super Mario Galaxy	Wii	2007	11.24 million

Source: VGChartz as of 20 April 2015

Tips 'n' Tricks

Struggling to get started in *Super Mario 3D World*? Then take the hidden red warp pipe on World 1-2 straight to World 2. First you have to pick up a Cat Suit in World 1-1. Then, when you near the end of the underground part of 1-2, you'll find a pipe that divides into two parts, with one loop filled with coins. On the next platform, leap into the air to reveal some invisible blocks that will take you up to a ledge with a patrolling Koopa. Halfway along the ledge, use the Cat Suit to scramble up the wall to a hidden platform and the red warp pipe.

Most KOs on *Super Smash Bros.*

Super Smash Bros. was the first videogame that Klayton Schaufler (USA) bought, and it instantly appealed to his competitive nature. On 16 October 2014, Klayton (pictured above as Sonic) achieved a record-breaking 20 KOs in the game.

He also holds the record for the **most KOs on *SSB Brawl*,** with 51 achieved on 8 February 2013.

"It's nice to have respect from other record holders in other countries..."

Klayton Schaufler

D.Y.K.?

Ken's *SSBM* signature move is the "Ken Combo", a spike set-up he discovered with Marth: single jump, forward aerial, mid-air jump, down aerial.

Highest-earning *Super Smash Bros. Melee* player

As of 20 January 2015, gamer "SephirothKen" (aka Ken Hoang, USA – seen below as Marth) had earned $36,175 (£23,886) from playing *Super Smash Bros. Melee*. Despite retiring from the game between 2008 and 2012, Ken remains a popular professional eSports player and is known as "The King of Smash" to his fans. In 2008, he appeared as a contestant on the US reality TV show *Survivor: Gabon*, where he finished in a respectable fifth place.

GUINNESS WORLD RECORDS

SUPER SMASH BROS.

60

Playable characters appearing across the *SSB* franchise, including Captain Falcon, Donkey Kong, Jigglypuff, Kirby, Link, Luigi, Mario, Ness, Pikachu and Samus.

Summary: Nintendo brings together characters from some of its most popular franchises – including *Mario*, *Pokémon* and *The Legend of Zelda* – in a showdown to see who really is the toughest. The result is a fun and highly playable fighting series.

Publisher: Nintendo
Developer: HAL Laboratory
Debut: 1999

Most trophies in a videogame

Since their first appearance in 2001's *Super Smash Bros. Melee*, trophies have become a much-loved feature of the series. They are collectible items representing characters, items and elements from other games. *Super Smash Bros. for Wii U* (2014) can boast 716 trophies to collect throughout the game, including everything from a trophy of Mario to a bonus fruit from the *PAC-Man* series – adding up to the most trophies in any videogame. Although collection of these goodies is optional, watch out for the Birdo and Pidgit trophies in *Super Smash Bros. Melee*, both of which unlock a special multiplayer stage.

NINTENDO GAMECUBE.

SUPER SMASH BROS. Melee

PAL Nintendo

Highest earnings in a *Super Smash Bros.* tournament

Playing as *Star Fox* character Falco, Christopher "PC Chris" Szygiel won $10,000 (£5,150) on 19 November 2006 at the *Super Smash Bros. Melee* Singles National Tournament in Las Vegas, Nevada, USA.

Strongest character in *Super Smash Bros. Brawl*

Match-ups predict how different characters will fare in a bout when pitched against one another. When Smash World Forums published their third annual Match-up Chart on 9 July 2013, it was *Kirby's* Meta Knight who came out on top with a hefty 252 points.

Longest average play time for a Wii game

According to statistics compiled by gamer website Kotaku from data released on the Nintendo Channel, 2008's *Super Smash Bros. Brawl* kept the average player entertained for an impressive 66 hr 32 min.

Longest solo home-run in *Super Smash Bros. Brawl*

The home-run is a mini-game in which players beat up a sandbag before hitting it as far as possible. The longest solo home-run is 6,426 m (21,084 ft), achieved with the Ice Climbers by Japanese gamer "Teitoku06142" and validated by allisbrawl.com on 19 December 2014.

Best-selling fighting game

Released in 2008, *Super Smash Bros. Brawl* is the king of the ring according to VGChartz, with 12.56 million global sales as of 4 March 2015. The *Super Smash Bros.* series has spawned five popular sequels to date, the latest two being the Nintendo 3DS and Wii U editions in 2014. With total sales of 34.07 million, it is the **best-selling fighting series on Nintendo hardware**, as of 4 March 2015.

Most knockouts on *Super Smash Bros. Melee*

US gamer "anthony11293", aka Jeremy Anthony, left his opponents reeling with 41 KOs in a single match on 28 April 2015, beating the previous record by three.

Highest score on *Super Smash Bros. Brawl* "Multi-Man Brawl"

On 17 September 2014, Spanish gamer "Kresnik" scored a total of 3,218 points on *Super Smash Bros. Brawl's* "Multi-Man Brawl" challenge on the "Endless" setting.

Fastest completion of *Super Smash Bros. for Nintendo 64*

Playing as Donkey Kong, Canadian speed-runner Ghillie Guide completed the entire game in just 5 min 43.77 sec on 9 August 2014 – breaking the previous record, which had stood for two years, by an astounding 3 min.

Largest *Super Smash Bros.* tournament

Apex is an annual eSports tournament held in New Jersey, USA, that specializes in *Super Smash Bros.* games. Despite a last-minute change of venue, Apex 2015 (30 January–1 February 2015) was the largest yet, attracting more than 1,000 entrants to register in a tournament featuring fiercely competitive singles and doubles events for all *Super Smash Bros.* games.

Largest *Super Smash Bros. Melee* tournament

On 11–13 July 2014, a total of 970 *Super Smash Bros. Melee* gamers competed at the EVO 2014 fighting tournament at the Westgate Las Vegas Resort & Casino, Nevada, USA. A total of 1,037 players were registered to participate at Apex 2015 on 30 January–1 February 2015 (see above), but an estimated 200 combatants failed to show owing to a late venue change.

First videogame compatible with Nintendo amiibo figurines

Launched on 21 November 2014, amiibo figurines are a set of interactive toys modelled on Nintendo stars. The first game to work with amiibo was *Super Smash Bros. for Wii U* (2014), with 12 figurines released in the first wave, including Donkey Kong, Link and Peach.

TEKKEN

D.Y.K.?

Despite his Swedish heritage, *Tekken 6: Bloodline Rebellion* debutant Lars Alexandersson (left) speaks Japanese in all his cutscenes. It's unusual for *Tekken* stars not to use their native tongue.

Summary: *Tekken* broke the fighting game mould, allowing players control of characters' individual limbs. The battle to decide the winner of the Iron Fist tournament has been raging since 1994, and shows no sign of stopping any time soon.

Publisher: Namco/Bandai Namco Games
Developer: Namco/Bandai Namco Games
Debut: 1994

Longest winning streak on *Tekken 6*

Eliot Smith-Walters (UK, inset top right) achieved a 68-match winning streak fighting human challengers on *Tekken 6* at the MCM Expo in London, UK, on 24 October 2009. Fighting under the moniker "Shadow Force", Smith-Walters lost only nine rounds and completed 25 perfects in the course of his streak. He used the character Lars (main image) for the majority of his fights, turning to Miguel, Dragunov and Lee when needed. Smith-Walters' high point came when he KO'd 2009 "Super vs. Battle" tournament champion Phil "Dinosaur" Mackenzie.

Largest screen at a game tournament

In September 2012, a *Tekken* qualifying tournament was held at the IMAX theatre in Sydney, Australia. Fans watched the action on a giant screen measuring 35.72 x 29.57 m (117 x 97 ft).

Best-selling fighting game series (excluding crossovers)

With sales of 36.69 million units as of 1 May 2015, *Tekken* ruled over its rivals with an iron fist. This figure includes the most recent numbered game for home consoles, *Tekken 6* (2007), as well as *Tekken Tag Tournament 2* (2011) and 2012's *Tekken 3D: Prime Edition* on the Nintendo 3DS.

First virtual card game conversion of a fighting game

Tekken Card Challenge was released for Bandai's handheld game console WonderSwan on 17 June 1999. Exclusive to Japan, it transferred characters from *Tekken 3* and applied them to a *Yu-Gi-Oh!*-style combat system.

First 3D fighting game playable in first-person mode

Tekken 2 (1996) contains an "Easter egg" (hidden feature) that allows gamers to play from a first-person perspective by holding down the L1 and L2 buttons while selecting their character. For this trick to work, however, players must first unlock all of the playable characters on the game's roster.

Most versions of a character in a fighting game series

He might look similar nearly every time you see him, but big-punching robot and *Tekken* mainstay Jack has, in fact, taken on eight different versions across multiple iterations of the series.

Longest marathon on a fighting game

Anthony "AJ" Lysiak (USA, inset) played *Street Fighter X Tekken* for exactly 48 hr at Game Emporium in Garrettsville, Ohio, USA, on 4–6 May 2012. The arcade in which the record took place was a small local business that ran two consecutive lock-in events to support AJ's attempt. Beginning his marathon at 2 p.m. on a Friday, he finished two days later having beaten the previous record by 16 hr.

First *Tekken* videogame to use the Unreal Engine 4

The powerful Unreal Engine 4 was used to develop *Tekken 7*, the latest iteration of the fighting series that hit Japanese arcades in March 2015. Epic Games' Taka Kawasaki commented: "This marriage is perfect – the most powerful engine in gaming along with one of the most enduring brands in fighting games."

First fighting game with simulated 3D

Tekken was the earliest fighting game to simulate a 3D effect. This feature did much to set it apart from existing fighting games such as *Street Fighter* and *Mortal Kombat*. The 3D trend continued with the Game Boy Advance version released in 2001, *Tekken Advance*.

Most viewed *Street Fighter X Tekken* match

As of 23 March 2015, a YouTube video of the two-versus-two final at the Evolution Championship Series on 8 July 2012 had been viewed 621,751 times. The hotly anticipated match featured Ricky Ortiz (USA) and Eduardo "PR Balrog" Pérez-Frangie (Puerto Rico) against the South Korean team of "Infiltration" (Lee Sun-woo; see also p.153) and Ryan "Laugh" Ahn. It was Lee and Ahn – playing as Rolento and Ryu respectively – who had the last laugh, sweeping the final and coming away as the victors.

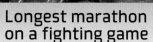

Best-selling 3D fighting game

According to VGChartz, *Tekken 3* (1997) had sold 7.16 million units worldwide as of 3 March 2015. *Tekken 6* (2009) had sold 2.71 million units worldwide by the same date, making it the **best-selling 3D fighting game for PS3**.

Most moves for a *Tekken* character

The jaguar-masked King is a professional wrestler who fights in the name of an orphanage for street children. In both his incarnations, King can draw upon a number of familiar wrestling moves and throws – in *Tekken Tag Tournament 2* (2011) he has a crowd-wowing 176 moves at his disposal.

TETRIS

Most variants of a videogame

Given the vast number of clones and legal grey areas, pin-pointing an exact figure for the number of *Tetris* variants is tricky. However, as of 1 May 2015, there had been a staggering 215 licenced and official variants of Alexey Pajitnov's classic puzzler recognized by The Tetris Company (USA). These ranged from the landmark Game Boy release (1989) to *Pokémon Tetris* (2002) and the multiplayer *Tetris Party* (2008).

196

Days in space spent by Russian cosmonaut Aleksandr A Serebrov from 1 July 1993 – accompanied by his Game Boy and copy of *Tetris*, the **first videogame in space**.

LEVEL

15

LINES TO CLEAR 9

Largest official *Tetris* cabinet

Debuting in Japanese arcades in December 2009, *Tetris Giant* is the largest officially licensed version of the game. The giant cabinet measures 1.6 m (5 ft 2 in) wide, 1.7 m (5 ft 6 in) deep and 2.2 m (7 ft 2 in) high. It also boasts two super-sized controller sticks and a 177-cm (5-ft 9-in) display.

Summary: A deliciously simple puzzle game that has sold millions of copies around the globe, *Tetris* challenges players to slot falling four-segment pieces – known as tetrominoes – into place. Fans of the game have created super-big, super-small and even super-hard versions.

Publisher: Various
Developer: Alexey Pajitnov
Debut: 1984

D.Y.K.?

The 2011 documentary *Ecstasy of Order* follows elite-level *Tetris* players such as Jonas Neubauer (above) as they prepare for the 2010 Classic *Tetris* World Championship in Los Angeles, California, USA.

Smallest game of *Tetris*

In November 2002, a game of *Tetris* was played using tetrominoes made of tiny glass spheres at Vrije University in Amsterdam, Netherlands. With each block measuring 1/1,000th of a millimetre, would-be puzzlers had to use an electron microscope to see the pieces.

First perfect score on *Tetris*

It took him four years of practice, but on 19 April 2009, Harry Hong (USA) became the first person to earn the maximum score of 999,999 on the NES version of *Tetris*. He told Twin Galaxies that achieving the feat had been "an adrenaline rush, to say the least".

Fastest time to achieve a perfect score on *Tetris DS*

Isaiah Triforce Johnson attained *Tetris* perfection in a time of 8 hr 10 min 22 sec on 19 August 2008. Triforce also holds the record for the **highest score in a *Tetris DS* standard marathon** – at a Twin Galaxies-refereed event on 5 July 2012, he scored an incredible 1,584,000 points.

Most expensive puzzle videogame

It might not be the rarest *Tetris* (see below right), but in April 2008 a 1990 Nintendo World Championships Gold Edition of *Tetris* was sold for $15,000 (£7,568).

Most difficult version of *Tetris*

The fiendish brainchild of Italian programmer Federico Poloni (above), "Bastet" replaces the usual random distribution of *Tetris* pieces with an algorithm that analyses the board before selecting the worst possible piece. Federico is proud of his twisted creation, even as he admits that "playing Bastet can be a very frustrating experience!"

Most lines cleared on *Tetris* for the NES

A dispute between Atari and Nintendo over gaming rights led to two different versions of *Tetris* for the NES. So while Ben Mullen (USA) claimed the record for **most lines on *Tetris* (NES Nintendo version)** with 296 verified on 20 March 2010, Bo Steil (USA) holds the record for **most lines on *Tetris* (NES Atari Tengen version)**, with a mighty 5,597 lines slotted together on 19 May 2013.

Fastest *Tetris* line race

On 16 August 2013, a video was uploaded to YouTube showing "keroco" completing 40 *Tetris* lines (otherwise known as a "line race") in 19.68 sec – which works out at 118.98 lines per min.

First playable videogame on an item of clothing

To celebrate the 30th anniversary of the release of *Tetris*, gadget fan Marc Kerger (Luxembourg) designed a playable T-shirt of the game. Kerger's invention used an Arduino Uno microcontroller board powered by four AA batteries and featured a 128-LED display area. His YouTube video had been viewed 266,909 times as of 27 April 2015.

Largest architectural videogame display

Frank Lee (USA) developed a version of *Tetris* that was played on the north and south facades of the 29-storey Cira Centre in Philadelphia, Pennsylvania, USA, on 5 April 2014. The display measured a whopping 11,111.2 m² (119,600 sq ft).

Highest score on *Tetris* by a team of two

Sharing one controller between them, Becca Caddy and Gerald Lynch (both UK) scored 23,552 points playing *Tetris* at the launch of *Guinness World Records Gamer's Edition 2012* at Liverpool Street Station in London, UK, on 18 January 2012.

D.Y.K.?

Steve Wozniak co-founded Apple Inc. (then known as Apple Computer, Inc.) with Steve Jobs and Ronald Wayne. Wozniak claims that he was once so good at *Tetris* that *Nintendo Power* magazine started refusing to list his high scores in their rankings – so he began spelling his name backwards as "Evets Kainzow".

Highest scores on *Tetris* for Game Boy

Player	Date verified	Points
Uli Horner	6 December 2011	748,757
Rob Cheung	28 November 2005	589,694
Harry Hong	29 November 2005	523,746
Steve Wozniak (see left)	26 July 1990	507,110
Rutherford Chang	3 October 2013	504,165
Phil S Strahl	6 October 2007	449,076
Brenda S Peavler	30 January 2006	441,790
Chris Scullion	20 April 2010	283,706
Robin J Smith	9 October 2009	283,408
Scott Kimberling	23 May 1999	212,835

Source: Twin Galaxies as of 31 March 2015

Rarest *Tetris* videogame

A legal dispute over rights led to the Mega Drive version of *Tetris* being withdrawn, leaving fewer than 10 Japanese copies of the game in existence. One was signed by creator Alexey Pajitnov and listed on eBay for $1 million in 2011, but was reportedly never sold.

Your New Favourite Games

Whether you want to design spectacular platformers, explore space or hone your Jedi powers, the next 12 months are bringing a smorgasbord of gaming excitement to your fingertips. Here's our pick of the big ones to watch.

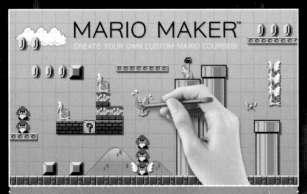

Mario Maker

ETA: September 2015 / Platform: Wii U

If you've ever dreamed of crafting your own Mario levels, *MM* will make them reality. By using a stylus, you'll move blocks, arrange enemies, drop coins and design everything else required to create your own 2D stages and challenges.

Scalebound

ETA: 2016 / Platform: Xbox One

Billed as the next great adventure from *Bayonetta* director Hideki Kamiya, *Scalebound* looks like a *Jurassic Park* nightmare for the dragon generation. Delicious visuals mix with nerve-jangling gameplay as you trawl a world populated with gigantic, scaly beasts.

Street Fighter V

ETA: 2016 / Platform: PS4, PC

The grand old overseer of fighting games returns, this time powered by the exotic delights of Unreal Engine 4. Cross-platform multiplayer action means you'll get to battle against PC-loving friends while playing on a PS4.

Edge of Eternity

ETA: 2016 / Platform: PC, Xbox One, PS4, Mac, Linux

Currently in development by French indie studio Midgar, space-bound RPG *Edge of Eternity* tips its hat to JRPGs, with an alluring mix of fantasy and sci-fi. It was a huge hit on Kickstarter, where it has been well backed by a growing army of admirers.

Deus Ex: Mankind Divided
ETA: TBC / Platform: PS4, Xbox One, PC
Set in 2029 and inspired by real-world transhumanist research, this action RPG plunges players into an era of modified humans. Players are challenged with making morally ambiguous choices while acquiring "superhuman" abilities.

Final Fantasy XV
ETA: 2016 / Platform: Xbox One, PS4
Any new *Final Fantasy* game release is a momentous occasion, but *FFXV* is the first built exclusively for Xbox One and PS4. Square Enix is reportedly using it to modernize the JRPG franchise with an open world, an action-focused battle system and a more mature narrative.

Metal Gear Solid V: The Phantom Pain
ETA: September 2015 / Platform: PS3, PS4, Xbox 360, Xbox One
Hideo Kojima's seminal stealth series has always pushed boundaries, but *The Phantom Pain* will be its first with a fully explorable open world. Players assume the role of Venom Snake as they travel around on foot, in tanks and on horseback.

Fire Emblem: If
ETA: June 2015 (Japan); 2016 (rest of world) / Platform: 3DS
The latest from the tactical RPG series lets players choose between two warring factions in a medieval fantasy world. Lavish visuals and strong plots will make this a cult favourite.

Star Wars: Battlefront
ETA: Late 2015 / Platform: PC, Xbox One, PS4
Expected at about the time of the *Episode VII* film, *Battlefront* will make *Star Wars* fans feel like multiple Christmases have come at once. This new sequel is being developed by EA Digital Illusions CE (the team behind *Battlefield*), who promise to add their own flavour to the series. Expect intense tactical action and a strong selection of engrossing multiplayer modes.

TOMB RAIDER

Best-selling gaming heroine

With lifetime sales of 36.88 million as of 16 April 2015, *Tomb Raider* remains the best-selling game franchise with a female lead. As well as two blockbuster movies, Lara Croft has appeared in TV ads, on magazine covers, and even "on stage" with rock band U2.

89

Percentage of voters who opted to name a new road in Derby, UK, "Lara Croft Way" in 2010. The city had been home to Core Design, which developed *Tomb Raider*.

D.Y.K.?

Lara Croft was once going to be a South American named Laura Cruz, before Core Design opted to make her quintessentially English by plucking her name from a Derbyshire phone directory.

Summary:
Intrepid archaeologist Lara Croft has become one of the most recognizable and iconic heroes of the gaming world, appearing in spin-off movies and earning *Tomb Raider* a series reboot in 2013.

Publisher: Eidos/Square Enix
Developer: Core Design/ Crystal Dynamics
Debut: 1996

Most critically acclaimed *Tomb Raider* game

As of 6 March 2015, the PlayStation edition of the original *Tomb Raider* (1996) had a GameRankings score of 90.02% and a Metacritic score of 91.

Fastest glitched single-segment *Tomb Raider* PS run

On 25 May 2007, Ali "AKA" Gordon blitzed through *Tomb Raider* in 1 hr 50 min 16 sec.

Most utilized weapon in *Tomb Raider*

Lara's twin pistols are almost as iconic as the character herself, yet the new bow weapon introduced in 2013's *Tomb Raider* has proven the most popular with players. In the first 16 weeks of the game's release across Xbox 360, PS3 and PC platforms, the bow accounted for 44% of all kills. Just 4% of kills came via melee combat.

First competitive multiplayer element in a *Tomb Raider* game

The 2013 *Tomb Raider* reboot featured four different game modes upon release, including a competitive multiplayer element. Players gained experience points for competing in matches that saw them progress through the ranks and unlock new items and weapons.

Best-selling action-adventure series for PS

As of 19 March 2015, the *Tomb Raider* series had sold 16.5 million units on the PS. The biggest-selling instalment is *Tomb Raider II* (1997), which had shifted 5.2 million units globally by the same date.

D.Y.K.?

Lara Croft's look has evolved with technology. Her original 1996 incarnation used just 540 polygons, compared with the 32,816 used in 2008's *Tomb Raider: Underworld*. By 2013, the rebooted Lara was sporting a younger, grittier look with a more realistic physique.

Fastest glitchless completion of *Tomb Raider III*

On 28 May 2009, speed-runner Shaun "MMAN" Friend (UK) completed *Tomb Raider III* in 2 hr 4 min 10 sec. The run saw Lara travel an in-game distance of 20.95 km (13.02 mi), taking her from Area 51 to the Lost City of Tinnos. "MMAN" had also set the **fastest glitchless completion of *Tomb Raider: Legend***, in just 54 min 19 sec on 22 January 2008.

First Oscar-winning actors to star in a game adaptation

Both Angelina Jolie and her real-life dad Jon Voight (both USA) had won Oscars by the time they starred in *Lara Croft: Tomb Raider* in 2001, as Lara and Lord Croft, respectively. Jolie's gong was for *Girl, Interrupted* (1999) and Voight's was for *Coming Home* (1978).

Most multiplayer wins on *Tomb Raider*

As of February 2015, gamer "Wasbeelt" (Netherlands) had recorded 16,253 wins on the 2013 *Tomb Raider* reboot. "Wasbeelt" was far ahead of the rest of the pack, with nearest rival "pmsom" (UK) on only 11,111 wins.

With 172,668 kills, "Wasbeelt" also holds the record for **most multiplayer *Tomb Raider* kills**.

Largest collection of *Tomb Raider* screenshots

More than 10,000 in-game screenshots can be found at "Katie's Tomb Raider Site", a fan-run website. Its owner, Katie Fleming (Canada), is one of the world's biggest *Tomb Raider* fans and writes short stories inspired by Lara Croft's adventures. In 2003, one of her stories took first prize in Core Design's *Tomb Raider* fan fiction competition.

Largest collection of *Tomb Raider* memorabilia

As of April 2014, Rodrigo Martin Santos (Spain) boasted a collection of 2,383 distinct *Tomb Raider* items.

Most official real-life stand-ins for a game character

Gymnast/model Alison Carroll (right), actress Rhona Mitra and model/TV presenter Nell McAndrew were among the 10 women hired as the official face of *Tomb Raider* heroine Lara Croft. In 2013, Crystal Dynamics ceased to use official stand-ins.

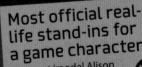

Fastest-selling *Tomb Raider* game

The success of 2013's *Tomb Raider* fully justified the decision to reboot the action-adventure series. The return of Lara Croft helped the game rack up global sales of 3.4 million by the end of March 2013 – the highest week-one sales in the history of the franchise.

Best-selling PS3-exclusive series

As of 2 April 2015, *Uncharted* had sold 18.04 million copies across its three titles, according to VGChartz. The best-selling individual title is *Uncharted 3: Drake's Deception*, with 6.64 million units sold. Series sales will grow further with the eagerly awaited fourth instalment, *Uncharted 4: A Thief's End* (above), due for release in spring 2016.

13,657,117,836

Number of kills from more than 9 billion multiplayer games of *Uncharted 3: Drake's Deception*, as recorded by Naughty Dog. More than 8 billion of these kills were head shots.

Summary: An epic action-adventure series exclusive to PlayStation, *Uncharted* follows the globe-trotting escapades of Nathan "Nate" Drake, a roguish fortune hunter with a ready quip. The original game was Naughty Dog's first title for the PS3, and it was soon clear that they'd struck gold.

Publisher: Sony
Developer: Naughty Dog
Debut: 2007

First game to use the Naughty Dog Engine

The rise of seventh-generation consoles saw developers abandoning their old software suites. The Naughty Dog Engine debuted on 2007's *Uncharted: Drake's Fortune* and has been used on all subsequent series' major titles, as well as the acclaimed *The Last of Us* (2013).

Most expensive game figure

ESC-TOY created a range of *Uncharted 3* figures including an uncoloured Nathan Drake signed by the game's staff. It sold for $4,250 (£2,629) on eBay on 31 December 2012.

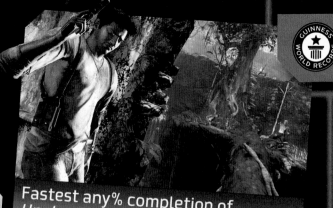

Fastest completion of *Uncharted 3: Drake's Deception*

On 2 November 2013, Greg "TheThrillness" Innes (UK) finished the game in 2 hr 35 min 37 sec. His segmented run was carried out on "Very Easy" mode, allowing him to avoid many time-consuming fights.

Most popular PlayStation 3 beta

Some 1.53 million users took part in the multiplayer beta trial for *Uncharted 3: Drake's Deception*. Between 28 June and 14 July 2011, more than 22 million matches took place, totalling 362 years of game time.

Fastest any% completion of *Uncharted: Drake's Fortune*

On 16 February 2015, German gamer "Marc118" jet-heeled through *Drake's Fortune* in just 46 min 44 sec. The intrepid explorer also finished the game while bagging all its glittery treasures in 1 hr 17 min 21 sec – the **fastest "All Treasures" completion**. This run was achieved on 19 October 2014.

Most critically acclaimed PlayStation 3-exclusive game

Released in 2009, *Uncharted 2: Among Thieves* had received a GameRankings rating of 96.43% as of 2 April 2015. This makes it the third-highest-ranking game for the PlayStation 3, behind only Rockstar Games' larcenous blockbusters *Grand Theft Auto IV* and *Grand Theft Auto V*.

First player to win a platinum trophy in *Uncharted: Golden Abyss*

On 20 December 2011, "se250tr" became the first player to win *Uncharted*'s platinum trophy by collecting all 55 in-game trophies. This feat was even more impressive for the fact that it was achieved just three days after the game's release.

Best-selling game for the PlayStation Vita

Uncharted: Golden Abyss was an exclusive for Sony's handheld, and saw Nate facing off against a rival treasure hunter in Panama. First released in Japan in December 2011, followed by the USA and Europe in 2012, it had sold 1.42 million copies by 15 April 2015. This placed it ahead of *Assassin's Creed III: Liberation* (sales of 1.24 million) and *Call of Duty Black Ops: Declassified* (1.21 million).

Rarest PlayStation 3 special-edition game

Copies of the "Fortune Hunter" edition of *Uncharted 2: Among Thieves* were awarded to US gamers who played the multiplayer demo or who won a special PlayStation Home challenge. Numbering just 200 in all, the special edition included a replica of the Phurba Dagger and was signed by the Naughty Dog development team.

First PS3 game to offer a platinum trophy

On 4 August 2008, Naughty Dog patched *Uncharted: Drake's Fortune* to offer a platinum trophy to players who had obtained all gold, silver and bronze trophies in a game. Every subsequent PS3 retail release has included this feature.

Most accurate *Uncharted 3: Drake's Deception* gun

Being a keen shot in the third *Uncharted* game is an invaluable skill – and that's no more evident than in its feisty online deathmatches. From multiplayer games tracked by Naughty Dog, the Para 9 has the most accurate hit rate (with 39%), followed by the Dragon Sniper (with 22%).

First TV reality show winner in a videogame

In a 28 September 2012 episode of *America's Next Top Model*, contestants undertook a challenge to be motion-captured for developers Naughty Dog. Winner Laura James (inset) was incorporated into *Uncharted 3* as the multiplayer taunt for Elena (above left) – and went on to win the entire TV series.

Tips 'n' Tricks

When taking on enemies in *Uncharted 3*, you have a range of options. Grenades are best used to take out enemies hiding behind cover – holding down the grenade button will enable you to throw more accurate arcs through doors and windows. Melee attacks allow you to get up close and personal and finish the job with your fists. Avoid head-on confrontations and creep up behind the enemy for a stealth kill. A blue "Ninja" icon will appear above your target's head, indicating that the stealth kill is on. One tap of the square button will take care of your opponent.

200

Approximate number of hours Senior Game Designer Damien Monnier estimates are needed to complete *The Witcher 3: Wild Hunt* if you do "everything" in the game.

D.Y.K.?

While many rock bands have been obsessed with J R R Tolkien and *The Lord of the Rings*, the same may also be said of *The Witcher*. The Polish folk-metal band Percival Schuttenbach is named after a gnome from the novels. A Russian group called ESSE once created a rock-opera based on Sapkowski's mythical yarns. And New York metallers Gwynbleidd are named after Geralt's nickname, meaning "White Wolf".

Most awards won by a videogame prior to release

Announced on 4 February 2013, *The Witcher III: Wild Hunt* had collected 206 awards up until 20 March 2015 – two months before its 19 May release. Highlights included multiple E3 gongs, including IGN's "Best reason to upgrade your PC" in 2013 and Golden Joysticks for "Most Wanted" in 2013 and 2014.

Summary: Based on the cult fantasy novels by Polish author Andrzej Sapkowski, *The Witcher* enjoys a fierce and dedicated following. The games follow the brutal exploits of Geralt, a mercenary monster-hunter blessed with supernatural powers and a flowing mane of white hair.

Publisher: Atari / Namco Bandai
Developer: CD Projekt RED
Debut: 2007

Fastest completion of *The Witcher 2* on "Hard"

On 25 August 2013, Germany's Tobias "Aphox" Baers ("TehLordson" on YouTube) completed Geralt's quest on the "Hard" difficulty mode in 2 hr 18 min 17 sec. One viewer observed that his time should really be 2 hr 16 min 25 sec, but a program flaw meant that the clock was running too fast.

Most downloaded mod for *The Witcher 2*

As of 28 January 2015, *The Witcher 2*'s "Full Combat Rebalance" had been downloaded 74,628 times. The mod was created by CD Projekt RED itself to improve the game's visuals, effects, combat balance and in-game mechanics.

Fastest completion of The Witcher 2: Enhanced Edition on "Insane" mode

The "Insane" mode is as tricky as it gets for hacking and slashing in Sapkowski's world. But on 12 April 2015, Héctor Ortega Avilés (Spain) took the challenge in his stride, completing a record-breaking speed-run of 2 hr 50 min 45 sec for PC.

Most viewed Witcher video

A total of 4,620,581 fans had viewed WeasleyJunior's "The Witcher 2 Gameplay – Internal video!" on YouTube as of 27 April 2015. The hugely popular five-min clip was released in September 2009 to show off the Witcher sequel and take viewers behind the scenes for its development.

Largest game of The Witcher

It's not unreasonable for a sequel to be "bigger" than its predecessors, but The Witcher III: Wild Hunt boasts an open-world playing area that is a colossal 35 times the size of The Witcher 2: Assassins of Kings. On 28 April 2015, gaming nexus NeoGAF calculated that the game's epic dimensions would stretch beyond 136 km² (52.5 sq mi).

Highest score on The Witcher 2: Enhanced Edition on "Arena" mode

With 2,147,483,647 points each as of 2 April 2015, five Steam champions – "eaxel", "¡SMÅLĽṿiĹĽɛı™", "blAke", "Mr. Faket" and "Michael Madsen" – reigned supreme in arena fighting. The Witcher 2's "Arena" was added in the sequel's Enhanced Edition, challenging players to defeat waves of enemies.

Most difficult achievement in The Witcher 2: Enhanced Edition

As of 2 April 2015, only 0.5% of PC players had unlocked the "Madman" achievement in The Witcher 2: Enhanced Edition – three years after the game was released in April 2012. The most elusive of 52 achievements available, unlocking "Madman" requires players to beat the game on its "Insane" difficulty level.

Largest distributor of DRM-free videogames

As of 28 January 2015, GOG.com – owned by The Witcher developer CD Projekt RED (Poland) – had 914 Digital Restrictions Management-free games available through its website. DRM laws are designed to prevent the unauthorized copying and distribution of digital products.

Most critically acclaimed game based on a book series

With a GameRankings score of 87.97% from 48 reviews, no other book series has translated into gaming as successfully as The Witcher 2. The Lord of the Rings MMO expansion Riders of Rohan carries 90%, but was only reviewed by three outlets.

Most matches won in The Witcher: Battle Arena

Released in January 2015, The Witcher: Battle Arena is a multiplayer online battle arena (MOBA) for iOS and Android, allowing players to tussle it out as the deadliest heroes from the Witcher world. As of 31 March 2015, iOS gamer "=Mracek=" led the game's leaderboards with 1,690 matches won.

The same gamer also held the record for **most kills in The Witcher: Battle Arena**, slaying 23,624 opponents and foes as of the same date.

Given the player's dedication, it's not surprising that "=Mracek=" also has the **most Experience Points in The Witcher: Battle Arena**, topping the leaderboard with 1,151,177 Experience Points.

Most critically acclaimed action RPGs for PC

Game	Publisher	Release date	Rating
Mass Effect 2	Electronic Arts	2010	94.52%
Diablo II	Blizzard	2000	=88.58%
Torchlight II	Runic Games	2012	=88.58%
Dark Souls II	Namco Bandai	2014	88.3%
The Witcher 2: Assassins of Kings	Atari	2011	87.97%
Freedom Force	Electronic Arts	2002	87.88%
Diablo III	Blizzard	2012	87.64%
The Witcher: Enhanced Edition	Atari	2008	86%
Dungeon Siege	Microsoft	2002	85.76%
Divinity: Original Sin	Larian Studios	2014	85.31%

Source: GameRankings as of 2 April 2015

Rarest edition of The Witcher 2

During a tour of Europe in May 2011, US President Barack Obama was presented with The Witcher 2: Collector's Edition by Polish Prime Minister Donald Tusk, signed by the game's development team. The gift also included the Andrzej Sapkowski books on which The Witcher was based, signed by the author himself.

WORLD OF WARCRAFT

Most popular subscription-based videogame

World of Warcraft had more than 10 million subscribers as of 14 November 2014 – the day after the launch of *Warlords of Draenor*. Although figures have declined since *WoW*'s 2010 peak of 12 million subscribers, the expansion's release triggered a spike of user activity.

5,500,000

Lines of code used in *World of Warcraft*. It took a team of 150 developers four years to write the code, create 30,000 items and build 1,400 locations.

D.Y.K.?

Quest-givers in the Un'Goro crater, "Larion" and "Muigin" dress in red and green and are a comic *World of Warcraft* homage to Nintendo's favourite plumbers.

Summary: A revolution for MMO gaming, the fantasy world of Azeroth has hosted countless adventures. Since *World of Warcraft* first appeared in 2004, more than 100 million unique accounts have been set up, with players from 244 countries and territories creating more than 500 million characters.

Publisher: Blizzard
Developer: Blizzard
Debut: 2004

Most viewed *World of Warcraft* video

In a YouTube video uploaded on 6 August 2006, Ben Schulz's *WoW* character Leeroy Jenkins ruins his guild's plans by charging into battle yelling his own name. As of 9 April 2015, the clip had been viewed 42,829,650 times.

Highest-earning *World of Warcraft* player

As of 13 April 2015, Canadian gamer Kelvin "Snutz" Nguyen had amassed winnings of $61,666 (£36,844) from various *WoW* tournaments. His biggest single win was at the 2012 Battle.net World Championship, where he won $35,000 (£22,058).

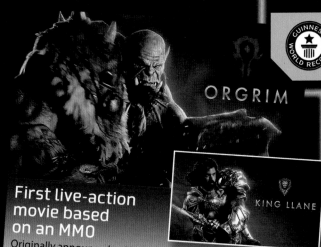

ORGRIM

KING LLANE

First WoW player to reach level 90 without a kill

On 12 October 2012, peace-loving gamer "Irenic" reached level 90 without taking a single life. The record took 12 days 4 hr 33 sec of in-game time to achieve, and necessitated Irenic's Tauren Druid character gaining experience points through exploration and completing professions such as archaeology and gathering.

Most critically acclaimed MMORPG

As of 9 April 2015, the expansion pack *World of Warcraft: Wrath of the Lich King* (2008) had a GameRankings score of 92.68%, ahead of the original full game *World of Warcraft* with 91.89%.

First live-action movie based on an MMO

Originally announced at BlizzCon in 2006, *Warcraft* is a live-action film based on the popular game series, directed by Duncan Jones and starring Travis Fimmel and Paula Patton. Principal photography was completed on 23 May 2014, and following a lengthy post-production period for digital effects the film is expected to be released in June 2016.

Longest marathon on an MMORPG

On 29–30 March 2014, Hecaterina Kinumi Iglesias (aka "Kinumi Cati") played *World of Warcraft* for 29 hr 31 min in Vigo, Spain. An avid fan of Japanese culture, Kinumi Cati also holds the record for the **longest JRPG marathon**, having spent 38 hr 6 min playing *Final Fantasy X* in Barcelona, Spain, on 26–28 July 2013.

First *World of Warcraft* players to reach level 100

Within hours of the release of *Warlords of Draenor* on 13 November 2014, dozens of players were able to reach the new level 100 cap. But the game's developers disabled the Realm First achievements for levelling, meaning the exact identity of the first 100-level player remains a mystery.

First MMO reality show

Debuting on the official *World of Warcraft* YouTube channel on 17 April 2014, *Azeroth Choppers* attracted 2 million viewers in its first week. In the show, two competing teams from a custom motorcycle workshop were given five weeks to create unique bikes based on the game's Alliance and Horde factions – with viewer votes deciding the winner.

Most honourable kills in *World of Warcraft*

An "honourable kill" is achieved when a player kills another player from an opposing faction who is in within 10 levels of their own. As of 11 January 2015, Dwarf Rogue character "Fartzwrgoben" had 1,967,242 honourable kills to his or her name.

First player to complete *World of Warcraft*

"Little Gray" (Chinese Taipei) completed all 986 in-game achievements listed in the *WoW* Armoury by 27 November 2009. Along the way he had killed 390,895 creatures, accumulated 7,255,538,878 points of damage and hugged 11 players.

Largest virtual beer festival

Once a year, the warring factions of the Horde and the Alliance put down their arms and get together for "Brewfest", the virtual homage to the Oktoberfest in Bavaria, Germany. The Brewfest lasts for a couple of weeks and offers the finest ales, meads and beers from breweries Thunderbrew, Barleybrew and the Ogres.

Largest MMO community donation

When a tsunami struck eastern Japan on 11 March 2011, the *WoW* community raised an incredible $1.9 million (£1.175 million) in aid. Blizzard Entertainment offered a special in-game feathered pet, the Cenarion Hatchling, which was bought by 190,000 players to raise money for the Red Cross.

WWE

21

Number of consecutive victories at WrestleMania by The Undertaker. But "The Streak" came to a shock end on 6 April 2014, when The Undertaker lost a tough match to Brock Lesnar.

D.Y.K.?

WWE wrestlers spent 40 days being motion-captured performing their moves for *WWE 2K15*. The sound of each impact on the mat was recorded to ensure added authenticity.

Best-selling wrestling franchise

There have been over 50 games based on the WWE and its predecessor brand, the WWF, and it is the *SmackDown!* series that has the rest in a submission hold. As of 23 January 2015, the franchise had amassed total worldwide sales of 58.8 million copies, according to VGChartz.

Summary: *WWE* (World Wrestling Entertainment) titles – formerly *WWF* – have been bringing some attitude to gaming since 1989, allowing players to take down their opponents with a mixture of dazzling aerial manoeuvres and devastating submission holds – and selling millions of games in the process.

Publisher: Various
Developer: Various
Debut: 1989

Fastest round-one victory on *WWE Day of Reckoning*

From his base in Aberystwyth, UK, Canadian gamer James "TwIsTeD_EnEmY" Bouchier scored a stunning victory in a blink-and-you'll-miss-it 11 sec on 17 May 2010.

Fastest completion of *WWF Royal Rumble*

On 18 June 2011, Richard Gibson (Canada) emerged triumphant from a battle royal on the 1993 Sega Mega Drive title in just 51 sec. He told SpeedDemosArchive, "I think this [time] is optimal and I would be very surprised to see someone pull off anything faster."

Fastest one-on-one match on *WWF Raw*

Daniel Lee Strickland Perea completed a match on the SNES in 36.4 sec on 7 January 2011.

Fastest victory in *WWF No Mercy* on Nintendo 64

On 22 September 2008, Matthew S Miller (USA) won an exhibition-mode match against an AI opponent on "Expert" level in 43 sec.

Most arenas in a sports combat videogame

WWE 2K14 features recreations of the official arenas for every TV show and pay-per-view event in the WWE calendar, as well as exact models of every WrestleMania – coming to an overall total of 46. The game's various "create-an-arena" tools mean that players can also build their own virtual sporting superdomes.

Fastest victory in *WWE Legends of WrestleMania*

On 4 May 2009, Carmelo Consiglio, from Encino, California, USA, took on an AI opponent with the "Difficulty" setting on "Legendary" and the "Disqualification", "Give Up" and "Pin" options all switched off. Consiglio not only came out of this hardcore match-up with the win, but did so in 55 sec.

Most-watched *WWE 2K15* match

On 10 December 2014, YouTube vlogger "H20Delirious" posted a video of an "Iron Man" match between himself and his friend and rival "Lui Calibre". A rematch of a previous bout, this contest saw "H20Delirious" come out on top. It had 870,318 views as of 30 March 2015.

WWE 2K14 user creation with most downloads

Curtis Axel may have been cut from *WWE 2K14*'s official roster of fighters, but his character model for PS3 – adapted from an Xbox 360 model by "GaMeVoLt" – had been downloaded 21,189 times as of April 2014.

Most prolific developer of combat sports games

As of 23 January 2015, Yuke's (Japan) had developed 83 commercially released titles.

First stereoscopic 3D wrestling game

The Nintendo 3DS version of *WWE All Stars* (2011) not only played out in stereoscopic 3D, it also included 13 WWE superstars that were available only as DLC on other consoles.

First WWE videogame with online multiplayer function

SmackDown vs Raw (2004) used the PS2's Network Adaptor so players could compete online in "One-On-One" or "Bra and Panties" matches.

Best-selling combat sports videogame

With more than 7.36 million copies sold across six console formats as of 12 May 2015, according to VGChartz, *WWE SmackDown vs Raw 2008* remains the most successful iteration of the series. The PlayStation 2 version alone shifted 2.34 million units.

Most WWE Superstar Challenge titles

Since 2003, the annual WWE 2K Superstar Challenge (formerly the THQ Superstar Challenge) has been hosted at WrestleMania, inviting WWE wrestlers to slug it out on the latest *WWE* game. Former WWE star Shelton Benjamin (USA) has won the title four times.

Most critically acclaimed combat sports videogame

The final WWF game to be released on the PlayStation, 2000's *WWF SmackDown! 2: Know Your Role* could claim a knockout Metacritic score of 90% as of 30 March 2015.

First *WWF* console game

WWF: WrestleMania hit the NES in 1989, introducing console users to the world of pro wrestling. Two years prior, *MicroLeague Wrestling* had been released for C64 and Atari ST, making the turn-based tie-in the **first videogame to feature WWF wrestlers**.

First female WWE Superstar Challenge winner

WWE Diva AJ Lee is as tough a fighter on the console as she is in the ring. On 30 March 2012, she defeated fellow wrestler Mark Henry in the final of the 16-person WWE Superstar Challenge gaming event in Miami, Florida, USA.

HARDWARE

Largest arcade machine

Verified on 23 March 2015 in Bensenville in Illinois, USA, the Arcade Deluxe is 4.41 m (14 ft 5 in) wide and 1.93 m (6 ft 4 in) tall, 1.06 m (3 ft 5 in) deep. It is fully functional and can play 250 classic games, including the perennial arcade favourite *PAC-Man*. Creator Jason Camberis (USA) wanted to remind gamers of the classic arcade experience, and spent a year-and-a-half building his mega machine. According to Jason, the hardest part was fashioning an illuminated, supersized, 40-cm (15.7-in) glass trackball, which was eventually cut out by a bowling ball company.

"When you play this game, it's like being a little kid again..."

Arcade Deluxe designer Jason Camberis

PS4

Summary: The PlayStation 4 has been a phenomenal success. In the USA alone it sold 1 million consoles in the first 24 hours, and in the UK 250,000 devices were sold in just two days. This makes it the **fastest-selling games console**. Despite this success, it took time for PS4 games to hit the standard expected of an eighth-gen console. However, strong, exclusive titles appeared in 2015, notably the action RPG *Bloodborne*.

Released in Japan in November 2013 and North America in October 2014, the PlayStation TV is about the size of a pack of playing cards, making it the **smallest PlayStation console**. It offers remote play, while the virtual-reality headset – given the working title of "Project Morpheus" by Sony – looks set to revolutionize console gaming.

Hacked off

On Christmas Day 2014, millions of gamers were unable to use either the PlayStation Network (PSN) or Xbox Live owing to hacking by a headline-baiting group calling themselves the Lizard Squad. This was not the first time that the PSN – launched in 2006 – had been attacked. In 2011, hackers stole the identities and log-in details of up to 77 million users. As of 2 January 2014, PSN had 110 million members – more than double Xbox Live's 46 million – making it the **largest console-based gaming network**.

45

Number of international markets in which the PlayStation 4 was sold in 2014. Microsoft's Xbox was only just behind with 42, while Nintendo's Wii U was a strong-selling third with 32.

Sharing is caring
The PS4 was the **first console to feature built-in game broadcasting**, allowing players to strut their stuff on platforms such as Twitch and Ustream. It also allows two online gamers to play the same copy of a title, although the developers of *Call of Duty*, *Tomb Raider* and *Minecraft* are among those restricting this Share Play service.

The dev's in the detail
Lucky game-dev students at the UK's Sheffield Hallam University have been given access to 34 PlayStation 4 development kits. As the South Yorkshire institution already has an extensive suite of PS3 and Vita dev kits, it can now boast the **largest PlayStation teaching facility** in the world. Greatness awaits...

D.Y.K.?
Brazil is the priciest place for PS4 purchasers. In March 2014, Bloomberg found import fees had pushed the cost of the console to $1,702 (£1,023).

Best-selling PlayStation consoles		
Console	Global sales	Launch date
PlayStation 2	157.68 million	March 2000
PlayStation	104.25 million	December 1994
PlayStation 3	85.41 million	November 2006
PlayStation Portable	80.82 million	December 2004
PlayStation 4	21.1 million	November 2013
PlayStation Vita	10.27 million	December 2011

Source: VGChartz.com as of 24 April 2015

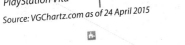

Home to bed
The virtual 3D social gaming platform PlayStation Home, which at its peak had 19 million users, was axed in 2015 owing to what Sony called "a shifting landscape". Meanwhile, a failed Kickstarter project to create a replacement called Neotopia – by developers who had worked on Home – attracted just 220 backers.

Anniversary special
To celebrate the 20th anniversary of the PlayStation, Sony created a special-edition PS4 in the 1994 original's colours. At a pop-up shop in London, UK, a total of 94 of these retailed for just £19.94 ($31.22) – the **lowest retail price for a PlayStation console**. One reportedly sold on eBay for £7,900 ($12,270).

The time is now
PlayStation's long-term vision is for content to be streamed to any networked device with a screen. Its PlayStation Now service – based on Gaikai streaming, created by *Earthworm Jim* designer David Perry – boasts more than 200 games.

XBOX ONE

Summary: With an ace library of games and regular updates to its system, Microsoft's eighth-gen unit continues to flourish. The interstellar *Halo* remains a major sci-fi franchise, while *Sunset Overdrive* (see right) and the acquisition of *Minecraft* developer Mojang are big weapons in Microsoft's armoury. Excitingly, developers can now access a seventh CPU core normally reserved for co-running the Xbox One's operating system. While this may come at the cost of certain features, it means added power for making even better games.

All hail to the chief

Although the file size for Xbox-exclusive *Halo: The Master Chief Collection* was 45 GB, it required an additional 15-GB update on its launch day – the **largest patch for a console game**. This was necessary because the Blu-ray disc containing the four *Halo* games was already full to the brim.

Sunset Overdrive

The critically acclaimed Xbox One game *Sunset Overdrive* won "Best Xbox One Game" at IGN's Best of E3 2014 Awards. A frantic and funny TPS set in the year 2027, it depicts a post-apocalyptic metropolis in which FizzCo's toxic energy drink has turned humans into mutants.

Lights out

Improving the Xbox 360 was a tough challenge that the Xbox One's design team met head-on with relish. They explored 75 different console prototypes and some 200 controller prototypes, eventually finalizing such innovations as reshaped joysticks, more vents for quieter running and controllers that dim when the room is dark.

12.02 Worldwide sales in millions of the Xbox One as of 24 April 2015, according to VGChartz. It still has a long way to go to overtake the Xbox 360, which had sold 84.7 million as of the same date.

Mega drives

With more games being played from hard drives rather than disks, hard-drive space is at a premium. When *Call of Duty: Advanced Warfare* was issued in 2014, it became the **largest download file size for an Xbox One game**, at 48.97 GB. A pack was released including an Xbox One with a one-terabyte hard drive – the **highest storage capacity for a videogame console**.

Box sets

Microsoft has positioned the Xbox One as a multimedia device. As well as offering games, they have struck deals with Sky and the BBC in the UK, and have become the first console to partner with Sling TV in the USA. However, Xbox Entertainment Studios, which launched to offer original TV programming, has now closed.

D.Y.K.?

The Xbox One has some of the longest game-install times of the eighth generation, with some games taking a thumb-twiddling 16 minutes.

Best-selling Xbox One videogames			
Game	Publisher	Release date	Global sales
Call of Duty: Advanced Warfare	Activision	2014	4.17 million
Titanfall	EA	2014	2.56 million
Assassin's Creed: Unity	Ubisoft	2014	2.55 million
Destiny	Activision	2014	2.51 million
Grand Theft Auto V	Rockstar	2014	2.43 million
Call of Duty: Ghosts	Activision	2013	2.37 million
Assassin's Creed IV: Black Flag	Ubisoft	2013	2.05 million
Halo: The Master Chief Collection	Microsoft	2014	1.94 million
Forza Motorsport 5	Microsoft	2013	1.92 million
FIFA 15	EA	2014	1.74 million

Source: VGChartz as of 5 March 2015

Eastern promise

In September 2014, the Xbox One became the first console to enter China since the country lifted its 14-year ban on console sales. Demand proved fierce for the Xbox One-Kinect bundle, which retailed at 4,299 yuan (£430; $698.35). One store in Shanghai reported a queue of more than 200 eager fans.

Going for gold

At the Games14 convention held in Dubai, UAE, on 11–13 September 2014, Italian company Gatti Luxury Lab unveiled an Xbox console encased in more than 220 g (7.7 oz) of 9-karat gold. The blinged-up box was priced at £8,448 ($13,699), making it the **most expensive Xbox One console**.

HANDHELD

Summary: Nintendo's DS line is more than 10 years old, with the 3DS XL being the company's latest attempt to beat competition from smartphones and tablets. It won't be easy. High-end Android tech and Apple's updates have unleashed console-quality graphics and innovative gameplay. For Sony, the PS Vita is likely to be the last handheld. Despite gems such as *Freedom Wars*, fewer first-party games are being made. But independent developers are creating acclaimed titles, sales are rising and the Vita remains a favourite for many gamers.

Shaky hands

Fringe handhelds are fighting for attention. The eNcade – a portable Raspberry Pi console (left) – attracted 84 backers and raised $6,629 on Kickstarter in December 2014, but it's a difficult market. Gizmondo, issued by Tiger Telematics in March 2005, sold just 25,000 units and was discontinued less than a year later. This makes it the **lowest-selling handheld games console** ever.

D.Y.K.?

Two of the three best-selling home consoles are handhelds (the Game Boy with 118.69 million and the Nintendo DS with 154.88 million).

14

Years that the Game Boy was on sale (from 1989 to 2003) in its original, Play It Loud, Pocket, Light and Color guises: the **longest period for a handheld to be commercially available.**

New Nintendo? XL-ent

Improvements abound on Nintendo's 3DS (for which *Pokémon X/Y*, left, is the best-seller). An added analog thumb controller is a step up from the CPU-hogging Circle Pad Pro. Plus, new ZL/ZR shoulder trigger buttons have been added, an upgraded processor makes it Nintendo's most powerful handheld, and its 3D capabilities include face-tracking technology that follows your line of sight.

Art work

The amazing visuals of Ustwo's 2014 iOS/Android BAFTA-winning puzzler *Monument Valley* have won critical acclaim for designer Ken Wong. His work has been compared to that of Dutch artist M C Escher, with each frame designed to be worthy of public display. As of January 2015, the game had been downloaded 2,440,076 times, earned $5.86 million (£3.93 million) and even featured in the Netflix show *House of Cards*.

Agents of Shield

Apparently aiming to take on PCs, Xbox One and PS4, the Nvidia Shield claims to have the fastest mobile processor. Geekbench tests suggest that Apple and Samsung may have it beat, but Shield runs Android *and* streams games such as *Crysis 3* and *Half-Life 2*.

D.Y.K.?

The first game console with a touchscreen was the Game.com, a short-lived handheld from Tiger Electronics, released in September 1997.

MEET UBERHERO

How much?

A Local Chaos Project (USA) has developed the **most expensive App Store game**. *BallAHolic HD* (2012) involves players navigating a character called Uberhero over a series of spheres and was retailing for an eye-watering $349.99 (£249.99) in January 2015.

Ker-ching!

The rise of free2play and casual titles such as *Angry Birds* and *Candy Crush* means that mobile games are projected to generate $30.3 billion (£20.3 billion) worldwide in 2015, according to Newzoo, compared with $26.4 billion (£17.7 billion) for console games.

Speed metal

iOS 8's Metal technology has unleashed console-style gaming on Apple products by improving performance on iPhone 5S and, later, iPad Air and iPad mini 2. Draw rates and load times are better, and titles such as *Modern Combat 5* and *Beach Buggy Racing* support it.

Controlling iOS

Apple touchscreens revolutionized the way we play, but iOS 7's support for controllers has paved the way for on-the-go gaming. Games including *BioShock* use MFi controllers (made for iPhone/iPod/iPad), such as the Mad Catz C.T.R.L. (left) and Razer Junglecat (above), and more arrive each month.

PC

Summary: PC gamers have never had it so good. With visually spectacular exclusives, closer ties with Xbox One and great support for virtual reality headsets, PC gaming remains perhaps the most diverse of all platforms. It boasts modern classics such as *Elite: Dangerous* and *The Witcher 3: Wild Hunt*, and – as a result of universal backward compatibility – can lay claim to the most games supported by one platform. But in the world of virtual technology it is the future that matters most, and with Microsoft throwing its support behind Windows-based gaming, things look bright for years to come.

A word on *The Witcher*

A hack-and-slash RPG series set in a medieval fantasy world, *The Witcher* is based on the books by Polish author Andrzej Sapkowski. Hero Geralt is described by level designer Miles Tost as "the silent badass you fear a bit, but deep down you know he'll do the right thing".

Worth the wait

The original space trading game, *Elite* was released way back in 1984. Sequels followed in 1993 and 1995, but fans of the series had to wait 19 years for the fourth instalment to appear – the crowd-funded *Elite: Dangerous*, which appeared in 2014. This amounts to the **longest development period for a videogame**.

Reality bites

Microsoft's augmented reality device HoloLens uses a camera to pick up the location of objects in front of the wearer and overlays them with virtual images. Users can control the headset via hand gestures, gazes and voice commands. When HoloLens was unveiled in January 2015, it showed incredible images of *Minecraft* being projected into a living room.

Open Windows

Tired of getting kicked off your Xbox One whenever someone else wants to use the TV? With Windows 10, this is less of a problem. Every copy of Windows 10 comes with a built-in Xbox app, allowing gamers to stream games directly from an Xbox One console to a PC or tablet via a home network, leaving the TV free.

56

Percentage of US game developers working on games for PCs, according to a 2014 GDC "State of the Industry" survey – higher than for any other platform.

Space investors

Trading and combat adventure game *Star Citizen* is not only the **most crowd-funded game project**, but also the **most crowd-funded project overall**. As of 6 March 2015, publisher Cloud Imperium Games had raised $74.98 million (£48.46 million) from 797,135 funders. Creator Chris Roberts (inset) says that the game will incorporate an FPS, a single-player campaign and a persistent online universe.

D.Y.K.?

Microsoft have given away the DirectX 12 programming add-ons for gamers upgrading to Windows 10 – the first free Windows release.

Best-selling PC games

Game	Year	Global sales
The Sims	2000	11.24 million
World of Warcraft	2004	10.09 million
Myst	1993	8.03 million
The Sims 3	2009	7.69 million
Microsoft Flight Simulator for Windows 95	1996	5.12 million
StarCraft II: Wings of Liberty	2010	4.65 million
Diablo III	2012	4.65 million
Warcraft II: Tides of Darkness	1995	4.21 million
Half-Life	1998	4.12 million
World of Warcraft: The Burning Crusade	2007	4.09 million

Source: VGChartz as of 23 March 2015. Note: VGChartz does not track Minecraft sales figures. If it did, Minecraft would rank first in this table – see p.102

Look sharp

Hardcore PC players are investing in pixel-packing 4K monitors that offer more than four times the resolution of 1080p. But Dell has produced a 5K monitor that is claimed to have more than 14 million pixels and a resolution of 5120 x 2880.

HARDWARE ROUND-UP

Summary: The big players – Sony, Microsoft and Nintendo – are only part of today's gaming hardware story. As well as US-based developer Valve Corporation continuing to promise big things with its impressive line of pre-built Steam Machines, it seems that everyone wants a slice of the console pie. Amazon's Fire TV, PlayJam's GameStick and Mad Catz's M.O.J.O. are just some of those vying for attention, with Android proving a popular operating system for fringe consoles such as Ouya. And, of course, it's all fuel to the fire of the PC-versus-console debate that will doubtless outlive us all…

Building up Steam

Valve Corporation, developers of *Half-Life* and *Portal*, blurs the boundary between PC and console gaming with its Steam Machines. These run SteamOS – based on Linux, the **most widely used free open-source OS** – and provide an interface made for big-screen play.

Back-in-the-day play

Hyperkin's Android-powered, multi-region RetroN 5 is the **most versatile home console emulator**. It runs original Genesis, Famicom, Game Boy Advance, NES and SNES cartridges, and Super Famicom, Mega Drive, Game Boy Color and Game Boy games.

Game on

The portable TV games console is reborn in USB form as the GameStick – another Kickstarter win.

M.O.J.O. risin'

The M.O.J.O.: a compact gaming and media centre whose initials don't actually stand for anything…

Woo hoo, it's Ouya

Ouya was one of the first Android-based consoles, and the $8,596,474 (£5,500,090) it raised on Kickstarter by 9 August 2012 made it the **most crowd-funded videogame console**. In 2015, Unreal Engine 4 support came to the Ouya – putting the critically acclaimed *TowerFall* (Matt Thorson) on the map.

Viva la Vega

By the end of a crowd-funding campaign on 30 January 2015, the Sinclair ZX Spectrum Vega had exceeded its target by 50%. The niche console – backed by the UK's Sir Clive Sinclair, who created the ZX81 home computer in 1981 – is capable of playing 14,000 different games produced for the machine.

Doting on *DotA*

Valve's MOBA title *DotA 2* is the **most actively played game on Steam**, with 842,368 playing it on 25 March 2015 – more than double that of FPS *Counter-Strike: Global Offensive*. On 14 February 2015, Steam Database also tweeted that it was the **first game to have more than 1 million Steam players online** at a time.

D.Y.K.?

The ill-fated 3DO, launched in 1993, was the first console to be based entirely on CD technology. *Time Magazine* named it "Product of the Year".

Full Steam ahead

Twelve years on from its debut, Valve Corporation's Steam is the **largest digital game distributor**. It survived the server-grinding *Half-Life 2* launch to achieve (by its own reckoning) more than 100 million active accounts on PC, Mac and Linux, and it has more than 3,700 titles available.

Amazon Fire TV

Fire TV connects your HDTV to online games, to be played with the Fire Game Controller.

178 Number of games created between 2008 and 2014 under the Increpare banner by the UK's Stephen Lavelle, making him the **most prolific independent game developer**.

i, caramba!

Apple's iPhone, iPod touch, iPad and Mac range helped the company to a profit of $18 billion (£11.8 billion) in the fiscal quarter ending on 27 December 2014 – one of the largest quarterly profits ever logged. The Apple Watch, released in April 2015, looks set to be another hit.

Twin Galaxies

Oldest videogame adjudication service

On 10 November 1981, a videogame arcade called Twin Galaxies opened its doors in Ottumwa, Iowa, USA. Its founder, Walter Day, sought to turn gaming into an international sport by creating contests, enforcing rules, crowning champions – and measuring world records. He began by collecting high scores for games from more than 100 arcades, releasing them as the Twin Galaxies National Scoreboard.

Since then, hundreds of thousands of videogame scores have been adjudicated and collected, with high scores logged and record holders honoured. Twin Galaxies has continued to improve its adjudicating methods to best-of-class and now features a state-of-the-art peer-review system adhering to GWR submission standards, ensuring that Twin Galaxies remains a gold standard for videogame adjudication. Submit your scores at: **www.twingalaxies.com**

Joel West, Jace Hall and Billy Mitchell give the thumbs-up to gamers worldwide

RYAN GENNO
Twin Galaxies Professional eSports Competitor
Current World Records: 66

Ryan Genno discusses his videogame collection

Actor Michael Rooker with Twin Galaxies staff ready for a competition

The 2007 documentary *King of Kong* followed the battle for the *Donkey Kong* high score

A sneak peek at the impressive technology behind Twin Galaxies

Joseph Jackmovich shows off his highly organized game library

Long live "The Originals"! Top players in 1982

A tense moment for a team playing in the games room at Twin Galaxies HQ

From left to right: Paul Dean, Patrick Wyrick, Richie Knucklez (back row), Ken Jong, Jack Gale, Mark Hoff, Billy Mitchell and Walter Day recognize gaming achievements

The Twin Galaxies/*LIFE* photo re-enactment in Ottumwa, Iowa, USA

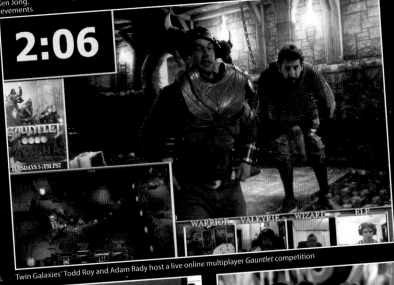

2:06

Twin Galaxies' Todd Roy and Adam Rady host a live online multiplayer *Gauntlet* competition

After Steven Kleisath announced his new *Mario Bros.* record, it was formally verified by Twin Galaxies on 10 January 2015

JOSEPH JACKMOVICH
Current World Records: 37

Walter Day, Ben Gold, Darren Olson and Todd Walker at Twin Galaxies' first videogame championship in 1983

TOP SCORE!

Steve Wiebe and Walter Day evaluate a game performance

Walter Day

Twin Galaxies HQ

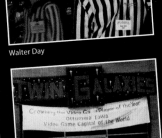

The original 1981 Twin Galaxies arcade in Ottumwa, Iowa, USA

A parade opened Twin Galaxies' inaugural videogame championship

Android · Arcade

Introduction: Listed over the next 10 pages are highlights from the thousands of records approved by gaming monitor Twin Galaxies as of 3 April 2015. All records are based on points achieved on Twin Galaxies' Tournament Settings, unless otherwise stated. Records are organized first by platform, then alphabetically.

Paperboy

Atari's 1985 arcade game *Paperboy* challenges you to deliver a week's worth of newspapers to the homes in a suburban American street, avoiding obstacles, angry dogs and speeding cars along the way. Topping the chart of highest-scoring players of "Easy Street" (the easiest level) is Edward Owen (USA), whose score of 168,372 points was verified on 17 March 2015.

D.Y.K.?

Super PAC-Man (1982) was the third game released in the *PAC-Man* series. In this version, the titular hero eats door keys instead of dots, and with the help of superpower pellets can transform into a bigger, faster Super PAC-Man.

Android

Game	Variation	Player	Record
2048	Endless Mode	Andrew Mee (UK)	16,768
Angry Birds	Poached Eggs – 1-1	Marc Cohen (USA)	34,570
Fruit Ninja	Arcade Mode [1:00] – Basic Dojo	Craig Rout Gallant (Canada)	269
	Classic Mode – Basic Dojo	Craig Rout Gallant (Canada)	103
	Zen Mode – Basic Dojo	Craig Rout Gallant (Canada)	147
Piano Tiles: Don't Tap the White Tile	Classic – 50 tiles	Don Atreides (USA)	9.25

Arcade

Game	Variation	Player	Record
1943: The Battle of Midway	Two Player	Brendan O'Dowd and Michael Sao Pedro (USA)	3,791,820
Altered Beast	One Player	Jamie Tibbetts (USA)	574,600
Bad Dudes vs. DragonNinja	One Player	Peter Hahn (USA)	999,999
Bubbles		Greg Elizondo (USA)	1,615,980
Bump 'n' Jump		John McNeill (Australia)	5,869,264
Death Race	Single Player	Robbie Lakeman (USA)	33
Donkey Kong	Hammer allowed	Robbie Lakeman (USA)	1,144,800
Donkey Kong II: Jumpman Returns	Three men to start	Roald Podevyn (Belgium)	185,900
Double Dragon II: The Revenge [World]	Two Player	Jérôme Pastorel and Régis Martzel (France)	166,410
Elevator Action	Normal – Difficulty 1	Steve Wagner (USA)	156,550
Hyper Sports		Hector Rodriguez (USA)	576,480
Mario Bros.	No POW Challenge [Single Player]	Steven Kleisath (USA)	2,134,120
	No POW Challenge [Two Player]	Steven Kleisath and Stephen K Boyer (USA)	627,480
	Two Player	Steven Kleisath and Stephen K Boyer (USA)	1,186,090
	Single Player	Steven Kleisath (USA)	5,424,920
Metal Slug – Super Vehicle-001	Single Player	Jacob Spring (Canada)	2,761,200
Missile Command	Marathon	Victor Sandberg (Sweden)	103,809,990
Ms. PAC-Man / Galaga: Class of 1981	Galaga [Fast Shot Speed]	Daniel Rodriguez (USA)	4,300,360
Off Road Challenge	Baja [Fastest Race]	Neil Hernandez (USA)	01:46.83
	Mojave [Fastest Race]	Neil Hernandez (USA)	01:45.45
Paperboy	Easy Street	Edward Owen (USA)	168,372
Primal Rage	Version 2.3 [Tournament Settings]	Peter Hahn (USA)	6,088,400
Space Zap		Bob Johnson (USA)	254,500
Super Contra	Single Player	Peter Hahn (USA)	10,788,700
Super PAC-Man	Marathon	Robbie Lakeman (USA)	12,111,640
Super Sprint		Rob Ross (Canada)	30,770

Arcade: Multiple Arcade Machine Emulator (MAME)

Game	Variation	Player	Record
Arm Wrestling		George Riley (USA)	605,450
Battletoads	One Player	Patrick Wheeler (USA)	1,124
Berzerk	Slow Bullets – One Life Only – Random Play (No Pattern)	Andrew Barrow (NZ)	31,810
	Fast Bullets – One Life Only – Random Play (No Pattern)	Mark Hoff (USA)	12,350
Black Widow	Marathon	Chris Point (USA)	357,975
Block Hole		Nick Vis (Netherlands)	798,940
Bubbles		Paolo Colman (Italy)	1,117,050
Bull Fighter		W Dietrich (USA)	171,340
Complex X		Eric Schafer (USA)	60,490,550
Cosmos		John McAllister (USA)	589,000
Dark Tower	One Player	Estel Goffinet (USA)	21,235,300
Defend the Terra Attack on the Red UFO		Brian Allen (USA)	45,160
Donkey Kong [US Set 1]	No Hammer Challenge	Jon Mckinnell (UK)	760,800
Donkey Kong Jr. [US]		Corey Chambers (USA)	1,323,200
Driver's Edge	Advanced Track [Fastest Lap]	Craig Rout Gallant (Canada)	01:06
	Easy Track	Craig Rout Gallant (Canada)	64,152
	Easy Track [Fastest Lap]	Craig Rout Gallant (Canada)	01:09.45
Enigma 2		Paul Kearns (UK)	10,380
Exerion		Spencer Roff (NZ)	2,288,200
Final Tetris		Don Atreides (USA)	245,200
Fire Shark	Two Player	Brendan O'Dowd and Michael Sao Pedro (USA)	390,960
Galaga [Namco rev.B]	Tournament	Andrew Barrow (NZ)	1,885,700
Hard Head	Single Player	Eric Schafer (USA)	1,479,100
Kung-Fu Master	Marathon settings	Paul Kearns (UK)	970,480
Mario Bros. [US]	Single Player: Medium	Stephen Boyer (USA)	4,260,210
Out Run [set 3]		Scott Cunningham (USA)	54,943,840
Parodius Da! [World]		Shahbaz Sadiq (Pakistan)	675,100
Pepper II		Max Haraske (USA)	1,136,630
Pooyan		Paolo Colman (Italy)	1,721,950
Power Spikes [World]		Bart Vanopstal (Belgium)	76,710
Primal Rage [Version 2.3]	Tournament settings	Peter Hahn (USA)	5,936,200
Puzzled/Joy Joy Kid		Nick Vis (Netherlands)	52,200
Road Fighter [set 1]	Marathon settings	Estel Goffinet (USA)	1,204,910
Scrambled Egg		W Dietrich (USA)	649,430
Snapper [Korea]		J Weaver Jr (USA)	304,800
Solar Fox [Upright]	Six lives to start	Brandon LeCroy (USA)	802,490
Space Invaders DX [US] v.2.1	Space Invaders mode	Paolo Colman (Italy) / Paul Kearns (UK)	11,340
Spin Master/Miracle Adventure	Single Player	Daniel Romero (Argentina)	752,000
Super Contra	Single Player	Peter Hahn (USA)	10,777,080
Taxi Driver		Dick Moreland (USA)	21,000
World Tennis		Craig Rout Gallant (Canada)	42,310
Zodiack		W Dietrich (USA)	123,700

Donkey Kong Junior

Corey Chambers (USA) set a record of 1,323,200 points – ahead of his nearest rival, George Riley (USA), with 1,308,000 points – as verified by Twin Galaxies on 5 February 2015. The **highest score on Donkey Kong Junior (arcade version)** is 1,412,200 points, achieved by Mark L Kiehl (USA) on 13 June 2013.

Nintendo

Game Boy

Game	Variation	Player	Record
Disney's The Little Mermaid II: Pinball Frenzy	Shark Chase	Tom Duncan (USA) / Andrew Mee (UK)	145,000,000
Elevator Action		Tom Votava (USA) / Rudy Ferretti (USA)	999,990
Game & Watch Gallery 3/Game Boy Gallery 4/Game Boy Gallery 3	Turtle Bridge – Classic	Andrew Mee (UK)	2,207
	Turtle Bridge – Modern	Jesse Porter (USA)	423
	Greenhouse – Classic	Andrew Mee (UK)	660
	Greenhouse – Modern	Jesse Porter (USA)	1,088
	Egg – Classic	Jesse Porter (USA)	153
Pinball Dreams	Graveyard	Andrew Mee (UK)	368,883,377
	Steel Wheel	Andrew Mee (UK)	11,640,240
Tetris	Game B – Level 0 High 5	Ben Mullen (USA)	7,623
Tetris Blast	Contest	Don Atreides (USA)	1,945
Tetris Plus	Classic	Don Atreides (USA)	999,999

Nintendo 64

(All records are NTSC)

Bust-A-Move '99	Arcade	Shawne Vinson (USA)	21,869,320
The Legend of Zelda: Ocarina of Time	Marathon Run	Matthew Felix (USA)	57
	Archery on Horseback	Alex Penev (Australia) / Jason Whalls (USA) / Matthew Felix (USA)	2,000
	Fastest Completion	Matthew Felix (USA)	04:56:49
	Dampé the Gravekeeper's Race	Matthew Felix (USA)	45
Mortal Kombat 4	Fastest Completion – Master II	Brendon Meares (USA)	06:59
Perfect Dark	Agent [Total Time]	Wayne Meares (USA)	42:38:00
	Chicago – Stealth – Secret Agent	Wayne Meares (USA)	01:24
	dataDyne Central – Defection – Agent	Wayne Meares (USA)	46
Puzzle Bobble 2/Bust-A-Move Again [Neo Geo]	Puzzle	Shawne Vinson (USA)	67,041,080
Space Invaders	Normal	Shawne Vinson (USA)	1,269,650

Nintendo DS

Big Brain Academy	Matchmaker – Hard	Don Atreides (USA)	379
Elite Beat Agents	NTSC/PAL – Sum 41 – "Makes No Difference" – Cruisin' – High Score	Andrew Mee (UK)	404,130
	NTSC/PAL – Steriogram – "Walkie Talkie Man" – Cruisin' – High Score	Andrew Mee (UK)	195,010
	NTSC/PAL – Freddie Mercury/Queen – "I Was Born to Love You" – Cruisin' – High Score	Andrew Mee (UK)	134,300
Super Mario 64 DS	Mario – Sort or 'Splode	Matthew Felix (USA)	225
	Mario – Mario's Slides	Matthew Felix (USA)	19
Tetris Party Deluxe	Master Mode, Endless	Don Atreides (USA)	109,850
	Master Mode, 150 Lines	Don Atreides (USA)	109,750
	Sprint Mode, Fastest Completion	Don Atreides (USA)	01:29.7

Perfect Dark

An FPS developed by Rare for the N64, *Perfect Dark* was released on 22 May 2000. Set in the year 2023, against a backdrop of interstellar war, it sees agent Joanna Dark take on the forces of the dataDyne Corporation. Wayne Meares completed the "Chicago – Stealth – Secret Agent" variation in 1 min 24 sec.

Nintendo Wii

Game	Variation	Player	Record
The Beatles: Rock Band	Single Player – Guitar – "A Hard Day's Night"	Marc Cohen (USA)	60,205
Furu Furu Park	Night Strike – High Score	Shawne Vinson (USA)	3,487,200
Guitar Hero III: Legends of Rock	6. The Hottest Band on Earth – "Cherub Rock" – 1 Player	Jared Oswald (USA)	188,930
Guitar Hero World Tour	NTSC – Bob Seger & The Silver Bullet Band – "Hollywood Nights" – Bass – Easy – 1 Player	Jared Oswald (USA)	155,000
The House of the Dead: Overkill	Director's Cut – The Fetid Waters – Single Player	Andrew Mee (UK)	131,075
	Story Mode – Overkill – Single Player	Andrew Mee (UK)	123,275
NBA Jam	Play Now Mode – Biggest Blowout – Single Player	Daniel Perea (USA)	104
Rock Band	NTSC – Blue Oyster Cult – "Don't Fear the Reaper" – Guitar – Medium – 1 Player	Marc Cohen (USA)	78,718
Super Smash Bros. Brawl	NTSC – Stadium – Boss Battles [Fastest Time]	Matthew Felix (USA)	02:09.93
	NTSC – Stadium – Home-Run Contest – Fox	Matthew Felix (USA)	1,963.1
Tetris Party Deluxe	Sprint Mode – Fastest Completion	Don Atreides (USA)	01:26.85
Wario Ware: Smooth Moves	Super Hard	Joe Jackmovich (USA)	44
Wii Fit/Wii Fit Plus	PAL – Training Plus – Obstacle Course – Advanced	Andrew Mee (UK)	628
Wii Sports	Training – Boxing – Working the Bag	Matthew Felix (USA)	49
Wii Sports Resort	Power Cruising – Beach	Andrew Mee (UK)	218.2
	Swordplay – Duel	Andrew Mee (UK)	1,460
	Table Tennis – Match	Craig Rout Gallant (Canada)	1,521
	Table Tennis – Return Challenge	Brandon Skar (USA) / Andrew Mee (UK) / Craig Rout Gallant (Canada)	999

Super Nintendo Entertainment System

(All records are NTSC unless otherwise stated)

Game	Variation	Player	Record
American Gladiators		Brendan O'Dowd (USA)	45
Bust-A-Move		Shawne Vinson (USA)	34,197,300
Chuck Rock		Tyler VanderZwaag (USA)	384,275
Donkey Kong Country Competition Pak	TGES	Charles Ahlert (Brazil)	4,081
Dragon: The Bruce Lee Story	Tournament Mode	Wayne Meares (USA)	11,316,000
ESPN National Hockey Night	Biggest Blowout	Rudy Ferretti (USA)	110
Firepower 2000		Ryan Genno (Canada)	176,475
NHL '94	Biggest Blowout	Raphael Frydman (USA)	58
Primal Rage		Wayne Meares (USA)	202,600
Super Bomberman		Ryan Genno (Canada)	553,170
Super Buster Bros.	Panic Mode	Mason Cramer (USA)	160,420
Super Ghouls 'n Ghosts	PAL	Jacob Spring (Canada)	246,300
Super Mario All-Stars	Super Mario Bros. [Minimalist Speed Run]	Andrew Gardikis (USA)	05:19
Super Star Wars: The Empire Strikes Back		Wayne Meares (USA)	126,205

3,722

Longest note streak on a *Guitar Hero* game, achieved by Danny Johnson (USA) playing "Through the Fire and Flames" on *Guitar Hero III* on 30 May 2009.

NHL '94

In sport, a blowout is a term for a large margin between the winning and losing score. Playing as All-Stars West vs. Anaheim on *NHL '94* on the SNES, Raphael Frydman (USA) won the game 59–1, giving him a blowout score of 58, as verified by Twin Galaxies on 28 January 2015.

PlayStation

PlayStation

Game	Variation	Player	Record
Bust-A-Move '99	NTSC – Arcade	Shawne Vinson (USA)	18,036,740
	NTSC – Challenge	Shawne Vinson (USA)	31,256,090
Buster Bros Collection	NTSC – Buster Buddies – Panic Mode	Shawne Vinson (USA)	527,800
Crash Bandicoot	NTSC – Fastest Minimalist Completion	Charles Ziese (USA)	01:16:07
Driver	PAL – Driving Games – Pursuit – Los Angeles 1 [Fastest Kill]	Andrew Mee (UK)	6.6
Extreme Pinball	PAL – Medieval Knights	Andrew Mee (UK)	15,163,000
Final Fantasy VII	NTSC – Gold Saucer – Snowboard Game [Course A – Fastest Completion]	Kevin Holst (USA)	01:26.64
Gran Turismo	NTSC – GT Mode – Licence A-8: A-Class Licence final test [Fastest Time]	Shaun Michaud (USA)	01:05.499
Intellivision Classic Games	NTSC – *Sharp Shot* – Football Passing	Matthew Miller (USA) / Tom Duncan (USA)	105
Madden NFL 2001	NTSC – Exhibition [Biggest Blowout]	Matthew Dauer (USA)	51
Metal Gear Solid: VR Missions	NTSC – VR Training – Special Mode – Variety Mode – Time Attack – Level 10 [Fastest Completion]	Ryan Sullivan (USA)	01:14.5
Resident Evil 2	NTSC – Leon "A" – All Weapons – Normal Difficulty [Fastest Minimalist Completion]	Austin Cook (USA)	01:14.06
Tetris Plus	NTSC – Classic Mode [Most Lines]	Don Atreides (USA)	120

PlayStation 2

Game	Variation	Player	Record
Gauntlet: Seven Sorrows	PAL – Entire Game – "Impossible" Difficulty – Two Players [Fastest Minimalist Completion]	Andrew Mee and Julie Mee (UK)	01:46:57
Guitar Hero III: Legends of Rock	PAL – 1. Starting Out Small – "Story Of My Life" – "Easy" Difficulty – 1 Player	Andrew Mee (UK)	157,435
Intellivision Lives!	NTSC – Buzz Bombers	Marc Cohen (USA)	75,500
Midway Arcade Treasures	NTSC – Defender – Marathon	W Dietrich (USA)	96,025
	NTSC – Defender – Tournament	W Dietrich (USA)	40,650
	NTSC – Satan's Hollow	Shaun Michaud (USA)	44,555
Midway Arcade Treasures 3	NTSC – Hydro Thunder – Castle von Dandy [Fastest Race]	Marc Cohen (USA)	01:48.72
Namco Museum	NTSC – Dig Dug Arrangement	Shaun Michaud (USA)	190,450
PAC-Man World Rally	NTSC – Time Trial Mode – Cherry Cup – Cloud Garden [Fastest Race]	Fred Bugmann (Brazil)	02:29.35
Sega Genesis Collection	NTSC – Vectorman	Jesse Porter (USA)	479,190
Snoopy vs The Red Baron	NTSC – Campaign – Aerodrome Island – Mission 1 [Fastest Completion]	Shaun Michaud (USA)	02:18.22
Taito Legends	NTSC – Exzisus	Shawne Vinson (USA)	522,630
Tony Hawk's Pro Skater 3	PAL – Rio Ruckus – Single Session	Andrew Mee (UK)	1,488,703
We Love Katamari	NTSC – Roll Up the Sun [Number of Celestial Bodies]	Joe Jackmovich (USA)	6,417
	NTSC – As Large as Possible – Racetrack [Diameter]	Joe Jackmovich (USA)	23.85

Crash Bandicoot

He was nearly called Willie the Wombat, but as Crash Bandicoot, Naughty Dog's lovable marsupial went on to become an iconic PlayStation character, notable for his success in the Japanese market. Series sales of 21.53 million as of 22 April 2015 make *Crash Bandicoot* the **best-selling platform series for PlayStation**.

D.Y.K.?

Starring Snoopy as a World War I pilot, 2006's *Snoopy vs The Red Baron* is the only time the popular cartoon beagle has been animated in 3D in any media, including TV and videogames.

PlayStation 3

Game	Variation	Player	Record
Batman: Arkham City	Challenge Mode – Blind Justice	Kevin Holst (USA)	37,410
Call of Duty: Modern Warfare 3	Special Ops – Solo – Missions – Stay Sharp – Fastest Completion	Adam Woodson (USA)	20.8
Green Day: Rock Band	Single Player – "Good Riddance (Time of Your Life)" – Microphone	Jackie Bartlett (USA)	118,000
	Single Player – "Pulling Teeth" – Microphone	Michael Sroka (USA)	119,474
Guitar Hero III: Legends of Rock	NTSC – 4. European Invasion – Even Flow – Easy Difficulty – 1 Player	Nik Meeks (USA)	119,379
	NTSC – 6. The Hottest Band on Earth – The Metal – Easy Difficulty – 1 Player	John Pompa (USA)	73,521
Pinball Hall of Fame: The Williams Collection	Whirlwind	Marc Cohen (USA)	76,222,110
	Sorcerer	Marc Cohen (USA)	11,437,130
Rock Band 2	NTSC – Panic at the Disco – "Nine in the Afternoon" – Guitar – Expert – 1 Player	Kevin Holst (USA)	57,810
Rock Band 3	Foreigner – "Cold as Ice" – 1 Player – Drums	Michelle Ireland (USA)	64,350
	Joan Jett & The Blackhearts – "I Love Rock 'n' Roll" – 1 Player – Guitar	Matt Siegfried (USA)	54,835
Sonic's Ultimate Genesis Collection/ Sega's Ultimate Mega Drive Collection	Sonic & Knuckles – Fastest Minimalist Completion	Jared Oswald (USA)	43:25:00
SoulCalibur IV	Arcade Mode – Fastest Completion	Jeremy Florence (USA)	04:51.6
Street Fighter IV	NTSC – Arcade Mode [Tournament Settings]	John Lapsey (USA)	906,800
Super Street Fighter IV	NTSC – Arcade Mode [Tournament Settings]	Rob Seymour (UK)	2,587,000
UFC Undisputed 2010	Exhibition Mode – Fastest Victory	Matthew Runnels (USA)	25

PlayStation 3 PSN

Lumines Supernova	Time Attack Mode – 600 Seconds – Most Blocks Cleared	Sophie Wormer (Netherlands)	440
Madden NFL Arcade	Play Now – Biggest Blowout	Terry Green (Australia)	35
PAC-Man Championship Edition DX	Championship I – Score Attack – 5 Minutes	Ethan Daniels (USA)	718,900
	Championship II – Score Attack – 5 Minutes	Marc Cohen (USA)	2,143,490
Zen Pinball	Eldorado	Marc Cohen (USA)	26,356,637

PlayStation Portable (PSP)

Atari Classics Evolved	Tempest Evolved	Dick Moreland (USA)	71,903
	Asteroids Evolved	Dick Moreland (USA)	38,160
Mercury Meltdown	Astro Lab – Stage 1	Andrew Mee (UK)	77,432
Midway Arcade Treasures: Extended Play	NTSC/PAL – Rampage	Ryan Sullivan (USA)	76,755
Namco Museum Battle Collection	Galaxian	John Brissie (USA)	19,090
	Ms. PAC-Man – 3 Lives	Perley Walsh (Canada)	36,680
PaRappa the Rapper	Stage 3 – "Easy" Difficulty	Andrew Palladino (USA)	291
Sega Genesis Collection	NTSC/PAL – Ristar	Jeremy Woodworth (USA)	65,900
Space Invaders Extreme	Stage 2	Terence O'Neill (USA)	982,850
Taito Legends Power-Up	Alpine Ski	Kevin Brisley (Canada)	63,532

D.Y.K.?

Warrior Mitsurugi is a mainstay of the *SoulCalibur* series, and in 2002 was voted into the top 10 favourite characters in a poll conducted by Namco.

PaRappa the Rapper

One of the quirkiest titles for the PSP, *PtR* features a rapping dog hoping to win the heart of flower Sunny Funny with his lyrical flow. Andrew Palladino (USA) scored 291 points on Stage 3 – "Easy" Difficulty, as verified by Twin Galaxies on 11 October 2011.

Xbox

45

Number of mini-games in *Fuzion Frenzy*, a launch title for the Xbox. Players were given a choice of six brightly coloured characters, from pink Jet to yellow Zak.

OutRun 2

Boasting an official licence from Ferrari, racer *OutRun 2* offers players a choice of eight cars from the classic Italian car manufacturer, including the Testarossa. Drivers can drift their way through the streets at incredible speeds, hoping their skills behind the wheel will increase the heart rate of their female passenger.

Xbox

Game	Variation	Player	Record
Amped 2	NTSC – Media Points – Millicent – Main Street	Katy Bride (USA)	1,027
Conflict: Desert Storm II	NTSC – 3 Player Speed Completion (Hard)	Joseph Baiocchi (USA) / Chris Bartella (USA) / Salvatore DiBenedetto (USA)	55:54:00
Crash Bandicoot: The Wrath of Cortex	NTSC – Time Trial 16 – Avalanche [Fastest Time]	Paulo Valmir (Brazil)	01:00.96
Defender	NTSC	John Pompa (USA)	16,655
FIFA Street	NTSC – Score [Easy Difficulty – Biggest Blowout]	Ryan McBride (USA)	11
Fight Club	NTSC – Survival Mode [Most Consecutive Wins]	Jeffrey Widzinski (USA)	2
Fuzion Frenzy	NTSC – Blast Man Standing [Fastest Time]	Katy Bride (USA)	01:03
Grand Theft Auto: Vice City	NTSC – Stoppie Distance	Mike Morrow (USA)	3,437
Gravity Games Bike: Street, Vert, Dirt	PAL – Career – Museum Competition	Andrew Mee (UK)	176,622
Intellivision Lives!	NTSC – *Reversi* – Board = 6x6 – Skill 1	Tom Duncan (USA) / Tee Jester (USA) / Troy Whelan (USA)	36
	NTSC – Night Stalker	Matthew Miller (USA)	2,555,500
Midway Arcade Treasures	NTSC – *Robotron*: 2084 [Points/Marathon]	Jeremy Woodworth (USA)	256,925
Namco Museum: 50th Anniversary	NTSC – *Xevious*	Paulo Valmir (Brazil)	52,540
Need for Speed: Underground	NTSC – Sprint Mode – To Liberty Gardens [Fastest Race]	Fred Bugmann (Brazil)	01:08.96
Need for Speed: Underground 2	NTSC – Circuit – Ambassador Ridge – Reverse Track [Fastest Race]	Fabiano Souza (Brazil)	03:10.96
	NTSC – Circuit – Freemount – Reverse Track [Fastest Race]	Fred Bugmann (Brazil)	01:31.18
OutRun 2	PAL – Out Run Challenge – Out Run Mission – Stage 0.4 Crazy Convoy [Fastest Time]	Andrew Mee (UK)	50.514
	PAL – Out Run Challenge – Out Run Mission – Stage 0.5 Cone Runner [Hearts]	Andrew Mee (UK)	94
	PAL – Out Run Challenge – Out Run Mission – Stage 3.5 Cone Runner [Hearts]	Andrew Mee (UK)	109
Project Gotham Racing 2	PAL – Time Attack – Circuit Challenge – Yokohama – Minato Mirai – Fastest Lap	Magnus Andersson (Sweden)	01:00.2
Taito Legends	NTSC – *The Ninja Kids*	Patrick Scott Patterson (USA)	471,050
Tetris Worlds	NTSC – *Hot-Line Tetris* – Highest Level Cleared	John Bieniek (USA)	3
	NTSC – *Tetris* – Highest Level Cleared	Patrick Scott Patterson (USA) / John Bieniek (USA)	10
Tony Hawk's Underground 2	NTSC – Pro Skater – High Combo	Michael Waks (USA)	653,643
	NTSC – Airport – High Combo	Michael Waks (USA)	4,833,375

Xbox 360

Game	Variation	Player	Record
2010 FIFA World Cup South Africa	Biggest Blowout	Frazer Braidwood (UK)	8
Call of Duty: Modern Warfare 2	Exhibition #5 – Terminal – 5/1/2010	Taylor Wilkerson (USA)	3,000
	Exhibition #6 – Overgrown – 5/8/2010	Douglas Simpson (USA)	3,000
	Triple Play #1 – 5/16/2010	George Filby IV (USA)	10,330
	Triple Play #2 – 5/23/2010	Alan Roskos (USA)	8,150
	Triple Play #3 – 5/30/2010	Douglas Simpson (USA)	3,450
	Triple Play #4 – 6/20/2010	Kevin Murphy (USA)	3,500
	Triple Play #5 (Map Packs) – 6/26/2010	George Filby IV (USA)	2,550
Dance Central 2	Bobby Brown – "My Prerogative"	Mary Mullen (USA)	269,938
	Far East Movement – "Like a G6"	Chaz Kaczor (USA)	239,433
	Nicki Minaj feat. Sean Garrett – "Massive Attack"	Destiny Knucklez (USA)	347,274
Fallout 3	Minimalist Completion [Fastest Time]	Anthony Walsh (USA)	55:00:00
Forza Motorsport 4	Camaro Club	Scott Kaczor (USA)	13,425
Gears of War 3	NTSC – Campaign (Arcade) Act I: One – Chapter 1: Anchored	Matt Siegfried (USA)	47,349
Guitar Hero Smash Hits/Greatest Hits	NTSC – The Reverend Horton Heat – "Psychobilly Freakout" – Bass – Easy – 1 Player	Gregrey Hall (USA)	68,814
Guitar Hero II	NTSC – 1. Opening Licks – "Tonight I'm Gonna Rock You Tonight" – Expert Difficulty – 1-Player	Tim McVey (USA)	73,776
Marvel vs. Capcom 3: Fate of Two Worlds	Arcade Mode	Victor Delgado (USA)	230,489
Mirror's Edge	Playground One – Time Trial	Daniel Collotte (USA)	01:01.51
Portal 2	Time Trial – Chapter 1-1: Courtesy Call	Matt Siegfried (USA)	43.76
Resident Evil 5	The Mines – Mercenary Mode	Guillermo Cepeda (USA)	31,740
SoulCalibur IV	NTSC – Arcade Mode – Fastest Completion	Jeremy Florence (USA)	03:45.81
Super Street Fighter IV	NTSC – Arcade Mode [Tournament Settings]	Jeffrey Lowe Jr (USA)	2,014,700
Super Street Fighter IV: Arcade Edition	NTSC – Arcade Mode [Tournament Settings]	John Lapsey (USA)	1,144,000

Xbox 360 Live Arcade

Game	Variation	Player	Record
Contra		Peter Hahn (USA)	1,395,600
Dig Dug		W Dietrich (USA)	272,500
Galaga		W Dietrich (USA)	327,160
Hexic HD	NTSC – Survival – Normal Difficulty	Andrew Mee (UK)	151,815
I MAED A GAM3 W1TH Z0MBIES 1N IT!!!1		Craig Rout Gallant (Canada)	914,950
NBA Jam: On Fire Edition	Biggest Blowout – One Player Only	Daniel Perea (USA)	43
PAC-Man		W Dietrich (USA)	109,810
Robotron: 2084		Mark Hoff (USA)	213,650
R-Type Dimensions	Single Player – R-Type – Classic Mode	Peter Hahn (USA)	707,500
Track & Field		Gil Limas (USA)	3,237,170
Xevious		W Dietrich (USA)	253,480

1,500

Number of *Marvel vs. Capcom 3* players competing at its only pro tournament – held at the Evo Championship Series in 2011.

NBA Jam: On Fire Edition

Featuring slam dunks so hot that basketballs literally catch fire, *NBA Jam: On Fire Edition* (2010) was another instalment in the beloved arcade sports franchise. When he racked up a winning margin of 43 points, Daniel Perea (USA) achieved the biggest blowout in the game.

Miscellaneous

36

Number of enemies and bosses in the notoriously tough *Ghouls 'n Ghosts* – from flying knights and weredogs, to demons such as Astaroth and Samael.

Teenage Mutant Ninja Turtles

In the early 1990s, developers Konami took the iconic heroes in a half-shell and developed three different tournament fighter games for them – for the NES, SNES and Sega Genesis/Mega Drive. On 10 March 2015, Jesse Porter (USA) racked up a bodacious score of 98,800 using tournament settings on the Sega version of the game.

Sega Dreamcast

Game	Variation	Player	Record
Sega Marine Fishing	NTSC – Original – Mini Game – Total Weight Training – Hideaway of Big Fish [Total Weight]	Troy Whelan (USA)	1,859.06
	NTSC – Original – Mini Game – Total Weight Training – Fishing Port [Total Weight]	Troy Whelan (USA)	1,896.38
	NTSC – Arcade – Coral Reef – Sailfish [Heaviest Fish]	Troy Whelan (USA)	260.56
Triggerheart Exelica	NTSC/J – Story Mode	Matthew Straka (USA)	3,009,541

Sega Genesis/Mega Drive

Game	Variation	Player	Record
Desert Demolition	NTSC – Fastest Completion [Wile E. Coyote]	Charles Ziese (USA)	10:40
Ghouls 'n Ghosts	NTSC	Clay Karczewski (Canada)	86,300
The Revenge of Shinobi	PAL	Andrew Mee (UK)	37,600
Road Rash II	NTSC – Alaska – Fastest Time	Marc Cohen (USA)	02:51.7
	NTSC – Hawaii – Fastest Time	Marc Cohen (USA)	02:58.2
Shaq-Fu	NTSC	Wayne Meares (USA)	294,138
Sonic the Hedgehog 3	NTSC – Fastest Total Completion – Sonic	Jared Oswald (USA)	43:48:00
	NTSC – Fastest Total Completion – Tails	Jared Oswald (USA)	47:35:00
Teenage Mutant Ninja Turtles: Tournament Fighters	NTSC – Tournament Settings	Jesse Porter (USA)	98,800
Twin Cobra	NTSC	Brendan O'Dowd (USA)	266,990
Vectorman 2	NTSC – Fastest Completion	Jesse Porter (USA)	25:21:00
Viewpoint	NTSC	Ryan Genno (Canada)	221,380
Winter Challenge	NTSC – Downhill – Fastest Time	Michael Sroka (USA)	01:50.12
	NTSC – Biathlon – Fastest Completion	Michael Sroka (USA)	04:53
	NTSC – Luge – Fastest Time	Michael Sroka (USA)	01:21.06

Sega Master System

Game	Variation	Player	Record
Altered Beast	NTSC	Clay Karczewski (Canada)	474,900
Dynamite Düx	NTSC	Ryan Genno (Canada)	627,790
Golden Axe	NTSC – Fastest Completion	Antonio Filho (Brazil)	17:32
Ms. PAC-Man	NTSC	Ryan Genno (Canada)	80,060

Sega Saturn

Game	Variation	Player	Record
Athlete Kings	PAL – High Jump	Jordi Schouteren (Netherlands)	2.16
	PAL – Long Jump	Jordi Schouteren (Netherlands)	9.35
Galactic Attack	NTSC	Estel Goffinet (USA)	896,300

PC

Game	Variation	Player	Record
Champ Kong	Default settings	Wes Copeland (USA)	135,200
Epic Pinball	Jungle Pinball	Andrew Mee (UK)	66,069,464
Pinball Master	Dino Island	Andrew Mee (UK)	294,699,786
Pro Pinball: Big Race USA	Combo Champion – Extra Easy	Juergen-Lucky Schroeder (Germany) / Henrik Orreblad (Sweden)	8
	Combo Champion – Hard	Augie Taylor (UK)	10
	Loop Champion – Extra Hard	Andreas Grabher (Austria)	10
Warblade	Skill 6 Meteorstorm	Todd Rogers (USA)	53,334,400
	Skill 4 Ace	Morningdove Mahoney (USA)	481,075

Amstrad CPC

Game	Variation	Player	Record
Donkey Kong		Stephen Anderson (UK)	43,900
Super Space Invaders	Single Player Only	Stephen Anderson (UK)	36,850
Xenophobe	EMU	Mike Morrow (USA)	1,115,885

Apple II

Game	Variation	Player	Record
Galaxian		Terence O'Neill (USA)	20,680
Mario Bros.		Terence O'Neill (USA)	408,050
*Q*bert*		Ryan Gavigan (USA)	9,850

Atari 2600

Game	Variation	Player	Record
Megamania	NTSC – Game 1, Difficulty B [Guided Missiles]	First achieved by Ron Corcoran (USA)*	999,999
Star Voyager	NTSC – Game 1, Difficulty A	Erik Kaufman (USA)	43

Commodore 64

Game	Variation	Player	Record
Impossible Mission	PAL	Peter Nadalin (USA)	31,635
LeMans	NTSC	Brendan O'Dowd (USA)	238,000
Pitstop	NTSC – Kyalami – 3 Laps – Fastest Time	Frankie Cardulla (USA) / Marc Cohen (USA) / Terence O'Neill (USA) / Fred Bugmann (Brazil) / Tom Duncan (USA) / Paulo Valmir (Brazil)	01:29
	NTSC – Le Mans – 3 Laps – Fastest Time	Frankie Cardulla (USA) / Marc Cohen (USA) / Terence O'Neill (USA) / Fred Bugmann (Brazil) / Tom Duncan (USA) / Paulo Valmir (Brazil) / Tee Jester (USA)	01:23
	NTSC – St Jovite – 3 Laps – Fastest Time	Fred Bugmann (Brazil) / Marc Cohen (USA) / Tom Duncan (USA)	01:30

Intellivision

Game	Variation	Player	Record
Donkey Kong	NTSC/PAL – Skill 1	John Pompa (USA)	249,100
Horse Racing	NTSC/PAL – Most Money Won	Jeff Coyle (USA)	9,999
Masters of the Universe	NTSC/PAL – Novice	Mark Stacy (USA)	764,900

Sinclair ZX Spectrum

Game	Variation	Player	Record
Alien Destroyer	EMU – Grandfathered [No More Scores Will Be Accepted]	David Magowan (UK)	6,920
ATV Simulator/All Terrain Vehicle Simulator	EMU – Grandfathered [No More Scores Will Be Accepted]	Gazz Halliwell (UK)	19,050
Summer Games II	EMU – Javelin – Grandfathered [No More Scores Will Be Accepted]	John Western (UK)	79.3
Turbo Esprit	PAL – Romford	Simon Bickerdike (UK)	12,120
	PAL – Minster	Simon Bickerdike (UK)	12,500
	PAL – Gamesborough	Simon Bickerdike (UK)	12,770

Pro Pinball: Big Race USA

A 1998 game published by Empire Interactive, *Pro Pinball: Big Race USA* took the idea of the classic American road trip and applied it to the pinball table. It was the third game in the series, following on from *Pro Pinball: The Web* and *Pro Pinball: Timeshock!*

*Subsequently achieved by Todd Rogers (USA), Bryan Wagner (USA), David Yancey (USA), Douglas Korekach (USA), Troy Whelan (USA), Natalie Purawec (Canada), Rich Semenza (USA), Frankie Cardulla (USA), Steve Germershausen (Canada), Marc Cohen (USA) and Greg Degeneffe (USA).

D.Y.K.?

Published by Epyx, 1984's classic C64 racer *Pitstop II* was one of the first 3D games with a split-screen two-player mode. No matter where racers found themselves on the track, the split screen would show them their individual positions.

Contributors

These are the experts who contributed to the *Gamer's Edition 2016*, sourcing and writing the records, facts, figures and trivia that go into the book. This year's *Gamer's Edition* includes writers who ply their trade at *Edge*, *Official PlayStation Magazine*, Eurogamer.net and GamesRadar.

DAVID CROOKES

David began his journalistic career freelancing for *Amstrad Action* in 1993 and he has spent the past 10 years writing for *Retro Gamer*. He has written dozens of features for *gamesTM*, *PLAY*, *X360* and the *Independent* newspaper, and also curated the huge Videogame Nation exhibition in Manchester, UK.

Which games did you play most in 2015?
FIFA 15, *Bloodborne*, *Grim Fandango Remastered*, *Life is Strange*.

What was the most exciting gaming event of 2015?
Aside from getting hold of the Retron 5 retro gaming console earlier in the year, the possibilities being offered by Microsoft's HoloLens are getting me giddy.

MATT BRADFORD

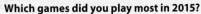

Matt is a Canadian freelancer and life-long gamer who has covered the industry for a number of websites and publications since the 1990s. His ramblings on gaming and pop culture can be heard on the weekly *Video Game Outsiders* and *Zombie Cast* podcasts.

Which games did you play most in 2015?
Aside from an addiction to *Hearthstone*, *Alien: Isolation* and *Dragon Age: Inquisition* ate up a good chunk of my year.

What was the most exciting gaming event of 2015?
I'm cheating, but I'd have to say "all of them". It seems there's a new gaming expo, conference or community event to get excited about every week. Ask me again when virtual-reality devices such as Oculus Rift start hitting the mainstream market and I'll have a more specific answer…

ANDREW DAVIDSON

Andy is a veteran of kids' magazine publishing, having edited such titles as *Toxic*, *Moshi Monsters* and *Angry Birds Magazine*. In his free time, he likes to dust and maintain his collection of retro consoles.

Which games did you play most in 2015?
Captain Toad: Treasure Tracker (Wii U).

What was the most exciting gaming event of 2015?
Halo 5.

ROB CAVE

Rob's first gaming computer was the Acorn Electron, which introduced him to both gaming and programming – giving him a love of the former and deep respect for the latter. He writes about videogames and comics for Guinness World Records, working on *Gamer's Edition* since it was launched in 2008.

Which games did you play most in 2015?
I played a lot of *Battlefield* this year.

What was the most exciting gaming event of 2015?
The news that Nintendo characters were coming to iOS and Android devices, and the *Call of Duty Online* beta in China.

IAN DRANSFIELD

Ian is a freelance journalist, researcher, video editor and consultant. His relationship with the gaming industry began over 10 years ago, while his maddening addiction to *Football Manager* began over 20 years ago. He regrets neither.

Which games did you play most in 2015?
Bloodborne.

What was the most exciting gaming event of 2015?
Football Manager Classic coming to Android – now I'm never without it!

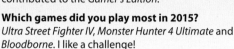

MATTHEW EDWARDS

Matthew is a community manager at Capcom UK. Prior to that he spent five years as a freelance writer, penning articles for the likes of Eurogamer.net, *gamesTM* and *Edge*. This is the third year that he's contributed to the *Gamer's Edition*.

Which games did you play most in 2015?
Ultra Street Fighter IV, *Monster Hunter 4 Ultimate* and *Bloodborne*. I like a challenge!

What was the most exciting gaming event of 2015?
The whole Capcom Pro Tour. With $500,000 [£333,925] on the line, the competition to win the Capcom Cup has never been fiercer.

TYLER HICKS

Tyler is a freelance game reviewer and eSports pundit, expressing his opinions through blogging, livetweeting and articles. He's spent thousands of hours across the *Halo* and *Diablo* franchises, including coaching MLG *Halo* teams, but now focuses his attention on *League of Legends*.

Which games did you play most in 2015?
My time has been balanced evenly between *League of Legends* and *Halo: The Master Chief Collection*, but the early access of *Offworld Trading Company* is starting to eat into that percentage.

What was the most exciting gaming event of 2015?
The Intel Extreme Masters World Championship in Katowice [Poland]. TSM finally did it!

ELLIE GIBSON

Ellie is an award-winning games journalist who began her career writing manuals and went on to spend nearly a decade working for Eurogamer.net. Ellie can be regularly seen as a talking head on the TV shows *Videogame Nation* and *Console Yourself*.

Which games did you play most in 2015?
QuizUp on the iPhone. I love quiz games and this one is so fast-paced and fun. Challenge me if you dare…

What was the most exciting gaming event of 2015?
New *Tomb Raider*, new *Metal Gear*, new *Halo*… 2015 was a good year for fans of classic franchises.

JOHN ROBERTSON

John has been working in videogames since 2007, contributing to both national and international publications as well as working as a consultant for some of the most respected developers in the industry. He is currently in the process of writing a new book, as well as working on a plan for promoting academic discussion on videogames.

Which games did you play most in 2015?
OlliOlli 2, *Bloodborne*, *PES 2015*.

What was the most exciting gaming event of 2015?
The launch of *Independent by Design*, the most in-depth book on the workings of independent videogame developers ever written.

STACE HARMAN

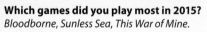

Stace is a freelance writer, editor and videogame consultant. Over five years he's written hundreds of articles for dozens of different publications, and is constantly looking for new ways to include games as part of broader cultural conversations.

Which games did you play most in 2015?
Bloodborne, *Sunless Sea*, *This War of Mine*.

What was the most exciting gaming event of 2015?
The launch of indie project *Independent by Design*.

MATT WALES

Matt is an experienced freelance writer, editor and consultant for the likes of IGN, Eurogamer, Kotaku, CVG and Prima Games.

Which games did you play most in 2015?
This was mostly a year for masochism as I plotted a tear-stained path through From Software's *Bloodborne* and *Dark Souls II: Scholar of the First Sin*. Elsewhere, I brought down behemoths in *Monster Hunter 4 Ultimate*, caused urban chaos in *Cities: Skylines* and lived a life of high adventure in inkle's amazing *Sorcery!* series of game books. Oh, and I found time to put the finishing touches to my geometrically terrifying haunted house of horrors in *Minecraft* too.

What was the most exciting gaming event of 2015?
Bloodborne's long-awaited arrival on PlayStation 4 was a real highlight, as was spending over 200 hours maiming things in *Monster Hunter 4 Ultimate*.

Games & Developers

1943: The Battle of Midway
Capcom, 1987

2010 FIFA World Cup South Africa
EA Canada, 2010

2048 Gabriele Cirulli, 2014

Alien Destroyer Kuma Computers, 1984

Alien: Isolation The Creative Assembly, 2014

Alone in the Dark Infogrames, 1992

Altered Beast Sega, 1998

American Gladiators Incredible Technologies, 2001

Amped 2 Indie Built, 2003

Angry Birds Rovio, 2009

Animal Crossing Nintendo, 2001

Ape Escape SCE Japan Studio, 1999

Arm Wrestling Nintendo, 1985

Assassin's Creed Ubisoft Montreal, 2007

Assassin's Creed II Ubisoft Montreal, 2009

Assassin's Creed III: Liberation Ubisoft Sofia/Milan, 2012

Assassin's Creed IV: Black Flag Ubisoft Montreal, 2013

Assassin's Creed: Brotherhood Ubisoft Montreal, 2010

Assassin's Creed: Project Legacy Ubisoft Montreal, 2010

Assassin's Creed: Revelations Ubisoft Montreal, 2011

Assassin's Creed: Unity Ubisoft Montreal, 2014

Asteroids Atari, 1979

Atari Classics Evolved Stainless Games, 2007

Athlete Kings Sega, 1996

ATV Simulator/All Terrain Vehicle Simulator Codemasters, 1987

Baby PAC-Man Bally Midway, 1982

Bad Dudes vs. DragonNinja Data East, 1988

Baldur's Gate BioWare, 1998

Baldur's Gate II: Shadows of Amn BioWare, 2000

Banjo-Kazooie: Nuts & Bolts Rare, 2008

Banjo-Tooie Rare, 2000

The Banner Saga Stoic, 2013

Barcelona vs Madrid Alina Avdeeva, 2012

Batman Ocean, 1986

Batman: Arkham Asylum Rocksteady, 2009

Batman: Arkham City Rocksteady, 2011

Batman: Arkham Knight Rocksteady, 2015

Batman: Arkham Origins Warner Bros. Games, 2013

Batman: Arkham Origins Blackgate Armature Studio, 2013

Batman Begins Eurocom, 2005

Batman: Dark Tomorrow HotGen, 2003

Batman: Rise of Sin Tzu Ubisoft, 2003

Batman: Vengeance Ubisoft, 2001

Battletoads Rare, 1994

Battlefield: Bad Company DICE, 2008

Battlefield 2 DICE, 2005

Battlefield 2: Modern Combat DICE, 2005

Battlefield 2: Special Forces DICE, 2005

Battlefield 3 DICE, 2011

Battlefield 4 DICE, 2013

Battlefield 4: Naval Strike DICE, 2014

Battlefield 1942 DICE, 2002

Battlefield 2142 DICE, 2006

Battlefield: Hardline Visceral Games, 2015

Beach Buggy Racing Vector Unit, 2014

The Beatles: Rock Band Harmonix, 2009

Berzerk Stern Electronics, 1980

Beyond: Two Souls Quantic Dream, 2013

Big Brain Academy Nintendo EAD, 2005

BioShock Irrational Games, 2007

Black Widow Atari, 1982

Block Hole Konami, 1989

Bloodborne From Software, 2015

Borderlands Gearbox, 2009

Borderlands 2 Gearbox, 2012

Borderlands: The Pre-Sequel! 2K/Gearbox, 2014

Brave Frontier A-Lim, 2013

Broken Age Double Fine Productions, 2014

Bubbles Williams Electronics, 1982

Bull Fighter Alpha Denshi, 1984

Bump 'n' Jump Data East, 1982

Bust-A-Move Taito, 1994

Bust-A-Move '99 Taito, 1997

Bust-A-Move Again Taito, 1995

Buster Bros Collection Capcom, 1997

Call of Duty Infinity Ward, 2003

Call of Duty: Advanced Warfare Sledgehammer, 2014

Call of Duty: Black Ops Treyarch, 2010

Call of Duty: Black Ops: Declassified nStigate Games, 2012

Call of Duty: Black Ops II Treyarch, 2012

Call of Duty Online Activision/Raven Software, 2015

Call of Duty: Ghosts Infinity Ward, 2013

Call of Duty 4: Modern Warfare Infinity Ward, 2007

Call of Duty: Modern Warfare 2 Infinity Ward, 2009

Call of Duty: Modern Warfare 3 Infinity Ward/Sledgehammer, 2011

Candy Crush Saga King, 2012

Castle of Illusion Starring Mickey Mouse Sega, 1990

Chambara Overly Kinetic, 2014

CHAMP Kong CHAMProgramming, 1996

Child of Light Ubisoft Montreal, 2014

Chrono Trigger Square, 1995

Chuck Rock Core Design, 1992

Clash of Clans Supercell, 2012

Colony Wars Psygnosis, 1997

Complex X Taito, 1984

Conflict: Desert Storm Pivotal Games, 2002

Contra Konami, 1987

Cosmos Century Electronics, 1981

Counter-Strike: Global Offensive Valve/Hidden Path Entertainment, 2012

Crash Bandicoot Naughty Dog, 1996

Crash Bandicoot: Wrath of Cortex Traveller's Tales, 2001

The Crew Ivory Tower/Ubisoft, 2014

Crossy Road Hipster Whale, 2014

Crysis Crytek, 2007

Crysis 3 Crytek, 2013

Dance Central Harmonix, 2010

Dance Central 2 Harmonix, 2011

Dance Dance Revolution Konami, 1998

Dance Dance Revolution X2 Konami, 2010

Dark Souls II From Software, 2014

Dark Tower Game Room, 1992

de Blob Blue Tongue, 2008

Dead Island Techland, 2011

Dead or Alive Team Ninja, 1996

Dead Space Visceral Games, 2008

Death Race Exidy, 1976

Defend the Terra Attack on the Red UFO unknown, 1979

Defender Williams Electronics, 1980

Descent: FreeSpace – The Great War Volition, 1998

Desert Demolition BlueSky, 1995

Despicable Me: Minion Rush Gameloft, 2014

Destiny Bungie, 2014

Deus Ex: Mankind Divided Eidos Montreal

Diablo Blizzard, 1996

Diablo II Blizzard, 2000

Diablo II: Lord of Destruction Blizzard, 2001

Diablo III Blizzard, 2012

Dig Dug Bandai Namco, 2006

Discworld Teeny Weeny/Perfect 10, 1995

Disney Infinity Avalanche Software, 2013

Disney Tsum Tsum LINE corp, 2014

Disney's The Little Mermaid II: Pinball Frenzy Left Field, 2000

Divinity: Original Sin Larian Studios, 2014

Donkey Kong Nintendo, 1981

Donkey Kong II: Jumpman Returns Jeff Kulczycki, 2008

Donkey Kong Country Competition Pak Rare, 1994

Donkey Kong Jr. Nintendo, 1982

Don't Tap the White Tile Umoni Studio/Hu Wen Zeng, 2014

Doom id, 1993

DotA Blizzard/"Eul"/"Guinsoo"/"IceFrog", 2005

DotA 2 Valve, 2013

Double Dragon II – The Revenge Technōs Japan, 1988

Dragon: The Bruce Lee Story Virgin Interactive, 1995

Dragon Age II BioWare, 2011

Dragon Age: Inquisition BioWare, 2014

Dragon Age: Origins BioWare, 2009

DRIVECLUB Evolution Studios, 2014

Driver Reflections Interactive, 1999

Driver's Edge Strata, 1994

Dungeon Siege Gas Powered Games, 2002

Dungeon Siege III Obsidian Entertainment, 2011

Dynamite Dux Sega, 1989

Edge of Eternity Midgar Studio, 2016

The Elder Scrolls: Arena Bethesda, 1994

The Elder Scrolls II: Daggerfall Bethesda, 1996

The Elder Scrolls Adventures: Redguard Bethesda, 1998

The Elder Scrolls Online ZeniMax Online Studios, 2014

The Elder Scrolls III: Morrowind Bethesda, 2002

The Elder Scrolls IV: Oblivion Bethesda, 2006

The Elder Scrolls V: Skyrim Bethesda, 2011

Elevator Action Taito, 1983

Elite David Braben and Ian Bell, 1984

Elite: Dangerous Frontier Developments, 2014

Elite Beat Agents iNiS, 2006

Enigma 2 unknown, 1981

Epic Pinball Digital Extremes, 1993

ESPN National Hockey Night Stormfront Studios, 1994

ESPN NFL 2K5 Visual Concepts, 2004

E.T. The Extra-Terrestrial Atari, 1982

EVE Online CCP Games, 2003

Everybody's Golf: World Tour Clap Hanz/SCE Japan, 2007

The Evil Within Tango Gameworks, 2014

Exerion Jaleco, 1983

Extreme Pinball Epic Games, 1996

Fable Simbiosis Interactive, 1996

Fable Big Blue Box, 2004

Fable II Lionhead, 2008

Fable III Lionhead, 2010

Fable Legends Lionhead, 2015

Fable: The Lost Chapters Lionhead, 2005

Fallout Interplay, 1997

Fallout 3 Bethesda, 2008

Fallout: New Vegas Obsidian Entertainment, 2010

Far Cry Crytek, 2004

Far Cry 2 Ubisoft, 2008

Far Cry 3 Ubisoft, 2012

Far Cry 3: Blood Dragon Ubisoft, 2013

Far Cry 4 Ubisoft, 2014
Far Cry Instincts: Evolution Ubisoft, 2006
Far Cry: Vengeance Ubisoft, 2006
Farm Heroes Saga King, 2013
FIFA 12 EA, 2011
FIFA 13 EA, 2012
FIFA 14 EA, 2013
FIFA 15 EA, 2014
FIFA Street EA, 2005
Final Fantasy Square, 1987
Crisis Core: Final Fantasy VII Square Enix, 2007
Final Fantasy III Square, 1990
Final Fantasy IV Square, 1994
Final Fantasy VII Square, 1997
Final Fantasy VIII Square, 1998
Final Fantasy IX Square, 2000
Final Fantasy X Square, 2001
Final Fantasy X-2 Square, 2003
Final Fantasy XII Square Enix, 2006
Final Fantasy XIII Square Enix, 2009
Final Fantasy XIII-2 Square Enix, 2011
Final Fantasy XV Square Enix, 2016
Final Tetris Jeil Computer System, 1993
Fire Emblem: If Intelligent Systems, 2016
Fire Shark Toaplan, 1989
Firepower 2000 SCi Games, 1992
Football Manager 2015 Sports Interactive, 2014
Forza Horizon Playground Games/Turn 10, 2012
Forza Horizon 2 Turn 10/various, 2014
Forza Motorsport Turn 10, 2005
Forza Motorsport 2 Turn 10, 2007
Forza Motorsport 3 Turn 10, 2009
Forza Motorsport 4 Turn 10, 2011
Forza Motorsport 5 Turn 10, 2014
Forza Motorsport 6 Turn 10, 2015
Freedom Force Sunsoft, 1988
Freedom Wars various, 2014
Fruit Ninja Halfbrick, 2010
FTL: Faster Than Light Subset Games, 2012
Furu Furu Park Taito, 2007
Fuzion Frenzy Blitz Games, 2001
Galactic Attack Taito, 1995
Galaga Namco, 1981
Galaxion Namco, 1979
Game Boy Gallery 3 Nintendo, 1999
Game Boy Gallery 4 TOSE, 2002
Game of Thrones Telltale Games, 2014
Game of War: Fire Age Machine Zone, 2013
Game & Watch Gallery 3 Nintendo, 1999
Gauntlet: Seven Sorrows Midway Games, 2005
Gears of War Epic Games, 2006
Gears of War 2 Epic Games, 2008
Gears of War 3 Epic Games, 2011
Gears of War: Judgment Epic Games/People Can Fly, 2013
Ghouls 'n Ghosts Capcom, 1989
God of War SCE, 2005
God of War: Ascension SCE, 2013
God of War: Chains of Olympus Ready at Dawn/SCE, 2008
God of War: Ghost of Sparta Ready at Dawn/SCE, 2010
God of War II SCE, 2007

God of War III SCE, 2010
Golden Axe Sega, 1989
Gran Turismo SCE/Cyberhead, 1997
Gran Turismo 3: A-spec Polyphony Digital, 2001
Gran Turismo 4 Polyphony Digital, 2004
Gran Turismo 4 Prologue Polyphony Digital, 2003
Gran Turismo 5 Polyphony Digital, 2010
Gran Turismo 5 Prologue Polyphony Digital, 2007
Gran Turismo 6 Polyphony Digital, 2013
Gran Turismo Concept: 2001 Tokyo Polyphony Digital, 2002
Gran Turismo PSP Polyphony Digital, 2009
Grand Theft Auto DMA (Rockstar), 1997
Grand Theft Auto IV Rockstar, 2008
Grand Theft Auto V Rockstar, 2013
Grand Theft Auto: Chinatown Wars Rockstar, 2009
Grand Theft Auto Online Rockstar, 2013
Grand Theft Auto: San Andreas Rockstar, 2004
Grand Theft Auto: Vice City Rockstar, 2002
Green Day: Rock Band Harmonix, 2010
Guitar Hero Harmonix, 2005
Guitar Hero II Harmonix, 2006
Guitar Hero III: Legends of Rock various, 2007
Guitar Hero Live FreeStyle, 2015
Guitar Hero Smash Hits/Greatest Hits Beenox, 2009
Guitar Hero World Tour Neversoft, 2008
Half-Life Valve/Gearbox, 1987
Half-Life 2 Valve, 2004
Halo: Combat Evolved Bungie, 2001
Halo 2 Bungie, 2004
Halo 3 Bungie, 2007
Halo 4 343 Industries, 2012
Halo 5: Guardians 343 Industries, 2015
Halo 2600 Ed Fries, 2010
Halo: The Master Chief Collection 343 Industries, 2014
Halo: Reach Bungie, 2010
Hard Head SunA, 1988
Haunted House Atari, 1982
Hay Day Supercell, 2012
Hearthstone: Heroes of Warcraft Blizzard, 2014
Her Story Sam Barlow, 2015
Hexic HD Carbonated Games, 2005
Hill Climb Racing Fingersoft, 2012
Homeworld Relic Entertainment, 1999
Horse Racing APh, 1980
House of the Dead: Overkill Headstrong Games, 2009
Hyper Sports Konami, 1984
I MAED A GAM3 W1TH ZOMBJES 1N IT!!!1 Ska Studios, 2009
Ikaruga Treasure/G.rev, 2001
Impossible Mission Epyx, 1984
Intellivision Classic Games Gray Matter, 1999
Intellivision Lives! Realtime Associates, 2002

Invizimals Novarama, 2009
Jade Empire BioWare, 2005
James Bond 007 series various, 1997–2013
Journey Thatgamecompany, 2012
Jr. PAC-Man Bally Midway/Atari, 1983
Just Dance Ubisoft, 2009
Just Dance 2 Ubisoft, 2010
Just Dance 3 Ubisoft, 2011
Just Dance 4 Ubisoft, 2012
Just Dance 2014 Ubisoft, 2013
Just Dance 2015 Ubisoft, 2014
Just Dance Kids 2 Ubisoft, 2014
Just Dance Wii Ubisoft, 2011
Kentucky Route Zero Cardboard Computer, 2013
Killzone Guerrilla Games, 2004
Kingdom Hearts Square, 2002
Kingdom Hearts: Chain of Memories Jupiter, 2004
Kingdom Hearts: Dream Drop Distance Square Enix, 2012
Kingdom Hearts HD 1.5 Remix Square Enix, 2013
Kingdom Hearts II Square Enix, 2005
Kingdom Hearts II: Final Mix Square Enix, 2007
Kingdom Hearts III Square Enix, 2016
Knack SCE, 2013
Kung-Fu Master Irem, 1984
Kung Fu Panda various, 2008
The Last of Us Naughty Dog, 2013
The Last of Us: Left Behind Naughty Dog, 2014
The Last of Us Remastered Naughty Dog, 2014
League of Legends Riot Games, 2009
Legend of the Brofist Outerminds, 2015
The Legend of Zelda Nintendo, 1986
The Legend of Zelda: A Link to the Past Nintendo, 1991
The Legend of Zelda: Link's Awakening Nintendo, 1993
The Legend of Zelda: Majora's Mask Nintendo, 2000
The Legend of Zelda: Ocarina of Time Nintendo, 1998
The Legend of Zelda: Ocarina of Time 3D Grezzo/Nintendo, 2011
The Legend of Zelda: Phantom Hourglass Nintendo, 2007
The Legend of Zelda: Skyward Sword Nintendo, 2011
The Legend of Zelda: Twilight Princess Nintendo, 2006
The Legend of Zelda: The Wind Waker Nintendo, 2002
LEGO Batman: The Video Game Traveller's Tales/TT Fusion, 2008
LEGO Batman 2: DC Super Heroes Traveller's Tales, 2012
LEGO Batman 3: Beyond Gotham Traveller's Tales, 2014
LEGO Dimensions Traveller's Tales, 2015
LEGO Harry Potter: Years 1–4 Traveller's Tales/TT Fusion, 2010
LEGO Harry Potter: Years 5–7 Traveller's Tales, 2011
LEGO Island Mindscape, 1997

LEGO Jurassic World Traveller's Tales, 2015
LEGO The Lord of the Rings Traveller's Tales, 2012
LEGO Marvel Super Heroes Traveller's Tales, 2013
The LEGO Movie Videogame Traveller's Tales/TT Fusion, 2014
LEGO Star Wars: The Complete Saga Traveller's Tales, 2007
LEGO Star Wars II: The Original Trilogy Traveller's Tales, 2006
LEGO Star Wars: The Video Game various, 2005
LeMans HAL Laboratory, 1982
Little Computer People Activision, 1985
Little Deviants Bigbig Studios, 2011
LittleBigPlanet Media Molecule, 2008
LittleBigPlanet 2 Media Molecule, 2011
LittleBigPlanet 3 Sumo Digital, 2014
LittleBigPlanet PS Vita Double Eleven/Tarsier Studios/XDev, 2012
Lumines Supernova Q Entertainment, 2009
Lumino City State of Play, 2014
Madden NFL 07 various, 2006
Madden NFL 11 EA, 2010
Madden NFL 13 EA/HB Studios, 2012
Madden NFL 15 EA Tiburon, 2014
Madden NFL 96 EA Tiburon, 1995
Madden NFL 2001 EA Tiburon, 2000
Madden NFL 2002 EA/Budcat, 2001
Madden NFL 2003 EA/Budcat, 2002
Madden NFL 2004 EA/Budcat, 2003
Madden NFL 2005 EA/Budcat/Exient, 2004
Madden NFL 09 All-Play EA, 2008
Madden NFL Arcade EA Tiburon, 2009
Marble Blast Ultra GarageGames, 2006
Mario & Sonic at the Olympic Games Sega, 2007
Mario Bros. Nintendo/Atari, 1983
Mario Kart: Double Dash!! Nintendo, 2003
Mario Kart 8 Nintendo, 2014
Mario Kart DS Nintendo, 2005
Mario Kart Wii Nintendo, 2008
Mario Maker Nintendo, 2015
Mario Party series various, 1998–
Mario Party 10 Nd Cube/Nintendo, 2015
Marvel vs. Capcom 3: Fate of Two Worlds Capcom/Eighting, 2011
Mass Effect BioWare, 2007
Mass Effect 2 BioWare, 2010
Mass Effect 3 BioWare, 2012
Masters of the Universe Intellivision, 1983
The Maw Twisted Pixel/Hothead, 2009
Medal of Honor DreamWorks, 1999
Medal of Honor: Allied Assault 2015, Inc., 2002
MegaMania Activision, 1982
Mercury Meltdown Ignition, 2006
Metal Gear Konami, 1987

Solar Fox Bally/Midway, 1981
Sonic Advance Sonic Team/Dimps, 2001
Sonic Advance 2 Sonic Team/Dimps, 2002
Sonic Advance 3 Sonic Team/Dimps, 2004
Sonic Adventure Sonic Team, 1998
Sonic Adventure 2 Sonic Team USA, 2001
Sonic & All-Stars Racing Transformed Sumo Digital, 2012
Sonic Generations Sonic Team/Dimps, 2011
Sonic: Lost World Sonic Team, 2013
Sonic Rush Sonic Team/Dimps, 2005
Sonic Rush Adventure Sonic Team/Dimps, 2007
Sonic the Hedgehog Sonic Team, 1991
Sonic the Hedgehog 2 Sonic Team, 1992
Sonic the Hedgehog 3 Sonic Team, 1994
Sonic the Hedgehog 3 & Knuckles Sonic Team, 1994
Sonic's Ultimate Genesis Collection Backbone Entertainment, 2009
SoulCalibur Project Soul, 1998
SoulCalibur II Project Soul, 2002
SoulCalibur IV Project Soul, 2008
South Park: The Stick of Truth Obsidian Entertainment/South Park Digital Studios, 2014
Space Invaders Taito, 1978
Space Zap Game-A-Tron, 1980
Spacewar! Steve Russell et al., 1962
SpeedRunners tinyBuild/Double Dutch Games, 2013
Spider-Man Neversoft/various, 2000
Spin Master/Miracle Adventure Data East, 1993
Spyro the Dragon Insomniac Games, 1998
Spyro 2: Ripto's Rage Insomniac Games, 1999
Stadium Events Bandai Co Ltd, 1986
Star Citizen Cloud Imperium Games/Behaviour Interactive/CGBot/voidALPHA, 2015
Star Fox Nintendo, 1993
Star Realms White Wizard Games, 2014
Star Voyager ASCII Entertainment, 1986
Star Wars: Knights of the Old Republic BioWare/Aspyr, 2003
Star Wars: Knights of the Old Republic II Obsidian, 2004
Star Wars: Battlefront Pandemic Studios, 2004
StarCraft Blizzard, 1998
StarCraft II: Wings of Liberty Blizzard, 2002
Street Fighter Capcom, 1987
Street Fighter II: The World Warrior Capcom, 1991
Street Fighter III Capcom, 1997
Street Fighter III: 3rd Strike Capcom, 1999
Street Fighter IV Capcom/Dimps, 2008
Street Fighter V Capcom, 2016

Super Street Fighter IV: 3D Edition Dimps/Capcom, 2011
Super Street Fighter IV: Arcade Edition Dimps/Capcom, 2010
Street Fighter X Tekken Dimps/Capcom, 2012
Subway Surfers Kiloo/SYBO Games, 2012
Summer Games II Epyx, 1985
Sunset Overdrive Insomniac Games, 2014
Super Bomberman Hudson Soft, 1993
Super Buster Bros. Capcom, 1990
Super Contra Konami, 1988
Super Ghosts 'n Ghouls Capcom, 1991
Super Mario 3D Land Nintendo, 2011
Super Mario 3D World Nintendo, 2013
Super Mario 64 Nintendo, 1996
Super Mario 64 DS Nintendo, 2004
Super Mario All-Stars Nintendo, 1993
Super Mario Bros. Nintendo, 1985
Super Mario Bros.: The Lost Levels Nintendo, 1986
Super Mario Bros. 2 Nintendo, 1988
Super Mario Bros. 3 Nintendo, 1988
Super Mario Bros. Special Nintendo, 1986
Super Mario Galaxy Nintendo, 2007
Super Mario Kart Nintendo, 1992
Super Mario Land Nintendo, 1989
Super Mario RPG: Legend of the Seven Stars Squaresoft, 1996
Super Mario Sunshine Nintendo, 2002
Super Mario World Nintendo, 1990
Super Mario World 2: Yoshi's Island Nintendo, 1995
Super PAC-Man Namco/Beam Software, 1982
Super Paper Mario Intelligent Systems/Nintendo, 2007
Super Smash Bros. HAL Laboratory, 1999
Super Smash Bros. Brawl Nintendo, 2008
Super Smash Bros. for Nintendo 3DS Sora Ltd/Bandai Namco, 2014
Super Smash Bros. for Wii U Sora Ltd/Bandai Namco, 2014
Super Smash Bros. Melee HAL Laboratory, 2001
Super Space Invaders Domark, 1991
Super Sprint Atari Games, 1986
Super Star Wars: The Empire Strikes Back Sculptured Software/LucasArts, 1993
Super Tetris Nintendo, 1991
System Shock Looking Glass Studios, 1994
Taito Legends Taito/various, 2005
Tales from the Borderlands Telltale Games, 2014
Taxi Driver Graphic Techno, 1984
Teenage Mutant Ninja Turtles: Tournament Fighters Konami, 1994
Tekken Namco, 1994
Tekken 2 Namco, 1995
Tekken 3 Namco, 1997
Tekken 3D: Prime Edition Arika/Namco Bandai Games, 2012

Tekken 6 Bandai Namco, 2007
Tekken 7 Bandai Namco, 2015
Tekken Advance Namco, 2001
Tekken Card Challenge Namco, 1999
Tekken Tag Tournament Namco, 1999
Temple Run 2 Imangi Studios, 2013
Tetris Alexey Pajitnov, 1984
Tetris Blast BPS, 1996
Tetris DS Nintendo, 2006
Tetris Giant Sega, 2009
Tetris Party Hudson Soft, 2008
Tetris Party Deluxe Nintendo/Hudson/Majesco, 2010
Tetris Plus Jaleco, 1995
This War of Mine 11 bit studios, 2014
Titanfall Respawn Entertainment, 2014
TOCA Race Driver Codemasters, 2002
Tomb Raider Core Design, 1996
Tomb Raider (2013) Crystal Dynamics, 2013
Tomb Raider: Rise of the Tomb Raider Crystal Dynamics, 2015
Tomb Raider: Legend Crystal Dynamics, 2006
Tomb Raider: Underworld Crystal Dynamics, 2008
Tomb Raider II Core Design, 1997
Tomb Raider III Core Design, 1998
Tony Hawk's Pro Skater 2 Neversoft/various, 1999
Tony Hawk's Underground 2 Neversoft/various, 2004
Torchlight II Runic Games, 2012
Track & Field Konami, 1983
Transformers Traveller's Tales/others, 2007
Transistor Supergiant Games, 2014
Triggerheart Exelica Warashi/Gulti/P.A. Works, 2008
True Crime series Luxoflux, 2003–05
Turbo Esprit Mike Richardson, 1986
Twin Cobra Toaplan, 1987
UFC Undisputed 2010 Yuke's, 2010
Ultra Street Fighter IV Dimps/Capcom, 2014
Uncharted: Drake's Fortune Naughty Dog, 2007
Uncharted: Golden Abyss SCE Bend Studio, 2011
Uncharted 2: Among Thieves Naughty Dog, 2009
Uncharted 3: Drake's Deception Naughty Dog, 2011
Uncharted 4: A Thief's End Naughty Dog, 2015
Valiant Hearts: The Great War Ubisoft Montpellier, 2014
The Vanishing of Ethan Carter The Astronauts, 2014
Vectorman 2 Blue Sky Software, 1996
Viewpoint Nexus Interact, 1994
The Walking Dead: The Game Telltale Games, 2012
Warblade Edgar M Vigdal, 2003
Warcraft II: Tides of Darkness Blizzard, 1995

Warcraft III: Reign of Chaos Blizzard, 2002
WarioWare: Smooth Moves Intelligent Systems/Nintendo, 2006
Wasteland 2 inXile Entertainment, 2014
WATCH_DOGS Ubisoft, 2014
We Love Katamari Namco/NOW Production, 2005
Wii Fit Nintendo, 2007
Wii Sports Nintendo, 2006
Wii Sports Resort Nintendo, 2009
Wing Commander Origin Systems, 1990
Winter Challenge Ballistic, 1991
The Witcher CD Projekt RED, 2007
The Witcher: Battle Arena CD Projekt RED, 2015
The Witcher 2: Assassins of Kings CD Projekt RED, 2011
The Witcher 2: Assassins of Kings Enhanced Edition CD Projekt RED, 2012
The Witcher III: Wild Hunt CD Projekt RED, 2015
The Wolf Among Us Telltale Games, 2013
Wolfenstein 3D id, 1992
The World Ends with You Square Enix, 2007
World of Goo 2D Boy, 2008
The World of Mystic Wiz COLOPL, 2013
World of Warcraft Blizzard, 2004
World of Warcraft: The Burning Crusade Blizzard, 2007
World of Warcraft: Warlords of Draenor Blizzard, 2014
World of Warcraft: Wrath of the Lich King Blizzard, 2008
World Soccer Winning Eleven 7 International KCET, 2004
World Tennis Original Game, 1982
WWE All Stars THQ San Diego, 2011
WWE Legends of Wrestlemania Yuke's, 2009
WWE SmackDown! Yuke's, 2000
WWE SmackDown vs Raw Yuke's, 2004
WWE 2K14 Yuke's/Visual Concepts, 2013
WWE 2K15 Yuke's/Visual Concepts, 2014
WWE Day of Reckoning Yuke's, 2004
WWF No Mercy Asmik Ace Entertainment/AKI Corporation, 2000
WWF Raw Sculptured Software/Realtime Associates, 1994
WWF Royal Rumble Sculptured Software, 1993
WWF SmackDown! 2: Know Your Role Yuke's, 2000
WWF Wrestlemania Rare Ltd, 1989
X-Men Konami, 1992
X-Men vs. Street Fighter Capcom, 1996
Xenophobe Bally Midway, 1987
Yie Ar Kung-Fu II Konami, 1986
Zelda II: The Adventure of Link Nintendo, 1987
Zen Pinball Zen Studios, 2009
ZombiU Ubisoft Montpellier, 2012

Index

Index

Index

Picture Credits

3 Mari Takahashi, Defy
6 James Ellerker/GWR; Ryan Schude/GWR; Paul Michael Hughes/GWR; Kevin Scott Ramos/GWR
9 James Ellerker/GWR
10 Madcatz
11 Marvel
12 The Independent
15 Alamy
16 Paul Michael Hughes/GWR
31 Matt Alexander
32 Moby Games
34 Jakob Wells
48 Paul Michael Hughes/GWR
51 Alamy
52 Paul Michael Hughes/GWR

58 Alamy
60 Reuters; Drew Gibson/Beadyeye; Alamy
62 Alamy; Reuters
64 Ryan Schude/GWR
71 Paul Michael Hughes/GWR; Ubisoft
76 Reuters
77 Jamie Simonds/BAFTA
80 Paul Michael Hughes/GWR
95 Alamy
98 James Ellerker/GWR
100 Paul Michael Hughes/GWR
101 BAFTA
102 Alamy
103 Getty; Alamy; AP/PA
104 Paul Michael Hughes/GWR

109 Alamy
119 Daniel Deme/GWR
123 Kevin Lynch
124 James Ellerker/GWR
128 Paul Michael Hughes/GWR
130 NAMCO
131 MJZ
144 Moby Games; IGN
148 Sculpture Studios
154 James Ellerker/GWR; Games Database
156 Ryan Schude/GWR
162 The Strong/National Museum of Play; Britain P Woodman
166 Moby Games; PA
169 Getty

171 Alamy
173 Paul Michael Hughes/GWR; GameSpot
175 Moby Games
176 Kevin Scott Ramos/GWR
180 Alamy
182 Alamy
184 AP/PA
186 Alamy

Acknowledgements

Guinness World Records would like to thank the following for their help in compiling the *Gamer's Edition 2016*:

2K Games (Matt Roche and Adam Merrett)

Activision Blizzard (Jonathan Fargher, Rachel Grant, Karen Ward and Sam Bandah)

Lewis Ayers (for his invaluable assistance with all things *Minecraft*)

Bandai Namco (Lee Kirton, David Greenspan, Shuhei Hokari and Tatsuya Kubota)

Sam Barlow

David Braben OBE

Mathew Callaghan

Capcom (Laura Skelly)

CD Projekt Red (Robert Malinowski)

Sami Cetin

Dead Good Media (Stu Taylor)

Defy Media (Liz Teschler)

Dotabuff

Electronic Arts (Tristan Rosenfeldt and Bryony Benoy)

Edelman/Microsoft (Dominic Carey)

GameRankings

Jace Hall

Jelly Media (Mark Bamber)

Koch Media (Suzanne Panter and David Scarborough)

Konami/Voltage PR (Steve Merrett)

Guillaume Leviach

Lick PR (Kat Osman and Lucy Starvis)

Arturo Manzarek Dracul

Franny Maufras

MCV (Alex Calvin)

Metacritic (Marc Doyle)

NetherRealm Studios

Premier PR (Will Beckett, Lauren Dillon, Gareth Williams, Yunus Ibrahim, Daniela Pietrosanu and Alison Payne)

Riot Games (Becca Roberts)

Rockstar Games (Hamish Brown, Patricia Pucci and Craig Gilmore)

Roll7

Tim Schafer

Sledgehammer Games

Smosh Games

Sony Computer Entertainment (Hugo Bustillos, Sarah Moffatt and Sarah Wellock)

Jessica Telef

Toys For Bob

TrueAchievements Ltd (Rich Stone and Dave Horobin)

Twin Galaxies

Ubisoft (Oliver Coe, Wayne Greenwell and Mark Bassett)

Vault Communications (Mark Robins)

VGChartz

Warner Bros. (Mark Ward)

Zebra Partners (Beth Llewelyn)

Glossary

100-percent completion Completing all tasks and missions in a game, often associated with speed-runs

AAA "Triple A" refers to a videogame that benefits from a large budget and development team and is expected to be hugely successful; the videogaming equivalent of a blockbuster movie

AI Artificial Intelligence: computer-generated NPCs that strive to react realistically to players' actions

Alpha The first phase of software testing, usually conducted exclusively by the developers

Any-percentage completion Completing a speed-run without finishing all goals within the game

Autoattack Default means by which a unit deals damage in *League of Legends*

Beta Phase of software testing that comes after alpha – usually open for public use

Chipset Part of a computer's integrated circuitry that relays data between the processor and other components on the motherboard, such as the memory disks and the external ports

Clan A team, guild or faction of gamers, usually at the same skill level, playing as an organized group; typically, a clan's members work together in multiplayer games such as MMORPGs and strategies

Cutscene Non-playable sequence in a game used to advance the plot

DAU Daily active users; often used to measure the popularity of Facebook games

DEV Short for "developer"

DLC Downloadable content

FPS First-person shooter, with action from the player's point of view

Fragfest A multiplayer deathmatch, most commonly referred to in shooters

Glitch A bug in the programming. Some can be exploited in speed-runs

HDD Hard-disk drive

Hit points/hp A metric in RPGs that determines how much damage a character can take before expiring

Easter egg

A joke, mini-game, bonus or hidden message implanted inside a game by the coders as a reward for those with the patience – or luck – to uncover it. *Saints Row 2* has a giant Easter bunny that rises up out of the ocean.

Kill-to-death ratio The number of enemies you eliminate divided by the number of lives you lose; also known as kill:death ratio

Machinima An animated film created by manipulating videogame graphics to establish a story-telling narrative. It is also the name of a popular gaming site

JRPG

Japanese role-playing games first appeared in the early 1980s, with titles such as *Donkey Commando* (1982). *Tales of Vesperia* (2008), the 10th game in the successful JRPG series *Tales*, follows Yuri Lowell's search for his friend Flynn.

MAU Monthly active users; often used to measure the popularity of Facebook games

Melee kill A kill achieved without the use of a gun, typically using a knife, sword or blunt instrument. Series such as *God of War* focus much of their gameplay around this kind of action

MMO Any kind of massively multiplayer online game – includes (and is often used interchangeably with) MMORPG. These "massive" games feature persistent "worlds"

MMOR A massively multiplayer online racing game, such as *Need for Speed: World*

Free2play

Games that are free for the most part, with extras generally available at a cost. Ubisoft's *Might & Magic: Duel of Champions* is a strategic online card game released in 2012; players choose a hero and build their deck to challenge others in epic battles.

MMORPG A type of MMO game that is specifically a role-playing game (RPG)

MOBA Multiplayer online battle arena, aka action real-time strategy

Mod Modification made to a game by a fan or a developer, from the smallest tweak to a complete new version (such as *Counter-Strike*, a take on *Half-Life*)

Motion-capture Mo-capping: the act of filming the movements of an actor or object for added realism. It is widely used in sports games, such as *FIFA* and *WWE*

NES Nintendo Entertainment System, known as the Famicom in Japan. Its successor was the SNES (Super Nintendo Entertainment System), known as the Super Famicom in Japan

NTSC National Television System Committee: the TV system used in North America

WHACK LUMBERJACKS
IN INTENSE ACTION DEFENSE!

20 30 30 40 115

Scroller

A game whose playing area is limited to a window through which the gamer moves, either horizontally (a "side-scroller", usually left to right) or vertically (a top-down view). Castle-defence game *Lumberwhack: Defend the Wild* (2013) offers a side-scrolling challenge in which monkey Koko Kornelius protects trees from axe-happy lumberjacks.

NPC

Non-playable character, controlled by the computer. Open-world RPG *Fable III* (2010) poses gamers a series of moral challenges and choices through interactions with its vast cast of NPCs, from Jasper the butler to the pirate-turned-businessman Reaver (right).

OS Operating system, such as Windows, Mac OS, iOS, Android or Linux – the software that runs the basic functions of a computer or device

Otaku Japanese term for a fanatic; most similar to the English words "geek" or "nerd", it refers typically to those people obsessed with manga, anime and videogames

PAL Phase Alternating Line: the TV system used in Europe; consoles are produced for both NTSC and PAL territories

Polygon A two-dimensional computer graphic that, when combined with vast numbers of other polygons, can create 3D-looking graphics. The higher the polygon count, the more realistic the final graphic will appear to be

Port The transfer of a game from one platform to another

PS PlayStation; can include PS2, PS3, PS4, PSP (PlayStation Portable), PSN (PlayStation Network) and PS Vita

RPG Role-playing game

RTS Real-time strategy

Sandbox Aka open-world, a game with an environment that can be explored and manipulated by the gamer, often with no objective in mind; in a more general sense, also refers to a game or level that has no artificial barriers

Speed-run A play-through of a whole game or a part of it, completed as quickly as possible

Story mode Used in fighting games to describe the single-player fighting battles as a narrative unfolds, perhaps through linking cutscenes

Taunt A movement that players use to antagonize opponents, most commonly within fighting games

Trophy In general terms, an award earned beyond an individual game (e.g., in a central, platform-wide network such as the Xbox 360's Gamerscore system) for completing a level, reaching a given score, securing a number of kills, and so on

Turn-based A game (such as *Hearthstone*) in which players are not active simultaneously but take turns to make their moves

UI User interface: the means by which a gamer interacts with a game, such as on-screen icons, buttons and messaging

UX User experience: a key concern for videogame developers

XP Experience points – gained through battles and achieving goals; they help to raise the level of a character, often in an RPG

Stealth

A genre of gaming in which the object is to achieve goals without being detected by the enemy. In Ubisoft's *Tom Clancy's Splinter Cell: Conviction* (2010), former Navy SEAL Sam Fisher has to draw on all his covert skills as he breaks into heavily armed compounds such as the headquarters of the Third Echelon.

Stop Press

Fastest completion of *Bloodborne*

Less than a month after its 24 March 2015 release, Florian "pr0Flo" Elmies (Germany) completed Sony's horror action RPG in 27 min 23 sec. Florian used the exploits "Forbidden Forest Skip", "DupeGlitch" and "Shadows of Yharnam Glitch" to nail his pace-setting time on 21 April 2015.

Most combined YouTube views for a videogame franchise

As revealed in YouTube rankings figures published by Newzoo and Octoly in March 2015, *Minecraft* is by far the most watched videogame on YouTube. The block-building creation sim had amassed a combined total of 3.9 billion views for all *Minecraft*-related videos that had been published on the channel. This placed it more than 2.5 billion views ahead of second-placed *Grand Theft Auto's* 1.3 billion views.

First videogame to win the "Best Persistent Game" BAFTA award

League of Legends set a gaming industry first in 2015 by winning the BAFTA British Academy Games Awards' first-ever "Persistent Game" award, beating fellow nominees *Destiny*, *EVE Online: Phoebe*, *RuneScape*, *WoW: Warlords of Draenor* and *World of Tanks*. The award was created to recognize games that have provided a lasting, dynamic world and significant updates.

Fastest time to reach level 70 in *Diablo III*

On 1 May 2015, "Dat Modz" (USA) power-levelled from 1 to 70 in record time using Cain's Scribe, Born's Privilege, Leoric's Signet and additional boosts within the rare Cow Level to reach max level in a super-fast time of 41 sec.

Fastest 120-star completion of *Super Mario 64*

In 2015, many famous *Super Mario 64* speed-runners returned to the spotlight. Leading the pack as of 5 April 2015 was Allan "cheese05" Alvarez, who managed to complete *Super Mario 64* with all 120 stars in a time of just 1 hr 41 min 16 sec.

Fastest completion of *Halo: Combat Evolved* (team)

On 21 February 2015, *Halo* veterans "Scurty", "Sol", "Vetro" and "Whistle" teamed up to set a speed-running record of 1 hr 7 min 4 sec. The segmented run of *Halo: Combat Evolved* was performed on the game's "Legendary" mode, the hardest possible.

Most "likes" on a Facebook videogame page

As of 20 May 2015, King's puzzle game *Candy Crush Saga's* Facebook page had received 75,187,303 "likes", making it the most popular page for a videogame on the popular social networking site. The game boasted a staggering 50 million Facebook players.

D.Y.K.?

Ori and the Blind Forest developer Moon Studios are based around the world, and the game's unveiling at E3 2014 was the first time many of them had met.

Fastest completion of *Ori and the Blind Forest*

Developed by Moon Studios, *Ori and the Blind Forest* is a haunting and visually dazzling eco-platform adventure released in March 2015. On 21 April 2015, Andy Laso braved the darkness and ancient dangers to complete the game on PC in a record time of 37 min 24 sec.

88 Overall rating for *Ori and the Blind Forest* on review aggregator Metacritic, as of 20 May 2015. The game scored the same for both of its available platforms – PC and Xbox One.

but while being predominantly *Minecraft*-focused, they also cover other games.

Most cards drawn in a *Hearthstone* turn

Some two weeks after entertaining *Hearthstone*'s vast fanbase with a 45-hr turn (see pp.68–69), Florian "Mamytwink" Henn (France) – the self-proclaimed "expert of useless *Hearthstone* challenges" – drew 14,745 cards on 8 April 2015. In the same 24-hr move, he also took 108,714,885 points of fatigue damage – the **most fatigue damage in a *Hearthstone* turn**.

Most expensive game package for an eighth-generation console

On 24 February 2015, Techland released a single "My Apocalypse Edition" of *Dying Light* through British retailer GAME for £250,000 ($380,517). It included a custom-built zombie-proof shelter, parkour lessons, a life-sized statue, an appearance in the game, collectables and the game itself.

Fastest completion of *Dying Light*

Open-world survival horror *Dying Light* was one of the year's first in-demand titles, with the game's official Twitter account announcing that 1.2 million people had played it in the week after its January 2015 release. US gamer "redemption99" brought peace to the zombie-infested city of Harran in the PC version of *Dying Light* in just 1 hr 47 min 26 sec, setting a world record speed-run on 21 March 2015.

First *Mortal Kombat X* tournament winner

On 11 April 2015, Dominique "SonicFox" McLean (USA) dominated the ESL *Mortal Kombat X* Fatal 8 Exhibition tournament, beating seven other gaming pros to claim the inaugural title.

Most popular Rockstar Editor *GTA V* video

Grand Theft Auto V arrived for the PC in April 2015 with the tools for players to create and share their own in-game movies. As of 19 May 2015, the video "Running, Man", created by Shoalts, Gordy Mills, Chaney and Sonny Evans, had 3,583 "likes" in the Rockstar Games Social Club.

First video made using *GTA V*'s PC video editor

The machinima "Running, Man" (see above) was the first video created entirely with *Grand Theft Auto V*'s PC video-editing tools. The two-minute short was commissioned by publisher Rockstar Games and stars *GTA V* gangster Trevor Philips. It was uploaded to the Rockstar Games Social Club on 12 April 2015.

Most views for a dedicated *Minecraft* channel

Since its launch on 14 July 2012, "TheDiamondMinecart" by "DanTDM" had uploaded 1,234 videos and accrued a total of 2,799,636,273 views as of 23 April 2015. The YouTube channels "stampylonghead" and "Lewis & Simon" have had a higher total number of views,

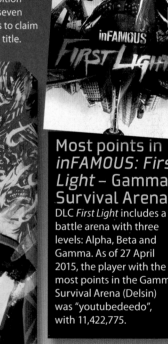

Most points in *inFAMOUS: First Light* – Gamma Survival Arena

DLC *First Light* includes a battle arena with three levels: Alpha, Beta and Gamma. As of 27 April 2015, the player with the most points in the Gamma Survival Arena (Delsin) was "youtubedeedo", with 11,422,775.

Fastest completion of *Hotline Miami 2: Wrong Number*

Released in March 2015, top-down shooter *Wrong Number* saw the violent conclusion of the saga of anti-hero "Jacket" and his homicidal phone calls. French gamer "Dingodrole" took the mayhem to the next level in setting a new speed-running record of 39 min 47 sec on 23 April 2015.

Most wins with a single character in *Evolve*

Since *Evolve*'s launch in February 2015, hunters and monsters have competed in deadly games of cat-and-mouse. As of 28 April 2015, Xbox One player "Yeti the God" had won 1,359 matches as the Kraken monster, the most victories with a single character.

THE ULTIMATE WORD IN RECORD-BREAKING!

GUINNESS WORLD RECORDS 2016

THOUSANDS OF **NEW** RECORDS!

AVAILABLE NOW